Delinquency in India

A Volume in the
Crime, Law, and Deviance
Series

Delinquency in India

A Comparative Analysis

Clayton A. Hartjen

S. Priyadarsini

RUTGERS UNIVERSITY PRESS
New Brunswick, New Jersey

Library of Congress Cataloging in Publication Data

Hartjen, Clayton A., 1943–
    Delinquency in India.

    (Crime, law, and deviance)
    Bibliography: p.
    Includes index.
    1. Juvenile delinquency—India—Tamil Nadu.
2. Juvenile justice, Administration of—India—
Tamil Nadu.
3. Juvenile delinquency—India—Tamil Nadu—
Public opinion. 4. Public opinion—India—Tamil
Nadu.
I. Priyadarsini, S., 1943–   . II. Title.
III. Series.

HV9399.T35H37   1983   364.3′6′095482   82-16693
ISBN 0-8135-0997-1

Copyright © 1984 by Rutgers,
the State University
All rights reserved
Manufactured in the United States of America

*To Our Mothers
Ruth J. Hartjen and
M. S. Rukmini*

Contents

List of Figures   ix
List of Tables   xi
Preface   xiii

PART ONE
The Study and Its Focus   1

1 *Introduction*   3
2 *Methodology*   13

PART TWO
**Delinquent Behavior:
Official and Self-reported**   37

3 *Delinquency Laws and Official Delinquency*   39
4 *Self-reported Delinquent Behavior*   57

PART THREE
**Official Control: Arrest, Judicial, and
Correctional Processing**   83

5 *Official Reaction*   85
6 *Judicial and Correctional Processing*   102

PART FOUR
Societal Perceptions and Reactions   123

7   Shaping Reactions: Crime and Delinquency News   125
8   Public Reaction   139
9   The Structure of Public Reaction   165

PART FIVE
Summary and Conclusions   193

10   Delinquency, Society, and Social Control   195

APPENDIXES

A   Self-report Questionnaire   215
B   Public Attitude Questionnaire   221
C   Factor Analysis of Self-report Survey   229
D   Factor Analysis of Public Attitude Survey   231

Bibliography   235
Index   249

Figures

2.1 *Map of India* 14

4.1 *Offense-scale Scores of Corporation, Private Aided, and Private High School Respondents* 73

7.1 *Average Number of Crime Stories per Month in Three Indian Newspapers* 129

7.2 *Percentage of Crime Stories by Story Type* 132

9.1 *Path Model of Sanction Choice Using Location as a Dummy Variable* 171

9.2 *Path Models of the Relationships among Knowledge, Opinion, and Attitudes* 173

9.3 *Path Models of Sanction Choice by Offense Type and Residence* 178

10.1 *Social Systems and Styles of Control* 209

Tables

2.1 *Percentage Distribution of the Socioeconomic Characteristics of High School and Approved School Respondents* 24

2.2 *Distribution of the Socioeconomic Characteristics of Rural and Urban Respondents* 31

3.1 *Recorded Violations of Indian Penal Code and Special and Local Laws in India, 1974* 48

3.2 *Recorded Violations of Indian Penal Code and Special and Local Laws in Tamil Nadu and Madras, 1974* 52

4.1 *Percentage Distribution of Self-reported Delinquent Behavior among High School and Approved School Respondents* 59

4.2 *Total and Average ($\bar{X}$) Admissions of High School and Approved School Boys by Offense Type* 64

4.3 *SES, Delinquency, Status-offense, and Theft-offense Scale Scores (Unweighted) by Schools* 68

4.4 *Pearson Product Moment Correlations between the Status-offense and Theft-offense Scale Scores by School* 70

4.5 *Differences in $\bar{X}$ SES, Delinquency, Status-offense, and Theft-offense Scale Scores of Pairs of Schools* 72

5.1 *Arrests of Juveniles for Violations of the Indian Penal Code and Special and Local Laws in India, Tamil Nadu, and Madras, 1974* 88

5.2 *Characteristics of Juveniles Apprehended in India, Tamil Nadu, and Madras, 1974* 93

xii   Tables

5.3   Percentage of Total Sample, High School, and Approved School Boys Admitting to Contact with Legal Authorities   95

5.4   Zero-order and Partial Correlations among the Judicial-contact, SES, Delinquency, Status-offense, and Theft-offense Scales   97

6.1   Dispositions of Juveniles Sent to Courts in India, Tamil Nadu, and Madras, 1974   103

6.2   Dispositions of Delinquent and Nondelinquent Cases by Tamil Nadu Juvenile Courts, 1971   105

7.1   Six-month Summary of Crime News in Three Indian Newspapers   128

7.2   Crime-news Coverage by Type of Story in Three Indian Newspapers   131

8.1   Percentage of Respondents Saying Act Should Be or Is Illegal by Offense/Offender   143

8.2   Percentage of Respondents Recommending Different Social Control Agents and Sanctions by Locality and Offense/Offender Type   150

9.1   Zero-order Correlations among Dimensions of Reaction by Offense Type and Locality   168

9.2   Direct, Indirect, and Total Effects of Locality on Knowledge, Opinion, and Attitudes   172

9.3   Direct, Indirect, and Total Effects of Knowledge on the Intervening and Dependent Variable with Combined and Separate Rural and Urban Samples   174

9.4   Effects on Choice of Sanction by Type of Offense and Locality   180

Preface

Most of the research and theory on crime and delinquency phenomena has centered on North America, particularly the United States, and Western European nations. While the amount of research conducted in other countries has increased in recent years, the limited attention devoted to criminal phenomena outside the Western Hemisphere has restricted both the scope of our knowledge and the depth of our comprehension. The few cross-national or comparative studies of crime and delinquency available today do suggest, however, that what we know about crime and the theories we have developed to explain it provide us with, at best, a very narrow and probably inaccurate understanding of the relationships among social structures, social processes, crime and delinquent behavior, and societal reaction to such behavior. Criminologists have, of course, long recognized the value of comparative inquiry and the extent to which our knowledge is enhanced by information derived from research in diverse societies; but there have been few opportunities to obtain such information.

Although no single study of delinquency outside the Western Hemisphere can address all the questions one might desire answered, the research reported in this book adds to the general body of cross-national information available to criminologists. Hopefully the analysis of a number of aspects of delinquency and its control in India will increase our understanding of crime and delinquency phenomena as such.

India is an ideal locality for conducting such an analysis. Poised on the brink of modernization and industrial development, the nation combines the socioeconomic characteristics of feudalism and modern individualism, of democratic government and the vestiges of colonial bureaucracy, of urban development and village social structure, of social heterogeneity and restricted social interrelationships. The country, then, is almost a natural laboratory for the investigation of many of the major theoretical and pragmatic questions posed by criminologists.

The present study was supported by the U.S. Subcommission for the International Exchange of Scholars under its Indo-U.S. Fellowship Foundation program in affiliation with the Departments of Psychology and Sociology of the University of Madras. Additional support was provided by the National Science Foundation; the Rutgers University Research Council; the Center of Alcohol Studies, Rutgers University; and N.I.A.A.A. All aspects of the research and writing were carried out jointly by the co-authors.

Of course no such study could be conducted without the aid of numerous individuals, too many to list individually. The support and encouragement of some of them, however, should not go unrecognized. We are grateful to Drs. T. E. Shanmugam and P. Rama Rao of the Department of Psychology and Drs. D. Sundaram and D. Palani of the Department of Sociology at Madras University for generously providing us with facilities, assistance, and guidance throughout the data collection process. The project would not have been possible without the dedication and enthusiasm of our project manager/secretary, G. Prema, and our research assistants, S. A. Anathakrishnan, A. Asha, K. Muralidaran, A. P. Raghupathy, T. O. Ranganathan, V. Saikumar, and S. K. Sundara Rajan. Lucile Duberman read and critiqued an early version of our manuscript, and David Greenberg offered encouragement and numerous insights, suggestions, and criticisms. We are also indebted to the citizens of Madras city and Thamaraikulam village who freely gave of their time in responding to our questionnaire. The many judicial, correctional, and high school officials we interviewed throughout India were also most gracious and helpful. The boys we surveyed in both the high schools and correctional facilities we studied were a researcher's delight. Without the cooperation of these individuals, this study could never have been completed. Although we are grateful to all the people who generously aided us in this analysis, we alone are responsible for its content.

PART ONE

The Study and Its Focus

CHAPTER 1

Introduction

Clothed in rags, the young boys stood at attention. They clearly suffered from malnutrition; some seemed close to starvation. Most of their bodies were covered with scabies. Their stunted growth belied their actual ages. None smiled or spoke. Their eyes, accentuated by malnourishment, were riveted on us.

Although none of the dozen or so boys standing before us had committed serious crimes, they were being admitted to the junior approved school (correctional facility) as offenders. Several had been found wandering in the streets without any means of support. Others had been arrested for petty pilfering. A few had been picked up in the train station for hustling money by illegally selling tickets or seat space (a form of scalping). All were "first offenders." Most had no home, did not know where they lived, or were no longer wanted by relatives. The school doctor said it would take about three months to bring them to health. By then, they would look like the other 400 or so boys incarcerated in the institution. Given their chances for survival on the outside, perhaps they were lucky; at least they would have food, clothing, shelter, the possibility of an education, and training for a trade. They will, however, carry the stigma of having been in a "jail school." Yet in India the stigma of delinquency does not necessarily have the same significance that it does in most "Western" (particularly American) societies.* Nor does the reality or meaning of delinquency compare with or have the same connotation that youthful misconduct has in the West. Indian officials rarely characterize

---

*The term "Western" is used here and throughout this book to indicate countries considered to be developed, postindustrial, modern, urbanized, and the like; i.e., we are referring primarily to the United States, Canada, and northern European countries, but we do not mean to limit the concept or analysis to these nations.

young offenders as "bad" and deserving of punishment, or "sick" and in need of therapy. The fear Westerners have of juvenile miscreants and their proclivity to "call the cops" when such youths are encountered are practically absent in India, even in major cities. Moreover, the occurrence of delinquent behavior, particularly that involving serious offenses against property or violence toward persons, is relatively infrequent compared to the West. In this respect, delinquency in India, in either a behaviorial or social-reaction sense, is not a social problem.

Delinquency as a Social Problem

Labeling the behavior of others as deviant is an instance of blaming activity—a way of locating a responsible-for-the act actor (Hartjen, 1981) and, thereby, accounting for the existence of the condition or event which the labeled behavior is thought to exemplify. Blaming, as an essential feature of deviance labeling, requires the "registering," "exemplifying," and "degrading" of some person or class of persons (Matza, 1969: 156). It requires, in effect, that some group or individual representative of the group be set apart socially and symbolically degraded as a threat to the integrity or well-being of the larger society. In this way the "deviant" actions or the conditions they exemplify are believed to be controlled and the power of society over those actions or the persons it deems responsible for them is confirmed. In this respect, labeling the behavior of others as deviant can be thought of as one way to create a "social problem." Calling the behavior of, or some members of, the juvenile population "delinquent" is one instance of deviant labeling—or the creation of a social problem.

As a result of the historical shifts in the conception of children and the socioeconomic changes that swept post-Civil War United States, in the name of salvation, youth in general, and delinquent youth in particular, became the objects of major public concern in much of the Western world by the middle of the twentieth century (Platt, 1969; Empey, 1982: 23–74). Due perhaps to the social and economic contingencies of the times, problem-causing youth emerged as the "youth problem." The official designation of youthful misconduct as "delinquent" behavior subject to formal control and correction by agents of the state served not only to subject an entire category of persons to intervention by state authorities, but also to create a "delinquency problem." Formally registered and degraded by special judicial and correctional systems as delinquent or otherwise in need of intervention work (correction, supervision, and control), youth in many Western countries were made to exemplify a category of miscreant to which innumerable resources and societal attention could be legitimately directed.

While largely etiological in character, the voluminous literature on problem children and the problems of youth in North America and some Western European nations suggests that delinquency was defined as, and is probably maintained as, a social problem independent of the actual conduct of young people. Undoubtedly many, if not all, youngsters sometimes act in ways considered offensive or threatening by adults in any society. But the delinquency problem in Western nations is the result of factors more socially profound than the actual behavior of individual young people. The very forces of industrialization, urbanization, and modernization that necessitated the separation of persons into age-generation categories provided the occasion for labeling the members of some categories as deviant (see Shelley, 1981a, 1981b). Being singled out as "special" warranted, and ultimately necessitated, the "special" treatment of young people by those adults in positions of control. Being part of, but not allowed to be participants in, the larger socioeconomic order, the young in Western nations increasingly became objects of attention and, consequently, their behavior became more and more the subject of concern and control (Friday and Hage, 1976; Friday, 1980). Why this occurred is a subject of debate with a paucity of empirical data. Until recently, sociological inquiry has centered on the behavior of young offenders rather than on the perceptions of and reactions to such behavior by others. While some attention has been devoted to judicial processing, law, public opinion, and other dimensions of societal reaction to delinquency in recent decades, little information is available on the broader societal or cultural factors that would produce a "social problem" out of delinquent behavior. Undoubtedly there is a correlation between the behavior of some category of persons (such as young people) and the reaction to that behavior, but it is not necessarily a direct or perfect relationship (Hartjen, 1977).

Young people in all societies and historical periods probably act, although with varying frequency and to differing degrees, in ways their elders consider harmful and/or threatening. But youthful misconduct is *not* universally considered equally threatening or treated and reacted to in the same ways (Clifford, 1976; Clinard, 1978). Even within a given society the behavior of young people, dependent upon class or power positions, is not uniformly a matter of concern. And the limited existing cross-national research suggests that wide differences exist in the ways youth is viewed and treated in various parts of the world (Clinard and Abbott, 1973; Vaz and Casparis, 1981; Zeldes, 1980 provide some examples). Perhaps, therefore, a broader conceptualization and scope of research are needed for a fuller understanding of delinquent behavior and the problem of delinquency.

Focus of the Study

In part, one goal of the present inquiry is to extend the scope of existing information regarding delinquency by investigating delinquent behavior and societal reaction to it in India. Specifically, we endeavored to carry out a number of studies on various aspects of delinquency in the South Indian state of Tamil Nadu, particularly in the state's chief city of Madras and in a village community reflecting the rural residents of the state. The objectives of this research were to explore aspects of delinquency phenomena in a non-Western, Third World society. Although such research has been carried out in several Third World countries (e.g., Weinberg, 1964; DeFleur, 1967; Cavan and Cavan, 1968; DeFleur, 1969; Chambers and Inciardi, 1971; Clinard and Abbott, 1973), sociological attention to juvenile delinquency in India is practically nonexistent. The data on juvenile delinquency in this large, heterogeneous, modernizing country are almost exclusively psychological (for a recent example see Shanmugam, 1980) with some commentary by social workers and representatives of the legal profession.*

While existing knowledge derived from the study of delinquency phenomena in Western nations and the few studies carried out in other countries may be applicable to India, the lack of data dealing directly with India made it difficult to devise research devoted to specific hypothesis testing. Consequently, although we were concerned with tapping specific aspects of delinquency phenomena in this undertaking, the lack of prior sociological research dictated that our inquiry be largely exploratory in nature.

Three basic issues became the focus of this research: (1) the types, relative amounts, and distribution of delinquent behavior (or youth crime) in India generally and specifically in one major city and village; (2) the reactions of the Indian public toward delinquency

*Both in India and the United States considerable effort was devoted to securing publications on delinquency and crime in India. Of the handful of works found, almost none were sociological in character and few were based on actual scientific research.

laws and youths who engage in behavior in violation of these laws; and (3) the judicial and correctional treatment of youngsters accused of delinquent acts. In short, we sought to study the occurrence of delinquent behavior and the reactions of adults and official agencies of control toward such conduct—in effect, to study the delinquency "problem" in India in terms of both its behavioral and societal-reaction components.

Comparative Research and the Case of India

Any social condition is potentially a social problem in the sense that some segment of a society or the group as a whole could organize to take collective action to change, ameliorate, or reduce its occurrence or effects. What the members of any society will react to as an adverse condition, the character or type of action they take, and the relative frequency with which they generate social problems are related to certain cultural and social-structural characteristics of the society (Hartjen, 1977; also see Spector and Kitsuse, 1977). Thus, it is likely that societies of similar social-structural and cultural characteristics would react to similar conditions (behaviors) in much the same way and with about equal frequency. Societies that are quite different in one or both of these respects would probably define different conditions as social problems and react to them in different ways and with different rates. It remains unclear, however, just what forces shape societal reactions to social conditions or why some conditions are defined as adverse in some societies but not in others. Little information is available with which to assess these varied possibilities.

One extensive inquiry (Newman, 1976), on which a portion of the present research is based, compared perceptions of "deviance" across six cultures. Considerable cross-cultural consensus regarding the disapproval respondents exhibited toward various acts of crime and deviance was found in this inquiry. However, wide variations in terms of the appropriate form of social control for specific acts occurred. As measured by choice of control agent, respondents in the six countries surveyed tended to group offense types into two general classes—"crime" and "deviance." Interestingly, with a few exceptions, the effect of variables such as age, sex, and occupation appears to be minimal on perceptions of deviance. This was also found to be true in our survey of public perceptions of "delinquency" in rural and urban Tamil Nadu. While there appears to be a cross-cultural consistency in perceptions of "traditional crimes," if not necessarily in perceptions of other forms of "deviance," it also appears that the extent to which people discriminate among various forms of deviance is positively related to economic development.

As with perceptions of deviance, social-problem creations are a function of cultural ideology and the structural arrangements of various interest groups. An analysis of societal reaction toward any specific condition or behavior could reveal the relative impact of ideological orientations and the place of claimsmakers within the stratification-power structure of the society. Such research might also reveal how some conditions come to be defined as matters for concern, made into public issues, and (in some instances) subjected to purposive change, while other conditions are not. But case-study analyses within specific historical and social epochs are inadequate for a more general theoretical understanding of social-problem phenomena.

Sociologists have long recognized the need for cross-national (societal, cultural) or comparative research and the value such research can have for advancing empirical knowledge and theoretical understanding (Marsh, 1967). And in criminology few would dispute the advances that might be gained through a greater number of cross-national studies. While the present study can best be characterized as a case study within a specific locality in India, it may provide information of more general comparative interest, if only by revealing the extent to which delinquency phenomena differ from or resemble one another in a social-cultural setting quite unlike that in which most criminological research has been carried out.

The minimal information available regarding delinquency in many countries, particularly the developing nations of Africa, Asia, and South America, compared with the extensive body of research and theory concerning delinquency in the United States and several European countries makes generalizing about the phenomena tenuous at best. Yet according to several surveys of the literature, a number of conclusions seem reasonable (see Friday and Hage, 1976; Toby, 1979; Friday, 1980; Gibbons, 1981). Although there are a number of exceptions, it appears that the extent of delinquency or youth crime is increasing and has grown considerably since the end of World War II in almost all countries throughout the world. The increase in delinquency rates tends to correspond to the extent of urbanization and industrialization a nation has experienced. Rates of delinquency are considerably higher in the more urban, industrial, affluent societies than in other nations, and regardless of country, rates of delinquency tend to be highest in urban areas. Most offenders are males, outnumbering females at ratios of 5 to 1 or more. Typically, offense behavior peaks in the mid-teens and decreases as individuals reach their early twenties. In most instances, offenders appear to "mature out" of criminality and to largely cease involvement by their mid-twenties. At least with regard to those who come to the attention of legal authorities, delinquents tend to come from slum neighborhoods and families that have a multiplicity of problems. In this respect, there appears to be a correlation between delinquency and a disrupted home environment, poor school performance, and unemployment or poverty. Although wide differences appear to exist with regard to specific forms of criminal activities, most delinquent behavior involves property crimes with personal or assault offenses constituting a small portion of the total.

On the surface, delinquency appears to be not only ubiquitous, it seems to be almost universal in form and the characteristics of those who are involved in it. However, limited research suggests that rather important variations are to be found both in the overall frequency of delinquency in various societies and in the specific forms of conduct in which young people are likely to be involved. First, the most important fact revealed by research in developing countries (see, for example, Cavan and Cavan, 1968; Clinard and Abbott, 1973) is that rates of delinquency are considerably lower in these countries than in the more economically advanced societies of Western Europe and North America. Second, while property crimes or petty acts of illegality make up the bulk of the "delinquency problem" in every society, the specific nature of the delinquency found in these societies is not necessarily identical. Thus, for example, Vaz's (1962) study of gang delinquency in Paris suggests that these gangs differ considerably in form and size from those found in the United States. Because of the lack of criminal syndicates in Paris, the likelihood that gang members would go on to become career criminals is reduced. Similarly, DeFleur's (1967) study of delinquency in Argentina shows that while offenders in Argentina resemble those in the United States in a number of respects, cultural differences between the two countries result in a number of variations in the forms and severity of their delinquency. For instance, while theft is common in both countries, it appears to involve more violence in the United States. Also, shoplifting is a common activity among females in the United States, while in Argentina theft from an employer is more frequent. Moreover, drinking activity varies greatly between the two countries as do the frequency and severity of assaultive behavior. In short, while a number of similarities in delinquent behavior exist throughout the world, important differences also exist.

To anticipate the findings of the present study, delinquency in India is both similar and dissimilar to that found in other nations, particularly the United States. As in other countries, delinquency involvement in India tends to be most heavily concentrated among males from slum neighborhoods or lower socioeconomic backgrounds. Commonly such conduct is pursued by youngsters from physically and otherwise disrupted homes (see, for example, Shanmugam, 1980) and mostly involves property violations. Although delinquent conduct appears to be found in all areas and social strata, official reaction to delinquency is most frequent in urban areas and is directed disproportionately toward minorities and youngsters from lower socioeconomic status groups (a pattern which Sundeen, 1981, found to be true also in Papua New Guinea). As reported by Newman (1976), officials and adults tend to be more concerned with "traditional crimes," such as robbery and serious assault, than with petty crimes or status offenses such as truancy. But overall, Indian officials, as well as the public in general, register little concern with youth crime and delinquency and prefer that such conduct be handled in an informal, nonpunitive manner. Perhaps this attitude reflects, in part, the country's relatively low rate of delinquency, but it may also reflect differences in cultural attitudes or the relative position of young people in the larger social system.

In short, delinquency in India is similar in many ways to general patterns found throughout the world; the types of conduct and characteristics of offenders most often involved in such conduct are particularly similar to those in economically advanced nations. However, delinquent behavior in India differs from that which exists in most other countries in terms of: (1) its relative frequency; (2) the specific forms or patterns of involvement; and (3) the manner in which it is perceived and reacted to by authorities. India thus is an ideal locality for conducting a comparative inquiry of delinquent behavior and the extent and character of societal reaction to it.

Although this book is not strictly "comparative" in a pure sense, our findings reported here do highlight the differences and similarities in the relative occurrence of delinquent behavior and societal reaction to it between a developing country and developed nations such as the United States. In addition, our study analyzes variations within India, particularly those between rural and urban communities.

Structurally India resembles the United States and several other Western nations, since it is a large, heterogeneous society. The bases for subgroup alignments may, of course, differ among these countries—with class being important in the United States while caste is still significant in India.* Were structural factors alone responsible for social-problem creations, we would expect to find similarities in how juvenile misconduct is perceived and reacted to in these societies mediated by, but not totally a function of, the incidence of such behavior. Our research suggests, however, that this is not necessarily the case. That is, juvenile misconduct is not perceived and reacted to the same way in India and, for example, the United States. In part, this may reflect differences in the relative occurrence of delinquent behavior. In effect, the "threat" posed by delinquency, either in terms of its frequency or seriousness, may differ between India and most Western societies. But if this were the case, different communities in India would react to such conduct in similar or different ways depending upon its relative incidence. However, reactions to delinquency in India do not appear to be any more closely related to the amount or type of such conduct that occurs than is true of the United States. Indeed, research shows that the members of different communities exhibit quite similar reactions to delinquency and crime independent of the objective threat they pose (e.g., Stinchcombe et al., 1980). Thus, cultural factors would seem to be related to the variability in societal reaction as much as, and possibly more than, the frequency or types of delinquent behavior found in any locality or the structural relationships among its members. In short, Indians simply do not seem to perceive the "world" in the same terms as Westerners do. They do not, therefore, react to it in the same way.

Although India has been dominated for over two centuries by European nations, Western culture and alterations in the stratification-power arrangements of the country are only today having wide impact. While the nation is still fundamentally "Indian" in character, modernization is taking place at an accelerated rate. As it continues, one can expect increased conflict among subgroups (not necessarily the traditional ones). In this regard, Indians are also likely to exhibit a greater tendency to resemble Westerners by defining certain conditions as adverse and reacting to them as social problems. Although juvenile delinquency may never command the proportions

---

*It should probably be noted that while Indian society is nationally heterogeneous, a good deal of homogeneity exists in local communities. However, even within villages, caste, subcaste, religious, and class differences are quite obvious and well recognized by the residents.

of concern it does in many Western or developed nations, it is quite likely that it will become increasingly a matter of public concern in India in the decades ahead. Thus, as an attempt to document the dimensions of delinquent behavior and the extent and character of societal reaction to it, this study might be read as a case analysis of an incipient social problem.

CHAPTER 2

Methodology

It is the purpose of this chapter to describe the localities in which this research was carried out, the various instruments and data sources utilized, and the methodological procedures followed in conducting the inquiry. To recapitulate the goals of the research, three basic issues were of central interest: (1) the types, relative amounts, and distribution of delinquent behavior in India generally and, specifically, in a major city and village; (2) the perceptions and reactions of Indian adults toward delinquency laws and youths who engage in violations of these laws; and (3) the judicial and correctional treatment of youngsters accused of delinquent acts.

Research Sites

For readers with limited knowledge of contemporary India or the state of Tamil Nadu in which much of our research was conducted, this section provides brief descriptions of some aspects of each research site.

INDIA

Created as a nation in 1947, India is now a federation of twenty-two states and nine union territories (areas governed directly by the Central Government). While united as a nation, India is politically and socially anything but a unified, homogeneous country. Fifteen different languages are recognized by its constitution and over a hundred distinct languages and several hundred dialects not officially recognized are spoken by various groups. Almost 80 percent of

FIGURE 2.1. **Map of India**

the population are Hindus, with Muslims (11 percent) the largest minority. However, not only is Hinduism regionally varied, but scores of subcastes (*jatis*) are regionally recognized throughout the country. While discrimination based on caste or *jati* is illegal, centuries-old relationships and customs are still prevalent (see Gough, 1955; Mandelbaum, 1970; Mencher, 1970; Maddison, 1971). In recent years, in addition to caste and religion, social class has begun to add a new dimension to India's system of stratification.

With over 600 million inhabitants, India is the second most populous nation in the world. In spite of mandatory education, the literacy rate is only slightly over 30 percent. And even though the country is the tenth largest industrial nation in the world, it is predominantly rural, with almost 80 percent of its inhabitants residing in villages and hamlets (Nyrop et al., 1975). Fewer than one-third of the total population are employed, and unemployment and underemployment are major facts of life for most Indians of working age. The population is predominantly young, with over 50 percent below age twenty-one. The birth rate is high (approximately 35 per 1,000), and with a death rate of 11 per 1,000 the country is confronted with a seemingly irreversible population growth rate of over 2.4 percent (*Europa Year Book*, 1978).

Since independence, India has been caught in the throes of nationalism and modernization. It is a land of contrasts and paradoxes wherein modern and traditional mix and sometimes collide. Indeed, it is the mix of the traditional and modern, the ascendance of class over caste and religious affiliation, the increase in industrialization and urban growth with a corresponding increase in rural population density, the conflict of the demands of familism with the liberty of individualism, that is the reality of India in the last quarter of the twentieth century. It is this mix that must be borne in mind if we are to comprehend the nature of delinquency in modern India.

TAMIL NADU

The state of Tamil Nadu (literally, "land of the Tamil speakers") was chosen as the site for this study for two reasons. First, as far as the social and economic characteristics of the several Indian states are concerned, Tamil Nadu appears to represent the mode. Second, one of the authors is a native Tamilian, thus the region presented no language barrier.

The state is located on the southeastern coast of India, approximately eight to fourteen degrees north latitude. Its population, residing in 15,000 villages (20 percent of which have fewer than 500 inhabitants), is predominantly rural, like that of most of India. Approximately 40 percent of the state's 41 million inhabitants are literate, and its population density (317 per sq. km.) is about 50 percent greater than that of the nation in general (*Census of India: Tamil Nadu, Series 19,* 1973). Tamil, one of the Dravidian languages, is the dominant language. Like other southern states, Tamil Nadu was largely spared the Mongol, Mughal, and other Muslim invasions that swept the north. As a result, it and the remaining southern states are socially and culturally quite different from the north. Generally recognized as conservative, the state evidences the political, social, religious, and economic diversity of the nation as a whole.

MADRAS CITY

Founded by the British East India Company in the early 1600s, Madras is today one of the major urban centers of India and the south, and the chief city of Tamil Nadu. The city's population of over 3 million persons within a 128 sq. km. area boasts a literacy rate of over 62 percent. As would be expected, over 99 percent of the working population is engaged in nonagricultural occupations. But the city has a large dependent population, since fewer than 30 percent of its residents are classified as employed (*Census of India: Tamil Nadu, Series 19, 1973*). While the city's population growth is substantial, it appears that most of the growth is a result of internal population increase rather than cityward migration (Nyrop et al., 1975).

Ecologically, the city is unlike any to be found in North American or European countries. There are several major shopping and various residential districts, but the dwellings reflect the wide economic diversity of the city's population. Every manner of housing, from the skin tents of gypsies to mansionlike dwellings, can be found. Street-dwellers are comparatively less visible than in cities like Bombay and Calcutta, but beggars, lepers, street-urchins, and similar individuals abound. And the ever-present cow (and occasionally other animals) can be found on just about any street.

Perhaps of greatest importance sociologically is the blend of different residential dwellings. Neighborhoods are not necessarily homogeneous in that households of every description are found within them. Indeed, the range of housing can be best understood in terms of permanence of dwelling rather than geographic location (Weinstein, 1976: 268). Nevertheless, nearly one-third of the city's residents are classified as slum-dwellers. But, as Wiebe (1976) found, the Madras slum does not resemble the slums found in cities in the United States and other developed countries. According to Wiebe, most Madras slums have a high degree of social integration, political organization, and family solidarity. Family living has remained the prevalent form of life and children are generally well cared for and supervised and often work along with their parents in some type of family enterprise. Poverty and deprivation are certainly facts of life for large segments of Madras' population. But the "culture of poverty" portrayed by several sociologists as promoting despair, crime, and its own perpetuation seems to be absent. Still the contrasts that pervade India prevail also in Madras.

Yet, in spite of the blatant incongruity of life-styles, the wide gap between the rich and the poor, and the assault on tradition demanded by an urban, industrialized environment, urban life in India remains essentially family life; and kinship, traditional values and customs, and the patterns of relationships found in village India have by no means been lost to the urban dweller.

THAMARAIKULAM VILLAGE

Nestled against a low, gently sloping hill, the village of Thamaraikulam is located about 400 miles southwest of Madras in the arid, windswept plains of southcentral Tamil Nadu. Selected in consultation with Indian sociologists and researchers at Madurai University and Gandhigram Institute, the village is not necessarily a "typical" Tamil village, but it has characteristics that make it "representative" of rural Tamil Nadu.

Almost 4,000 people reside in 700 households in the village. Of these households, fewer than 300 have electricity, none have toilet facilities, and very few have running water. The only telephone in the village is located in the tiny sub-post office. Water, a precious commodity, is drawn from the several private wells in addition to the centralized supply via street taps. Caste, religion, and *jati* segregation do appear to be factors as far as settlement patterns are concerned.

Information provided by various village officials allows for a crude statistical picture of the village. With a total population of 3,800, it is one of the larger of Tamil Nadu's villages. The majority of the adults are married, and over 25 percent are over sixty years of age with 37 percent below age eighteen. The estimated per-capita income, per year, is Rs.400–500, an amount that is low compared to city incomes. Almost all workers are employed in agricultural pursuits.

The average landholding is about three acres and, of the inhabitants, only 125 are classified as landowners, a fact which suggests that much of the village land is owned by a small group of families. No Brahmins reside in the village and there are eleven *jatis* among the caste Hindus.* A large community of Muslims reside in their own quarter and Harijans ("untouchables") are physically isolated in a section on the outskirts of the village.

The main governmental authority is the *panchayat* (an ancient institution that was revived in India after independence). The power of the *panchayat* is largely limited to economic matters, but the informal authority of the organization is substantial. Concerns of relevance to the whole village or disputes that cut across *jati* or religious lines are typically arbitrated by the *panchayat*, and it is not uncommon for a parent to bring a wayward youngster before the body for discipline. Membership in the *panchayat* is by direct popular vote. Since the village is divided into wards of unequal size and the *panchayat* members are elected proportionate to the ward's population, it is not surprising that the largest ward dominates the organization and the *panchayat* president resides in that ward.

Since the similarities and differences between delinquency phenomena within rural and urban cultural and social environments are of special interest to this research, these localities provide settings for a number of comparisons. To the extent that Madras city is reflective of the urban population of India and Thamaraikulam residents not unlike the rural population, the findings of this study may have implications for understanding aspects of delinquency beyond the specific localities studied.

Data and Research Methods

Five sources of data provided information regarding the various aspects of delinquency investigated in this study. First, a self-report questionnaire was constructed and administered to samples of urban and rural high school and institutionalized boys to measure the types, amount, and distribution of illegal activity. Second, to tap public sentiment toward delinquency laws and juvenile misconduct, a survey of urban and rural adults was carried out employing an instrument created specifically to measure their opinions, know-

―――――――――
*Hindus who are not Harijans ("untouchables").

ledge, and attitudes. Third, the judicial and correctional treatment of apprehended juveniles was investigated through in-depth interviews with officials in these fields and through extensive observations of several correctional facilities. Fourth, a content analysis of three newspapers with large circulation was carried out in order to gain some understanding of why the public holds particular opinions regarding juvenile delinquency. Finally, a variety of available data was collected, including census reports, official statistics on crime and delinquency, media discussions, and numerous interviews with people in all walks of life as well as recognized experts on crime and delinquency in India.

SELF-REPORT STUDY

Essentially there are three ways to estimate the extent and distribution of various forms of illegal behavior within any group or population (see Empey, 1982, for a discussion of these measures in relation to delinquency research). Most typically, official counts (if collected) of known or detected crimes have been used by criminologists to make and test hypotheses regarding the epidemiology (or incidence) of illegal conduct. Although such official statistics were used in this study, it must be noted that they suffer from a number of drawbacks and are, at best, questionable measures of the actual incidence of criminal or delinquent behavior occurring in a population. Particularly in Third World countries where the compilation of relevant statistics may be lacking or inaccurate, estimates on the extent of delinquent behavior based on this source alone are highly unreliable. Moreover, comparisons among countries may be impossible because of differences in recording practices, categorization, laws, and similar factors.

Victimization surveys provide a second source of delinquency data. However, these also tend to be unreliable. In many cases the victim may not know the age of the perpetrator or may estimate the age erroneously. An alternative means to judge the actual extent of illegal behavior on the part of juveniles has been found in self-report studies. Beginning with the work of Porterfield (1943), a substantial number of self-report investigations have been undertaken, especially in the United States, Canada, and England (Murphy et al., 1946; Short and Nye, 1958; Reiss and Rhodes, 1961; Dentler and Monroe, 1961; Akers, 1964; Voss, 1966; McDonald, 1969; Batta et al., 1975; Shapland, 1978). The results of these inquiries have been surprisingly similar. They show that delinquent conduct is widespread, is found (although with somewhat different frequencies and involving different types of behavior) among all social classes and ethnic groups, and tends to be higher among adjudicated offenders, although it is common among all youth.

Asking someone to admit to their illegal behavior may, of course, raise a number of questions regarding validity. Subjects may under- or over-report their conduct. Outright lying or simple lapse of memory pose problems whether a questionnaire or interview technique is used. Second, the significance of various acts may not be the same for different populations of young people. Questions regarding defying parents, engaging in gangfights, and the like could produce quite different results depending upon how respondents interpret the questions. This is an especially acute problem when cross-national comparisons of self-report findings are attempted.

Nevertheless, a large number of studies concerning the issue of validity do seem to indicate that on the whole self-report investigations, regardless of technique, do solicit reasonably accurate responses, at least with regard to the types of acts typically included in this kind of research (see Clark and Tifft, 1966; Gibson et al., 1970; Blackmore, 1974; Hardt and Hardt, 1977; Hindelang et al., 1981). As a measure of the overall occurrence and distribution of delinquency, self-report studies cannot be used alone since few of them cover the totality of acts for which young people could be adjudged delinquent, and the samples so far studied have been too small to generalize for the entire population of young people within any country (Elliott and Ageton, 1980). However, as a basis for estimating the relative occurrence and distribution of delinquent behavior within a population or the subgroups of a population, self-reported delinquency is apparently a useful measure.

In light of previous research, it seems reasonable to assert that self-reported delinquency does provide a basis for an accurate estimation of the relative involvement of various groups of young people in delinquent conduct—at least in those acts included in the specific instrument—and that one can generalize the relative types, frequency, and distribution of delinquent acts for the larger population from samples of respondents. Thus, if one were to find that substantial differences in reported behavior occurred for any subgroups within a population, it would be legitimate to conclude that these subgroups are, in fact, likely to be involved in different types of misconduct with different frequencies. Moreover, to the extent that significant variables affecting the reporting of behavior are controlled, randomized, or operate with equal force across populations (e.g., cross-culturally), self-report studies offer a viable means of comparing delinquency in different populations.

Instrument: The questionnaire used in this study was based on earlier research among American youngsters (e.g., Short and Nye, 1958; Akers, 1964). The instrument was originally constructed in English and then translated into Tamil. It was then "back translated" into English for verification (Schachter, 1954) and reviewed by several Tamil scholars and lay judges for usage and phraseology. Since formal Tamil and colloquial Tamil are quite different, the colloquial usage was followed throughout. The questionnaire covered the spectrum of activities (see Appendix A) ranging from status offenses, property and personal crimes of varying severity, to "morals" offenses such as drinking alcohol and using drugs. Nowhere on the instrument or at no time during the course of its administration was it suggested that any of these acts were illegal. In this respect, one might argue that what was being measured was self-perceived involvement in behavior rather than self-perceived involvement in delinquent behavior (Gibson, 1971).

Respondents were asked to indicate their involvement in each of the offenses by placing a check mark before one of four ("no," "once or twice," "several times," and "often/frequently") possible choice categories. The ordering of response categories was reversed on several questions to avoid "patterned" responses or systematic choice of a particular category (Warwick and Lenninger, 1975: 147). Since younger respondents (fourteen years of age or younger) would not have been susceptible to judicial processing below the age of eleven for several of the offenses, a time frame of the three years preceding the survey was set in which any of the acts could have occurred. Four questions concerning the youngsters' involvement with judicial authorities were included and basic demographic data such as age, education, and guardian's occupation were solicited at the beginning of the questionnaire.

Sampling Procedures: Completed questionnaires were received from 517 high school boys and 306 inmates of boys' approved schools in Tamil Nadu. Girls were excluded from the study, since few of them were to be found in correctional institutions (less than thirty at the time of this study) and according to our informants, most of those who were institutionalized were apprehended for prostitution.

Approximately 8,000 youngsters (almost all of them male) were in the various juvenile correctional facilities called "approved schools," both public and private, of Tamil Nadu. From a list of these schools provided by the Directorate of Correctional Administration and Approved Schools, four schools (two private and two public) were selected. Although several other schools in the state were visited in the course of the research, these four schools were purposively selected because they housed youngsters in the age category of interest and were within reasonable access to Madras. Limited time and resources prohibited self-report research in schools located beyond commuting distance from Madras. From our observations and interviews, however, we have no reason to believe that the schools selected are in any way atypical of approved schools throughout the state.

The two private approved schools are designated (as were all private approved schools) "junior" approved schools. Of the public schools, one is a junior and the other a senior approved school. In all four schools, all the boys of ninth and tenth standard (grade) age (approximately fourteen years old) present at the school during the survey period who were willing to participate in the study were asked to complete the questionnaire. In all but one instance a census of all available boys was obtained, and none refused to participate and complete the questionnaire. Since very few boys in any of the institutions were unavailable (being in the hospital, on home leave, etc.), we were able to administer the instrument to almost all boys of the target age. Although sample sizes differed substantially among the four schools (they ranged from 120 to 26), they were large enough for statistical analysis.

To compare the behavior of these "official delinquents" with that of boys not in correctional institutions, ninth and tenth standard boys in six Madras city high schools for boys and the eighth standard (there being no higher grade) students in Thamaraikulam village were surveyed. The Director of Public Instruction for Tamil Nadu (the official in charge of elementary and secondary schools) provided a list of all schools under the Directorate's jurisdiction. These consisted of corporation (or public) schools and private aided schools (schools that receive some state aid). Since there are reasons to believe that the mostly industrialized northern and mostly suburban southern parts of the city are substantially different in their socioeconomic composition, two corporation and two private aided schools were randomly selected from each of the two areas. Corporation schools (which include the village school) tend to recruit students from somewhat lower socioeconomic groups than do private aided schools, and closely resemble city schools in the United States. Families able to manage the minimal tuition costs are more likely to send their children to private aided as opposed to corporation schools.

The majority of youths from upper-middle-class and professional families attend private (nonaided) schools that teach in English and tend to be associated with some religious organization. For this reason, two private schools, one each from the northern and southern areas of Madras, were chosen in order to cover the spectrum of social classes.

Since the schools varied both in their number of students and their number of ninth and tenth standard sections, either a census of all ninth and tenth standard students present on the day of the survey was obtained or one ninth and one tenth standard class from schools having more than one section was selected using a table of random numbers. In one private school, however, a random selection was impossible since the assistant headmaster simply assigned us two classes that had their free period during our scheduled visit. We have no reason to assume that these respondents differed in any substantial way from the other students in the school. The sample sizes drawn from each school ranged from a high of 111 to a low of 31.

As with the institutionalized respondents, subjects were given the option of participating in the survey and, with only one or two exceptions (because they could not read or write Tamil), all those present completed the questionnaire. Table 2.1 presents the socioeconomic characteristics of the samples drawn from the combined high schools and approved schools.

Administration of Instrument: Factors beyond our control (physical facilities of the schools, administrative considerations, etc.) made it impossible to follow identical procedures in administering the questionnaire. In all schools, however, we were present during the survey and were aided by two or more research assistants. Standardized procedures were followed as closely as possible. The research staff paid considerable attention to preventing teachers from overseeing the boys answering the questionnaire and to ensuring that boys did not look at or try to influence the responses of others. In the vast majority of instances, each boy was interviewed immediately following the completion of the instrument to verify answers and ensure completion.

While we cannot know to what extent, if any, procedural variations, presence of teachers, or the "help" some boys may have given

TABLE 2.1. **Percentage Distribution of the Socioeconomic Characteristics of High School and Approved School Respondents**

Characteristic	High school	Approved school
Age		
8–10	0.0	0.7
11–13	19.1	28.4
14–16	68.7	55.6
17 +	12.2	15.4
	(517)	(306)
Education		
3 years or less	0.0	0.3
4–6 years	0.0	45.4
7–9 years	84.1	51.3
10–12 years	15.9	2.9
	(517)	(306)
Occupation of guardian		
Professional	5.5	1.7
Manager	30.4	2.5
Clerical	15.0	4.1
Skilled worker	19.4	20.2
Unskilled worker	25.1	47.1
Farm owner	0.6	3.7
Farm worker	4.0	5.8
Petty-shop keeper	0.0	14.9
	(506)	(242)
Annual income of guardian		
Less than Rs.2,000	30.5	62.6
Rs.2,000–Rs.4,999	32.3	25.6
Rs.5,000–Rs.9,999	21.5	10.5
Rs.10,000 +	15.7	1.3
	(511)	(238)
Religion		
Hindu	82.2	80.7
Muslim	6.2	5.9
Christian	9.5	12.1
None/Don't Know	1.7	1.0
	(515)	(305)

Note: Number in parentheses = total number of respondents.

others biased or influenced the results, we felt reasonably confident after our conversations with the boys that they generally gave candid answers to the questions and that the extent of over- and under-reporting was either minimal or random.

On the whole, the administration of the questionnaire went smoothly. Since such "objective" tests are a rather new phenomenon in India, the boys seemed to consider the survey an interesting and exciting activity. The presence of a (white) foreign professor lent an air of importance to the event. The general rapport established between the research staff and the students and the fact that some strangers were showing an active interest in the boys both facilitated our carrying out the survey and increased our confidence in the validity of the responses.

PUBLIC ATTITUDE SURVEY

Although they are surely related, there is no necessary direct correlation between the frequency or seriousness of youthful misconduct and the extent, nature, or severity of the public's reaction to it. That is, any group might exhibit considerable concern over and attempt to "do something about" social conditions which do not objectively warrant such concern. The reverse is also possible (see Becker, 1966; Spector and Kitsuse, 1977).

In democratic societies such as those of the United States and India, public policy ideally reflects the wishes, attitudes, and opinions of the electorate. While literacy levels may affect the number of informed participants and the extent to which members of a society are likely to become aware of public issues, phenomena of general social relevance—such as youthful misconduct—are likely to be things about which most individuals hold opinions. In recent years a number of studies in the United States have been designed to measure or assess public knowledge of and sentiments toward criminal offenders, law, and correctional and judicial procedures, and several surveys have been conducted on the issue of public fear of crime (see Hartjen, 1978: 45–49 for a summary). Much of this research has sought to determine the relationship between public policy and public opinion or to evaluate the validity of fears concerning crime by comparing survey results with data on the occurrence of crimes and victimizations. However these investigations can also be interpreted as measuring the extent to which people perceive of crime and delinquency as matters of concern (i.e., social problems) and deserving of societal reaction.

Since it is our purpose here not only to assess the character and occurrence of juvenile delinquency in India, but also to investigate the extent to which juvenile misbehavior is considered a problem by the Indian populace, a public attitude survey was designed and administered to samples of urban and rural adults. It was our intention to tap the following four dimensions of public perceptions: (1) opinions regarding delinquency laws; (2) knowledge of these laws; (3) attitudes regarding to whom the offenders should be reported; and (4) attitudes as to what penalty should be imposed upon the offenders. We wanted to compare these results to delinquency statutes, judicial and correctional practices, and where possible, similar information obtained from other research. In addition, we sought to measure the divergence in knowledge and attitudes in terms of social demographic variables. This was done for two reasons: to determine the unanimity or disparity in public sentiments regarding juvenile delinquency, and to enable us to draw theoretically relevant conclusions regarding societal perceptions of and reaction to a social condition that is generally considered a serious problem in the Western world.

Instrument: The schedule designed for this study was modeled after an earlier instrument used in a cross-cultural study of public attitudes toward deviance (see Newman, 1976); however, the specific questions asked and the forms of behavior included were changed for the present study. An English language version of the instrument was translated into colloquial Tamil and was critiqued by both Tamil scholars and Tamil-speaking sociologists. In addition, several laypersons were asked to review the instrument for readability and cultural relevance. It was then "back translated" for verification.

The initial questionnaire was pretested on a sample of thirty adults from three randomly drawn census tracts of Madras city. A female respondent was interviewed for every male respondent contacted, a younger person for each older repondent, and for every middle-class or upper-class respondent a person of apparent lower class was interviewed. We solicited as much feedback about the instrument as possible. Each of the pretest interviews, therefore, took two or more hours to complete. In both the pretest and final version of the instrument, response categories were randomized to prevent automatic response patterns.

Based on our tallies of the responses to the original instrument and the respondents' comments regarding specific questions, we eliminated nine scenarios from the original thirty-six and generally revised the instrument in terms of wording, story construction, and offenses included. This resulted in a total of twenty-five abridged, hypothetical situations covering the same spectrum of offenses as the pretest version. Some of these acts are explicitly prohibited as crimes by the Indian Penal Code; others fall under one or another provision of the Madras Children Act and are largely status offenses forbidden only juveniles. Some acts (e.g., truancy) are not specifically prohibited, but could be grounds for a "delinquency" disposition under the "uncontrollable" and other omnibus provisions of the Children Act.

The projective scenarios included in the instrument were chosen according to the following criteria: (1) they had to be flexible enough to introduce culturally relevant stimuli for the respodents (i.e., they could be committed by different types of offenders or occur under varied circumstances); (2) they had to allow for individualized responses but at the same time they must enable the classification of responses into standardized categories; and (3) they had to make sense to the respondents (i.e., they had to involve activities or situations that could, in fact, happen).

Each scenario was followed by four questions: (1) *Should* this act be prohibited by law (a measure of opinion)? (2) *Is* this act prohibited by law (a measure of knowledge)? (3) To *whom*, if anyone, would you report the person engaged in this act? and (4) *What*, if anything, should be done to the person engaged in this act? The latter two questions are measures of attitudes or likely reactions to the offense.* In addition, standard demographic information was solicited from each respondent.

Since it was assumed that reactions to illegal behavior might vary depending upon personal victimization, respondents were asked if they had been victims of crimes, if they had reported any victimizations, and, if not, why. Since fewer than 5 percent of the total sample reported having been crime victims, the results of these items have been largely excluded from the analysis of the data obtained from this survey.

Conceptualizations of acts as criminal or delinquent offenses require conceptualizations of some agent or person as an offender (Hartjen, 1981). Public attitudes or reactions toward juvenile misconduct, therefore, are not only likely to vary depending upon the char-

---

*This term is defined in a multitude of ways (Allport, 1967; Chein, 1967; Katz and Braly, 1967), most of which suggest that attitudes include one or more of the following components: (1) they are learned; (2) they are habitual and not ad hoc behaviors; (3) they can be toward any object such as persons, groups, values, or behavior; and (4) they vary in degree of affectivity. Here attitude is defined briefly as a predisposition to respond to juvenile misconduct in a patterned way.

acteristics of the specific act but also in terms of the characteristics of the person engaged in the activity. Thus, while respondents might generally agree that armed robbery, for instance, should be illegal and should be punished by some judicial authority, in concrete cases the actual attitudes of respondents or their reactions to a particular offense might be mediated by the social characteristics of the person who had engaged in it (Newman, 1974). For this reason, the twenty-five scenarios included in the instrument consisted of brief descriptions of some illegal act, the circumstances of its occurrence, and the social characteristics of the offender. For twenty of the twenty-five offenses, the social characteristics of the offender were varied in terms of age, sex, or social class so that in one instance the offender was described as a girl while for an identical offense the offender was depicted as a boy. Similar paired variations were used for the age and social class of the protagonists. Where no variation in offender characteristics was being measured (the offense itself being the factor of interest), the age and social class of the person were left ambiguous and the offender was simply described as a boy (see Appendix B). The distribution of paired-variation stories in the questionnaire was randomized.

Sampling Procedures: The 1971 (most recent) Census of Madras city divides the city into 120 enumerated census tracts or districts. Using a table of random numbers, a random starting point was chosen and a systematic one-sixth (twenty tracts) sample of the census tracts was then selected. From these twenty selected tracts, a proportionate multistage, random sample of 603 adults (about .02 percent of the city's population) was drawn for the urban subsample of the target population. This provided a total sample of about one out of every 5,000 residents.

Respondents were selected by means of the following procedure. The Census enumerates all the blocks or streets located within each tract and lists the door numbers of each dwelling or building (some of which are multifamily dwellings) on each street. The populations of the selected tracts varied from 12,072 to 38,330. Therefore, on the basis of its population, a proportionate, random sample of streets was drawn from each of the twenty census tracts. This was accomplished by dividing each tract's population by the total population of the twenty selected tracts and multiplying the fraction by our target sample size of 600. Two respondents were selected from each of the streets included in the sample. The sample sizes per tract, thus, varied from eighteen to forty-eight respondents.

The interviewers were instructed to pick respondents only from the houses or door numbers listed in the Census for each street included in the sample. Although allowed to interview any two adults from a selected street, interviewers were told to survey an equal number of men and women, older and younger persons, and persons of apparent higher and lower income. This allowed for an adequate diversification of the sample population for comparative purposes.

In each designated area interviews were conducted on various days of the week at varied times of the day so that employed and unemployed persons, and individuals who might not be accessible during certain hours, could be contacted. Interviewers were trained by the investigators and frequent meetings were held to discuss any problems related to the survey. Spot checks were made of each interviewer to verify that they were following procedures and were, in fact, carrying out the interviews.

Based on interviews of the survey team, we estimated that the rejection rate in general was below 5 percent, and the interviewers reported little reluctance on the part of respondents to answer the questions and spend the one and one-half hours it typically took to complete the interview. Since survey research is comparatively new in India and since being asked for their "opinion" is a novelty that few Indians have ever experienced, the survey was remarkably easy to carry out and resulted in an amazingly high response and completion rate.* Because of the problem of illiteracy, it was necessary that the questionnaire be read verbatim by the interviewers to each respondent. This allowed some control over interviewing error (Hudson and Brady, 1959) as well as probes when respondents chose the "other" or "don't know" categories as answers. Any potential respondent who did not understand Tamil or who was not a resident of the city was excluded from the sample. The investigators conducted in-depth interviews with about twenty-five of the respondents throughout the city. These persons were randomly chosen from a list of respondents' addresses noted down by interviewers on the reverse of the completed schedule. This procedure helped verify the information recorded on the questionnaires and enabled us to obtain a firsthand "feeling" for the survey data.

---

*There were two exceptions. Muslim women (because of cultural restrictions) were reluctant to speak to male interviewers and a female interviewer was assigned to contact these respondents. The fishermen in one area (who were politically active at the time of the survey) refused to be interviewed, so a second district had to be substituted.

As in the city, the sample of Thamaraikulam village was a random, proportionate sample. The limited size of the village population and the physical structure of the village allowed for a more rigorous sample design and procedure. The total population of the village of 3,653 people resided in 700 households. The village *panchayat* provided information on the number of persons residing in each household and their ages. The village was divided into four electoral wards. Wards one and four each consisted of two blocks of houses, while the second and third wards had a block of houses each. Three hundred of the seven hundred households were located in ward one. There were 101, 174, and 125 households respectively in wards two, three, and four. Each ward tended to be more or less homogeneous in *jati* and class. Using a random starting point, every third household in each ward was selected for the sample. If no respondent was available in a designated household, the next immediate household was substituted. Since the wards reflected the caste, religious, and class composition of the village, this systematic, proportionate sample gave a fairly representative group of village respondents.

The sample size for each ward was determined by dividing the number of households in the ward by the total number of households in the village and multiplying that fraction by the target sample of 200 respondents. Thus, samples of households proportionate to each ward's contribution to the village were drawn. One adult per household was interviewed. An equal number of males and females were included. Interviewers were instructed to vary the selection of respondents by age. Very few rejections were encountered by the two male interviewers. Interviews were conducted at different times of the day so that men and women working in the fields could be included in the sample.

As with the urban survey, the questionnaires were read verbatim by the interviewers to each respondent. For some reason, this took somewhat longer in the village than in the city, averaging approximately two hours per interview. Villagers exhibited a somewhat greater tendency to "get off the track." Indeed, it was not unusual for respondents to describe instances of behavior they had known in actual life that were similar to those depicted in the survey instrument. Interestingly it was always some neighbor's child who was the miscreant, never one of the respondent's children.

Table 2.2 provides details of the demographic characteristics of the respondents sampled in Madras city and Thamaraikulam village.

TABLE 2.2. **Distribution of the Socioeconomic Characteristics of Rural and Urban Respondents**

Characteristic	Thamaraikulam		Madras		Total	
	N	%	N	%	N	%
Sex						
Female	100	50.0	272	45.1	372	46.0
Male	100	50.0	331	54.9	431	54.0
Age						
18–29	73	36.5	212	35.3	285	36.0
30–39	55	27.5	191	31.6	246	31.0
40+	72	36.0	200	33.1	272	33.0
Education						
None	84	42.0	50	8.3	134	17.0
1–8 years	87	43.5	188	31.1	275	34.0
9–11 years	22	11.0	180	29.8	202	25.0
Some college	3	1.5	81	13.4	84	10.0
B.A.	4	2.0	83	13.7	87	11.0
M.A.+	0	0.0	18	2.9	18	2.0
No answer	0	0.0	3	0.4	3	0.4
Occupation						
Professional	9	4.5	79	13.1	88	11.0
Mgr./proprietor	14	7.0	94	15.6	108	13.0
Clerical	9	4.5	120	19.9	129	15.0
Skilled worker	23	11.5	125	20.7	148	19.0
Unskilled worker	16	8.0	129	21.4	145	18.0
Farm owner	33	16.5	3	0.5	36	5.0
Farm worker	87	43.5	1	0.2	88	11.0
Petty-shop keeper	7	3.5	30	5.0	37	5.0
No answer	2	1.0	22	3.6	24	3.0
Income (per month)						
Less than Rs.200	99	49.5	142	23.5	241	30.0
Rs.201–Rs.400	63	31.5	122	20.2	185	23.0
Rs.401+	33	16.5	314	52.1	347	43.0
No answer	5	2.5	25	4.2	30	4.0
Religion						
Hindu	182	91.0	515	85.4	697	87.0
Muslim	15	7.5	33	5.5	48	6.0
Christian	2	1.0	51	8.5	53	7.0
No answer	1	0.5	4	0.6	5	0.6
Crime victim						
Yes	20	10.0	17	2.8	37	5.0
No	174	87.0	579	96.0	753	94.0
No answer	6	3.0	7	1.2	13	1.0

MEDIA ANALYSIS

The images a person has of the world and his or her place within it are sustained by the various groups with which one is in immediate contact. In literate societies, the influence of peers, family, and community is accompanied by an additional force—the mass media. In this respect, mass media provide a framework or reference source by which members of a society acquire perceptions of social reality. As Allport (1958) argued, the media play a significant role in creating and reinforcing one's images of the world and the various groups in one's society.

While the effects of mass media have been investigated to some extent in Western societies, their role in Third World countries has not as yet been fully assessed. Lerner's (1958) classic work on the Middle East, however, does show the importance of newspapers on the lives of at least class-conscious individuals. Similarly, Mishra's (1970) research on the impact of the media in a New Delhi slum suggests that the media play a key role in raising the political consciousness of some individuals. To the extent that the media influence general consciousness and awareness (see Lee, 1946; Klopper, 1960), they likewise serve to shape images of specific conditions as social problems. Ross and Staines (1972), for example, argue that as vehicles of propaganda, the media not only shape public consciousness as to what conditions are to be thought of as adverse, but also characterize the problematic nature of various conditions and the degree of concern people should have with regard to such conditions. This is particularly true with regard to crime and delinquency. Although limited research is available, public concern over crime and delinquency as social problems quite clearly reflects the attention paid to illegality and the manner in which such conduct is portrayed by the media (Davis, 1952; Quinney, 1974; Hubbard et al., 1975; Winick, 1978).

In developing, as in developed, countries relatively few people have any direct and immediate experience with crime and delinquency. Thus one principal source of information about these phenomena is the mass media. In India and other Third World countries, the main vehicle of social awareness in this respect is the press.* An adequate understanding of public perceptions of and reactions to crime and delinquency requires that sociologists pay attention to the kinds and amounts of information made available to people regarding these phenomena.

*As in the United States, the press in India is a "free" press.

Three large-circulation newspapers available to Tamilians were selected for this analysis. *The Hindu* (circulation 270,000) and *The Indian Express* (circulation 212,600)), both of which are English language morning dailies, and the *Dina Tanthi* (literally, the "Daily Telegraph," circulation 252,300), which is a Tamil language (morning) daily. *The Hindu* is published in Madras and circulated throughout the south of India. The other two papers are published in various locations, with *Dina Tanthi* limited in circulation to Tamil speakers. Of the six newspapers regularly published in the region, these three have the largest circulation. Actual readership is probably considerably greater than circulation figures suggest for at least two reasons: (1) as in most poor countries, each copy of a newspaper may be read by several people; and (2) it is quite common for a literate person to read a newspaper aloud to an audience of persons unable to purchase or read a newspaper. The three papers listed were also selected for their wide spectrum of style—conservative to sensational.

All news relating to crime, criminal justice, law, and related matters was recorded by the investigators each day for two three-month periods. The following details were recorded: (1) page location of the story (front versus other); (2) the number of lines devoted to each story; and (3) the number of pages in each issue of the paper. This allowed us to compare the volume of coverage for these papers over time both in regard to crime and matters relating to it (e.g., the passage of criminal laws, reorganization of the police force, etc.) Brief descriptions of each story were recorded for categorization and future reference.

The stories were categorized according to their predominant focus and the most serious offense they described. Thus, for example, if a specific story concerned a robbery and murder, it was categorized as a "personal" offense. If a description or report on a robbery alone was covered, it was categorized as a "property" offense. The following eight categories were used to sort stories into types: (1) riots/demonstrations; (2) prohibition offenses; (3) political crime; (4) personal crime; (5) property crime; (6) news concerning the criminal justice system; (7) news concerning criminal law; and (8) other. All coding of the stories was carried out individually by the investigators and the coding of one was verified by the other.

The time frame for this analysis was determined by the period in which the research was undertaken. Our original intention was to analyze all news for a three-month period, from mid-February to mid-May. We hoped this work would provide us with a basic understanding of the characterization of delinquency as a social problem in

India before we embarked on other phases of the research. Once we started reading the papers, however, we realized that in the aftermath of Indira Gandhi's defeat, much of the space devoted to "crime" news consisted of rather long and detailed discussions of Gandhi's alleged illegal behavior. Consequently, we decided that another three-month period, that following our return to Madras from fieldwork in the village, would be studied. This period covered the months of September, October, and November. As we anticipated and subsequently found to be true, as coverage of Gandhi's "political" crimes decreased, greater attention was devoted to the more traditional forms of criminal behavior and crime-related issues. While a content analysis of crime news for the entire period of this research would have been desirable, the extremely time-consuming and tedious nature of the work, coupled with the other demands of our inquiry, restricted the amount of attention that could be devoted to media analysis. Nevertheless, the findings of this study do cast some light on the extent and kinds of information on crime made available to Tamilians and, thereby, add to our understanding of their opinions of and reactions to delinquent behavior.

INTERVIEWS WITH OFFICIALS

The manner in which juvenile offenders are handled in India was assessed through in-depth interviews with judicial and correctional personnel as well as extensive site visits to eight correctional facilities and the Madras city juvenile court. Within Tamil Nadu, four approved schools (three male and one female) and three private (two male and one coed) institutions housing some approved wards as well as orphans and destitute youngsters were observed. In addition, the approved school in the city of Hyderabad (located in the neighboring state of Andhra Pradesh) was investigated. The judicial and correctional systems of this state are quite similar to those found in Tamil Nadu.

The interviews with officials were free-format interviews but solicited information on a predetermined set of issues as well as other topics. Since we sought in-depth information on staff attitudes regarding a number of diverse topics concerning the treatment of delinquents, a relaxed, informal approach wherein rapport could be maintained was thought best. To avoid losing desired information through informal chitchat, the interviews were directed to discussions of the programs, facilities, and "treatment" policies of the various institutions. In addition, we sought to gain insights into the ideology and attitudes of judicial and correctional personnel as far as delinquent behavior and its treatment were concerned. During the course of the interviews, notes on specific details (such as budget, population of inmates, staff composition, and the like) regarding the institutions were recorded with the consent of the respondents. Field notes concerning the information received from the conversations, the physical characteristics of the institutions, the physical condition of the wards, and similar matters were recorded immediately after each interview. Both investigators were present at the interviews and in several instances the project director was also present.

Similarly, staff members of the six high schools in which self-report questionnaires were administered were interviewed concerning the behavior of the youngsters within each of the schools and the actions school officials take with "misbehaving" students. In all instances, any specific data regarding the school was noted during the course of the interviews and extensive field notes were written immediately after each visit. Besides information obtained from interviews, observations and impressions of research staff were also incorporated in the field notes.

In all, more than twenty-five persons were interviewed, including institutional and school officials, local criminologists, lawyers, judicial personnel, and various experts dealing with juvenile offenders or young people in general.

MISCELLANEOUS INFORMATION

In addition to the above data, a variety of information was collected from libraries and other sources. These include census data, official statistics on crime and juvenile delinquency, documents and statistics on correctional programs, published studies and accounts of crime and delinquency, and other available data. Finally, numerous discussions regarding adolescents and juvenile crime were carried out with people from different social strata.

Conclusion

This study relied upon diverse methods and data bases in order to gain a variety of information regarding juvenile delinquency in India generally and in urban and rural localities in the state of Tamil Nadu specifically. The major questions addressed in the research were explored through a self-reported delinquency study of young people in high schools and approved schools, a public attitude survey among rural and urban residents to measure their perceptions of various forms of behavior, and a content analysis of three regional newspapers for their portrayal of crime- and delinquency-related news. Samples in both the self-report and attitude surveys were random samples and the instruments used were pretested and adapted to suit the Indian context. In addition, a large amount of interview data were obtained and other available data were collected from diverse sources.

PART TWO

Delinquent Behavior: Official and Self-reported

CHAPTER 3

Delinquency Laws and Official Delinquency

Societal reaction to behavior considered deviant is predicated on a perception of threat—a judgment by reactors that the behavior in question is in some way detrimental to their values, interests, or well-being. Often the interests felt to be threatened are reflected in the norms of the group and may be codified in formal law. Norms or, more specifically, laws can themselves be seen as a form of societal reaction to perceived threats and serve to legitimize more-direct, instrumental action to control the behavior of groups considered threatening (see Gusfield, 1963; Chambliss and Seidman, 1971). The enactment of specific laws and collective action taken with respect to them can thus be understood as instances of social-problem production. The laws passed and the scope (frequency and extent) of their enforcement draw the boundaries of the problem. Thus, it is appropriate to begin our analysis of delinquency in India by describing delinquency laws and the amount and kinds of juvenile behavior authorities record in violation of these laws.

Laws Applicable to Juveniles

Since much of India was under British rule during the colonial period, contemporary Indian law closely resembles British law. However, many areas of the country were independent kingdoms and after independence the various states chose to enact legislation independently, particularly in regard to juvenile crime. Hence, as in the United States, laws concerning juveniles vary somewhat from state to state. While most delinquency laws are similar to those in the United States and England, several states in India have not yet enacted such legislation and in some places where it does exist, little serious effort has been made to enforce the provisions of the law. Because they are directly ruled by the Central Government, Union Territories come under the provisions of the Indian Criminal and Procedure Codes and the Indian Children Act enacted in 1960. While the Criminal and Procedure Codes also apply in the various states, Children Acts and a variety of special and local laws may or may not exist in specific states.

LEGAL HISTORY

Separate legislation for children in India began with the Apprentice Act of 1850. This law, which provided for the bonding of female and male children between the ages of ten and eighteen, stipulated that a father or guardian could bond a child to an employer for a period of seven years (not to continue past the age of twenty-one) for the purpose of learning a trade or craft. Specifically intended to benefit orphaned or poor children dependent on public charity, the law also pertained to children accused of petty offenses and authorized a magistrate to commit such children to an employer as apprentices (Central Bureau of Correctional Services, 1970).

Enacted in 1860, the Indian Penal Code detailed the age limitations of criminal culpability, and the Reformatory School Act passed in 1876 and modified in 1897 established distinctive machinery for dealing with youthful offenders. This law empowered the court to send youthful offenders (boys only) under fifteen years of age who had been sentenced to transportation or imprisonment to a reformatory school for a period of not less than three or more than seven years. It also established regulations concerning the standards for and administration of such schools. In conjunction with this law, the Code of Criminal Procedure, written in 1861 and modified several times thereafter, contained three sections (298, 399, and 562) which provided for the trial of any person under age fifteen and their confinement in a reformatory or placement on probation.

The first Children Act was enacted in Madras province (now Tamil Nadu) in 1920. Bengal and Bombay provinces enacted similar laws in 1922 and 1924 respectively. These laws explicitly provided for the custody, trial, and punishment of youthful offenders as well as for the protection of children and young persons (see below for definitions of these terms). Several other states followed the Madras example in the ensuing years, but it was not until after independence that Chidren Acts were passed in many of the newly created states. The All India Children Act, passed in 1960, introduced some new features, the most important of which provided for the separate handling of destitute and delinquent children. It was not until 1969, however, that the idea of separate procedures for and laws pertaining to juveniles spread throughout most of the Indian subcontinent.

CONTEMPORARY LAWS

All states and Union Territories in India are covered by the Indian Penal Code and Code of Criminal Procedure. However, all states are free to enact specific legislation for children and at this writing all but four states have passed their own Children Act. In Union Territories the All India Children Act of the Central Government applies and stands as a model for the various states. Uniformity in terms of age limitations for criminal culpability and the procedures to be followed in processing juvenile offenders is provided by the Indian Penal Code and Code of Criminal Procedure. The Children Acts of the various states, however, are quite diverse in their provisions and coverage. Age designations, for example, vary considerably. Three states define a "child" as any person below the age of eighteen. Age sixteen has been established as the upper limit in five states. Four states, as well as the Central Government, differentiate age limits for boys and girls; the central government and the laws of three states define a boy as a child below age sixteen and a girl as a child below the age of eighteen. One state stipulates these ages as eighteen and twenty respectively. Tamil Nadu differs from the other states in that it distinguishes between a "child" and a "young person." According to Tamil Nadu law, a child is any person below the age of fourteen, while a young person is between the ages of fourteen and eighteen. As explained below, these distinctions are pertinent to the judicial processing of juveniles in Tamil Nadu.

The laws of eight states, as well as the All India Children Act, make provisions for "neglected" children; however, the specific wording of the various laws differs considerably. In general neglected children, as defined by the laws, include those who are begging, homeless, destitute, or orphaned; those who associate with unfit persons such as theives or prostitutes; and those whose parents are either unable or unwilling to support them or are in circumstances considered detrimental to the child's well-being.

Eight states and the All India Children Act also include provisions for uncontrollable children. Although these laws differ in specifics, their wording is quite similar; parents or guardians of a child can petition the juvenile court or magistrate that they cannot control the child and can then ask that the child be either remanded for observation or treatment or placed in a correctional facility.

In addition to these statutes, the laws of seven states and the All India Children Act contain sections concerning offenses committed against children by (usually) adults. All these laws are quite detailed and specific and, with a few exceptions, cover much the same conduct. Thus, a person can be punished for cruelty toward a juvenile, for employing a juvenile as a beggar, for giving a juvenile dangerous drugs or liquor, for inciting a juvenile to gamble, for buying goods from a juvenile, for permitting a juvenile to be in a brothel or at the risk of seduction, for living on the earnings of a juvenile, or for abetting an offender's escape.

All the Children Acts contain sections providing for the establishment of "remand (detention) homes" and "approved (training) schools," juvenile courts and child welfare boards, the appointment of juvenile court magistrates, and the determination of court composition and court procedures. Again, however, the specific provisions of these sections vary considerably from state to state.

In short, special provisions for children have long existed in Indian law. It is only recently, however, that the provisions have been extended to take the form of the delinquency statutes typical of many Western countries. As in other countries, the laws of India establish minimum and maximum ages for criminal culpability, define as a "delinquent" any child or young person who has committed an offense which would be a crime if committed by an adult, provide for neglected and destitute children, stipulate penalties for offenses against children, and establish courts and correctional procedures for the handling of youthful offenders.

CONTEMPORARY TAMIL NADU LAW

In Tamil Nadu, in addition to a variety of special laws (e.g., the Prohibition Act), three major codes contain sections that pertain to children. These are the Indian Penal Code, the Code of Criminal Procedure, and the Tamil Nadu Children Act.*

Sections 82 and 83 of the Indian Penal Code read as follows (Ranchhoddas and Thakore, 1953: 156):

> Section 82: Nothing is an offense which is done by a child under seven years of age.
> Section 83: Nothing is an offense which is done by a child above seven years of age and under twelve, who has not attained sufficient maturity of understanding to judge of the nature and consequences of his conduct on that occasion.

Thus, children below the age of seven are excused from criminal culpability and those between seven and twelve can be culpable only if it can be shown that they are legally competent.

The recently amended Code of Criminal Procedure details court jurisdiction in cases involving juveniles (Natt and Malik, 1973). Section 27 of that code states:

> Section 27: Any offense, not punishable with death or imprisonment for life, committed by any person who at the date when he appears or is brought before the court is under the age of sixteen years may be tried by the court of a chief judicial magistrate or by any court specifically empowered under the Children Act, 1960 (60 of 1960) or any other law for the time being in force providing for the treatment, training and rehabilitation of youthful offenders.

Section 399 of the same code allows for the confinement of youthful offenders in reformatories rather than adult institutions. Subsection 1 of this section reads as follows (Singh, 1966):

> (1) When any person under the age of fifteen years is sentenced by any criminal court to imprisonment for any offense, the court may direct that such persons, instead of being imprisoned in a criminal jail, shall be confined in any reformatory established by the (State Government) as a fit place for confinement, in which there are means of suitable discipline and of training in some branch of useful industry or which is kept by a person willing to obey such rules as the (State Government) prescribed with regard to the discipline and training of persons confined therein.†

In brief, these sections of the Penal and Procedure Codes establish the minimum age of criminal culpability and designate the age

---

*This law was enacted in 1920 as the Madras Children Act and was amended in 1958 and 1960.
†An accused person sixteen or older is not entitled to the benefits of this act. However, the Children Act extends its provisions to persons beyond the age of fifteen.

requirements for treating a young person as a juvenile rather than an adult. In the latter case the law does not require special treatment for young persons but allows for such treatment by providing criminal court magistrates the option of waiving the case to a juvenile court or incarcerating an offender in a juvenile, rather than an adult, facility. Thus it should be noted that the law gives judges the discretion to deal with juveniles differently than adults, but it does not require that they do so.

The Tamil Nadu Children Act, in effect, modifies and extends some of these provisions. This law establishes definitions of "child," "young person," and "youthful offender" and details the sentences that can be imposed upon such persons, the institutions in which they can be confined, the procedures for dealing with them, and the categories of children not considered youthful offenders who can come under the court's jurisdiction (Krishnamurti and Alagamalai, 1975).

Specifically, the act defines a "child" as anyone under the age of fourteen. A "young person" is anyone from fourteen to eighteen years of age. The term "delinquent" is not used in the law; however, judicial and correctional personnel employ it with much the same meaning that it has in the West. The term "youthful offender" refers to any person under the age of eighteen who has been convicted of an offense punishable by imprisonment.

In Tamil Nadu two levels of correctional facilities—called approved schools after the British example—have been established for juveniles. A person between the ages of twelve and eighteen (overlapping the child and young person classifications) can be sentenced to a "senior" approved school, while a child who is ("apparently") under twelve years of age may be sent to a "junior" approved school. Those placed in an approved school who attain age eighteen before their sentences expire can be transferred to a Borstal school; but this, apparently, is considered undesirable by many of the correctional officials we interviewed. Sentences to a senior approved school cannot be for a period of less than two years or more than five. Such a sentence cannot extend beyond the time when a youthful offender attains the age of twenty-one. Similarly, youngsters sentenced to a junior approved school cannot, theoretically, be retained in that facility beyond age eighteen, at which time they are to be transferred to a senior facility.

Besides sentences to approved schools, the law allows for several alternative sentences. These are: (1) discharge with admonition; (2) placement in custody (under bond) of parent or guardian; (3) placement in the custody of a person named by the court; (4) placement in the custody of any suitable person willing to care for the offender; (5) payment of a fine by the offender or parent/guardian; (6) sentence (in the case of a young person) to imprisonment; or (7) "dealing with the case in any manner in which it may legally be dealt with."

In Tamil Nadu, then, a competent youth between the ages of seven and seventeen who has committed any act prohibited adults can be certified as a youthful offender (delinquent) by a juvenile (or other designated) court and remanded to a reformatory for a designated period of time. Or the delinquent might receive one or more of several alternative sentences deemed appropriate by the court.

Indian law, like that of the United States, provides for the care and custody of youngsters other than "criminal" offenders. Although Indian laws contain few, if any, of the juvenile-status offense designations commonly found in Western law, the omnibus character of the provisions of the Tamil Nadu Children Act (like other such acts in India) clearly allows that Indian youngsters can be made wards of the court for committing many of the kinds of offenses covered by Western laws. The opening description of the intent of the Tamil Nadu Children Act, for instance, clearly describes the purpose and scope of the law:

> An act to provide for the custody, trial, maintenance, welfare, education and character training of youthful offenders and the care, protection, maintenance, welfare, education and character training for children and young persons who are uncontrollable or in moral danger, or destitute, or in need of care and protection.

Thus, any authorized person can bring a juvenile below the age of sixteen before a court empowered to hear cases regarding a juvenile who:

> (a) is found wandering and not having any home or settled place of abode, or visible means of subsistence, or is found wandering and having no parent or guardian, or a parent or guardian who does not exercise proper guardianship; or
> (b) is found destitute, not being an orphan and having both parents or his surviving parent, or in the case of an illegitimate child his mother, undergoing imprisonment; or
> (c) is under the care of a parent or guardian who, by reason of criminal or drunken habits, is unfit to have the care of the child; or
> (d) frequents the company of any reputed thief; or
> (dd) is found in street or place of public resort begging or receiving alms whether or not there is any pretense of singing, playing, performing, or for the purpose of so begging or receiving alms; or

(e) is living in a house used for an immoral purpose or in any other circumstance calculated to cause, encourage or favor the seduction or prostitution of the child.

Children covered by these provisions may be placed in a junior approved school. Similarly, parents who consider their children to be uncontrollable can petition the court and such children can be placed in a junior or senior approved school.

In brief, juvenile laws in India, and in Tamil Nadu specifically, are not unlike those found in the United States in that they allow or stipulate that separate judicial procedures be followed in cases involving juveniles, designate correctional facilities for housing young offenders apart from adult criminals, stipulate that a youthful offender is anyone below a certain age who commits a "crime," and extend court jurisdiction to children who are uncontrollable, engage in or are subject to potentially dangerous or corrupting acts or lifestyles, or are destitute or neglected.

Recorded Delinquency

One way to estimate the volume or frequency of acts in violation of delinquency laws is by means of official records of the numbers of these offenses reported to or detected by law enforcement officials. The Central Government of India publishes this kind of information in a report called *Crime in India*. The report is similar to the *Uniform Crime Reports (U.C.R.)* compiled by the Federal Bureau of Investigation in the United States. Similar to the *U.C.R.*, *Crime in India* records the number of cognizable crimes of specific types known to the police for both adults and juveniles, the number of persons (both adult and juvenile) arrested for these crimes, the number of law enforcement personnel, and the number of police officers killed or injured. *Crime in India* lists offenses in violation of selected acts under the Indian Penal Code (I.P.C.) as well as arrests for these violations and provides a separate record of offenses or arrests for violations of a variety of special and local laws. *Crime in India* differs from the *U.C.R.* in terms of the categories of crime included and the system used to categorize offenses as well as localities and demographic characteristics of persons arrested. Lacking reliable population estimates for persons of different ages, the Indian report provides few rates, so it is difficult to gauge the relative incidence of delinquent behavior on the basis of the raw figures alone.

Direct comparisons of crime rates between India and the United

Delinquency Laws and Official Delinquency 47

States (or other countries) cannot be made from these reports. In spite of this and the limitations imposed by official statistics and the various difficulties criminologists recognize as endemic to official reports of crime (see, for example, Kitsuse and Cicourel, 1963), the reports do permit one to gain some idea of the relative incidence of delinquent and criminal behavior in India and to draw some comparisons between India and countries like the United States.

The following pages deal only with "known" crime, or the number of offenses recorded by the police. Arrest and disposition information and the formal processing of juvenile offenders are reported in a following chapter.

COGNIZABLE CRIME

Table 3.1 presents the total number of offenses recorded by police throughout all of India in terms of what are considered "major" violations of the Indian Penal Code and offenses against a variety of "special" and "local" laws. The number of offenses recorded as having been committed by juveniles (persons below age twenty-one) and the percentage of juvenile to total crime are also listed. Although relative rates for juvenile offenses are not provided in the report, we have sought to estimate these from available census data.

Total Crime: Even if one takes into consideration the difficulty of comparing such information across nations, analysis of Table 3.1 suggests that the overall volume of the kinds of crime recorded in India compared to most European and North American countries is low—close to 10 percent of the total number of (Index) crimes reported in the *U.C.R.* Indeed, the contrast between India and the United States in the total "known" number of murders, robberies, burglaries, and theft offenses is striking. Although the actual number of recorded murders is about equal for the two countries, the Indian rate is about one-third that of the United States. The robbery rate in India is about 2 percent of the American rate and the volume of burglary and theft in India compared to the United States is negligible. Thus, although about 4 million offenses considered serious enough to warrant attention by official agencies are recorded in India, in contrast to the United States "serious crime" is hardly a "serious" problem.

In making these comparisons it would be useful to note the differences and similarities in the kinds of offenses recorded in the two reports. Most of the offenses listed as violations in the Indian

48   Delinquency in India

report are recorded under arrest statistics in the U.C.R.. In the U.C.R. part I,(or Index) crimes known to the police exclude several of the offenses listed in the Indian tabulations (e.g., kidnapping and abduction, dacoity, riots, criminal breach of trust, cheating, and counterfeiting). The Indian report excludes aggravated assault and rape in "national" figures. Dacoity (an offense not found in the

TABLE 3.1. **Recorded Violations of Indian Penal Code and Special and Local Laws in India, 1974**

Violations	Total	Juvenile	% Juvenile
I.P.C.			
Murder	18,649	804	4.3
Kidnapping and abduction	10,543	426	4.0
Dacoity	13,697	288	2.1
Robbery	22,286	521	2.3
Burglary	199,878	7,238	3.6
Theft	436,918	16,153	3.7
Riots	80,547	3,729	4.6
Criminal breach of trust	22,274	272	1.2
Cheating (fraud)	15,380	252	1.6
Counterfeiting	718	2	0.3
Other	371,387	10,982	3.0
Total I.P.C.	1,192,277	40,666	3.4
Special and local laws			
Arms Act	40,798	429	1.0
Opium Act	11,813	207	1.8
Gambling Act	194,898	15,183	7.8
Excise Act	145,010	3,688	2.5
Prohibition Act	347,179	10,886	3.1
Explosives Act	1,575	7	0.4
Suppression of Immoral Traffic	14,825	2,139	14.4
Motor Vehicles Act	658,111	375	0.0
Customs Act	204	—	—
Prevention of Corruption Act	235	1	0.4
Railways Act	27,173	763	2.8
Other	1,138,319	28,096	2.5
Total special and local	2,580,140	61,774	2.4

Source: Bureau of Police Research and Development, *Crime in India, 1974* (New Delhi: Ministry of Home Affairs, Government of India, 1977), pp. 1–2, 68, 72.

U.C.R.) is probably unique to India and refers to offenses (usually armed robbery) committed by gangs of bandits who roam parts of the Indian countryside (notably the Chambal Valley) robbing trains, villages, and unwary travelers much like the desperadoes of the Old West. The rather large number of offenses categorized as riots in the Indian report attest to the common occurrence of such events throughout most of India. Thus, although it is similar in some ways, the crime "problem" in India differs from that in the United States both in magnitude and character, a fact which may perhaps reflect the cultural and structural similarities and differences of the two countries.

Juvenile Crime: In developed countries it is frequently observed that to a great extent the crime problem is a juvenile problem in that a large portion (considerably greater than the proportion of juveniles to the total population) of the offenses committed are thought to be the work of young persons. As indicated by Table 3.1, this does not appear to be the case in India.* Indeed, for violations of the I.P.C. the percentage of offenses recorded as having been committed by juveniles varies from a low of 0.3 for counterfeiting to a high of 4.6 for riots. On the whole, slightly more than 3.0 percent of all recorded crime under the I.P.C. is attributed to juveniles. Similarly, offenses against special and local laws show a small incidence of involvement by juveniles, with the highest percentage (14.4) being for violations of the Suppression of Immoral Traffic in Women and Children Act (a euphemism for prostitution). Since over 45 percent of the Indian population is below age twenty-one, these figures are even more striking in their magnitude. With the exception of prohibition violations and excluding the "other" category, much of the crime recorded as occurring in India involves property offenses, a pattern not unlike that found in the United States. Indeed, thefts account for almost 40 percent of the I.P.C. violations and gambling for about 25 percent of the special and local law offenses recorded for juveniles. The juvenile crime problem in India, in short, is largely a property crime problem, and crime as such is largely an adult phenomenon, with juvenile lawbreaking being a negligible portion of criminal activity.

*Since the *U.C.R.* do not provide estimates of juvenile involvement in known crime, it is not possible to directly compare the two countries. It is generally accepted among criminologists, however, that juveniles are disproportionately involved in crime in the United States.

VARIATIONS BY STATE

Since our inquiry was largely limited to the state of Tamil Nadu, it would be useful to put the state in perspective by comparing it with two others that also have large urban centers. For this purpose, official statistics regarding Maharashtra and West Bengal (in which respectively, Bombay and Calcutta are located) were examined.

The total number of violations of the I.P.C. recorded in the state of Maharashtra is almost twice that of Tamil Nadu and about 60 percent greater than the number recorded in West Bengal. The crime rates of Tamil Nadu and West Bengal are similar, being 182.1 and 181.1 per 100,000 population respectively. The Maharashtra rate is 282.5 per 100,000 population. The relative incidence of various types of crimes also varies widely.

The proportion of juvenile crime to all crime recorded in the three states is again low, but differs widely from state to state. Since we lack adequate population estimates for various age groups, it is difficult to discern if these variations are a function of differences in the numbers of young people in the states or (what is more likely) of a differential reaction to youthful offenses by the various state authorities. Again, property crimes constitute the bulk of recorded I.P.C. crimes for juveniles regardless of state. As far as special and local laws are concerned, gambling and prohibition violations make up the bulk of offenses in Maharashtra and Tamil Nadu, with the exception that excise offenses are also frequent in the former state. The only category of juvenile offenses of any frequency in West Bengal is violations of the Railways Act; the numbers of these offenses were negligible in the other states.

Thus, although the patterns of adult and juvenile criminality tend to correspond in the three states as far as types of offenses are concerned, considerable differences exist in the overall rates of offense behavior recorded. In particular, the relative proportions of all crime attributed to juveniles vary considerably from state to state with Tamil Nadu being between the other two states in this respect. Whether these figures reflect real differences in the actual offense activity of juveniles in the various states or, whether they are a function of differences in the recording practices of authorities or the treatment of young offenders (e.g., as adults or juveniles) is difficult to determine. From the information gathered in our interviews, we suspect that the differing reactions of law enforcement officials are probably more significant than behavioral differences on the part of juveniles. Thus, as far as actual crime is concerned, the differences in recorded offenses are more apparent than real.

TAMIL NADU AND MADRAS

When states and cities within India are compared in terms of recorded crime rates, considerable variations are found in the relative amounts and distributions of crime and in the proportions of crimes attributed to juveniles (see Table 3.2). However, as with the country as a whole, recorded crime (both adult and juvenile) in Tamil Nadu and the city of Madras consists largely of property offenses, acts in violation of some morals law (such as gambling and prohibition), or technical violations (such as traffic offenses). For the state of Tamil Nadu, the majority (over 50 percent) of the I.P.C. offenses consist of property crimes and less than 2 percent of all offenses constitute violent personal crimes. Together, gambling and prohibition violations make up over one-fourth of all special and local law violations. As with India in general, relatively small proportions of these offenses are attributed to juveniles; theft accounts for 70 percent of the I.P.C. offenses attributed to juveniles in the state, and (excluding "other") prohibition, gambling and excise violations account for the bulk of juvenile special and local law violations. Generally, the proportion of total crimes attributed to juveniles in Tamil Nadu is lower than for the county as a whole. The notable exception is involvement in burglary and theft; Tamil Nadu youths' proportions are double those of the nation.

Although only about 10 percent of Tamil Nadu's population resides in Madras city, over 23 percent of total crimes recorded for the state are listed as having occurred in Madras. Respectively, 21.6 percent of the state's I.P.C. offenses and 23.4 percent of its special and local law violations occurred in the city of Madras. Moreover, over 72 percent of the juvenile crime recorded for the state is listed as having taken place in Madras. Almost 33 percent of the I.P.C. offenses and over 77 percent of the special and local law violations attributed to juveniles occurred in Madras.* Thus, according to official reports, crime, especially juvenile crime, is an urban phenomenon in Tamil Nadu—as it appears to be universally. Interestingly, the relative

*It might be noted that Tamil Nadu is comparatively high in this respect in contrast to Maharashtra and West Bengal where about 5 and 10 percent of the juvenile I.P.C. and special and local law offenses recorded for the states take place in each state's major city.

TABLE 3.2. *Recorded Violations of Indian Penal Code and Special and Local Laws in Tamil Nadu and Madras, 1974*

	Tamil Nadu			Madras		
Violations	Total	Juvenile	% Juvenile	Total	Juvenile	% Juvenile
I.P.C.						
Murder	1,030	20	1.9	36	3	8.3
Other homocide	13	—	0.0	—	—	0.0
Rape	65	—	0.0	5	—	0.0
Kidnapping and abduction	275	2	0.7	27	2	7.4
Dacoity	30	—	0.0	1	—	0.0
Robbery	141	3	2.1	25	2	8.0
Burglary	8,212	586	7.1	622	83	13.3
Thefts	28,304	2,064	7.3	8,083	730	9.0
Riots	4,464	47	1.0	316	16	5.1
Criminal breach of trust	1,147	9	0.8	316	6	1.9
Cheating (fraud)	1,000	8	0.8	531	8	1.5
Counterfeiting	39	—	0.0	2	—	0.0
Total I.P.C.	79,862	2,910	3.6	17,257	955	5.5

	Tamil Nadu			Madras		
Violations	Total	Juvenile	% Juvenile	Total	Juvenile	% Juvenile
Special and local laws						
Arms Act	155	—	0.0	—	—	0.0
Opium Act	89	—	0.0	6	—	0.0
Gambling Act	59,954	1,363	2.3	5,981	1,320	22.1
Excise Act	61,510	1,569	2.6	5,058	408	8.1
Prohibition Act	136,381	2,011	1.5	17,168	1,114	6.5
Explosives Act	133	2	1.5	3	—	0.0
Suppression of Immoral Traffic	8,765	596	6.8	1,615	303	18.8
Motor Vehicles Act	143,257	—	0.0	33,896	—	0.0
Customs Act	42	—	0.0	—	—	0.0
Prevention of Corruption Act	—	—	0.0	—	—	0.0
Railways Act	13,294	—	0.0	—	—	0.0
Other	357,042	15,789	4.4	118,622	13,355	11.3
Total special and local	780,622	21,330	2.7	182,349	16,500	9.0

Source: Bureau of Police Research and Development, *Crime in India, 1974* (New Delhi: Ministry of Home Affairs, Government of India, 1977), pp. 6–7, 40–43, 73–74.

proportion of crimes attributed to juveniles is greater in Madras than in Tamil Nadu generally, although compared to the United States and most European countries these proportions are low. Wherever a ratio can be computed, in almost all instances, the percentage of juvenile crime to total crime is considerably greater in Madras than in the entire state. This further implies that delinquency of the kind recorded in these statistics is largely an urban phenomenon: Not only is the overall rate of crime and delinquency higher in the city, but the rate of delinquent behavior relative to total crime is also considerably greater.

To the extent that these statistics reasonably reflect the actual relative incidence of illegal behavior, it appears that India (and specifically Tamil Nadu) parallels the crime pattern found in developed countries in that (1) the bulk of recorded crime consists of property or technical violations; (2) the overall rate of crime, both for adults and juveniles, is greater in cities than other areas; and (3) the relative proportion of crime attributed to juveniles is greater in urban areas than in rural localities. India and Tamil Nadu depart from the epidemiological picture of crime and delinquency in most developed or Western countries, however, in that (1) the frequency of illegal activity appears to be more limited; and (2) the relative involvement of young people in criminal behavior is relatively lower. In other words, even in major cities crime and delinquency are hardly problems in India.

Conclusion

While differing in some respects, delinquency laws in India are similar to those found in many Western nations and provide an occasion for comparing the relative incidence of delinquent behavior in India with that occurring in countries such as the United States. Analysis of official reports of crime and delinquency in these countries suggest the following:

1. Both in terms of overall rates and rates for most types of crime, the amount of crime recorded in official statistics in India is substantially lower than that recorded for the United States.

2. Although crime is comparatively infrequent in India, its pattern is similar to that found in the West—i.e., property offenses or violations of regulatory laws such as prohibition are the most frequent crimes.

3. As in other large, heterogeneous countries, official statistics report considerable variation in the incidence of crime between regions and between rural and urban areas. In general, crime rates tend to be relatively higher in large cities than in other areas.

4. While a large portion of crime in developed countries is believed to be the work of young persons, the proportion of total crime in India attributed to juveniles is strikingly low. The infrequency of juvenile crime is even more pronounced when one considers the comparatively large proportion of the Indian population below age twenty-one.

5. Juvenile crime in India tends to emulate the pattern of adult crime; it consists largely of theft and regulatory law violations.

6. The relative rate of juvenile crime increases in urban areas.

In short, assuming that official reports of crime do, in fact, reflect the relative incidence of lawbreaking behavior within a population, the problem of delinquent behavior and youth crime which appears to be large and growing in most developed nations does not seem to exist in India.

In light of previous research on delinquency in other non-Western or developing countries, these findings are to be expected. The limited knowledge available on delinquency in Third World nations generally indicates that, compared to the West, delinquent behavior in these countries occurs with a relative infrequency and increases under conditions of economic and technological development (see Clinard and Abbott, 1973; Shelley, 1981a). Since India shares many of the characteristics of other developing countries (although India is larger and more heterogeneous), it is not surprising that the country exhibits low rates of delinquent behavior. The problem of explaining the differences in rates between developed and developing countries is, however, a matter that has so far received little attention from criminologists. It will be a topic for extensive discussion in the next chapter.

Still official statistics tap only certain aspects of crime or forms of criminal and delinquent behavior and are known to dramatically underestimate the actual frequency and diversity of illegal behavior that actually occurs. It could very well be that more delinquency exists in India than these reports indicate, and/or Indian youth could be frequently involved in various acts not recorded in official statistics. Indeed, it is possible that much of the divergence in crime and delinquency rates between developed and developing nations is a function of differences in their ability or desire to record violations of law. Therefore, before we speculate as to the extent of delinquency in India, it will be necessary to look at the alternative measure of delinquent behavior provided by the self-reported delinquency research described in the following chapter.

CHAPTER 4

Self-reported Delinquent Behavior

In addition to the actual frequency of illegal behavior they are supposed to record, official counts of known crimes reflect differences in reporting behavior and in the detection and recording practices of law enforcement officials. From research carried out in the United States, there is reason to believe that official statistics substantially underestimate the actual rates of illegal behavior. However, the consistency of this underestimate is not known. It is also likely that the amount of juvenile crime recorded in official reports in India is only the tip of the iceberg and that substantially more delinquent behavior takes place in India than the official reports would lead one to believe. Moreover, offense information in India, as elsewhere, is typically compiled from reports of limited types of conduct. Generally the more serious or flamboyant acts or those which are easily observed by authorities are listed. Thus, much of the behavior which is technically delinquent goes uncounted or is so hidden in the rather large category of "other" offenses that it is impossible to discern the range of behavior for which juveniles come to the attention of judicial authorities. Even if we are correct in assuming that Indian youths, overall, are relatively infrequently involved in serious offenses, we have no way of knowing from official records the extent to which they are involved in milder misbehavior. That is, young people in India, as in other localities, could be frequently involved in petty crimes or acts that are technically delinquent but are not often reported to, detected by, or recorded by officials. Indeed, a substantial body of research in the United States and other Western countries indicates that delinquency is much more widespread than official data would lead one to

58   Delinquency in India

suspect (see Gibbons, 1981: 16–54). It is possible that this is equally true in India.

One way to tap this "dark figure" of delinquency is to ask young people if they have or have not engaged in a variety of behavior for which they could be adjudged delinquent. Although limited in the amount and scope of offense behavior included, the bulk of the self-reported delinquency research carried out in Western countries suggests that delinquency is frequent and widespread among all social groups in these countries (Empey, 1978; Jensen and Rojek, 1980; Gibbons, 1981; see also Elliott and Ageton, 1980; Braithwaite, 1981). It would not be an exaggeration to say that most youngsters in these countries are, at least occasionally, involved in such conduct during their adolescent years. But to what extent the volume and distribution of delinquent behavior revealed by this research are unique to these countries is not known.

Given the unreliability of official statistics as measures of "actual delinquency," the self-reported delinquency study carried out as a part of this research attempted to estimate the relative involvement of Tamil Nadu youths in specific acts that are, or could be, defined by a juvenile court as delinquent. This chapter reports the findings from that inquiry and draws some conclusions from these findings and the findings from the official statistics discussed in the previous chapter.

The Frequency of Delinquent Behavior

Table 4.1 presents the percentages of high school and approved school boys surveyed who reported never having engaged in the fifteen offenses included in the survey as well as those who admitted to involvement in this conduct on one or more occasions. Several things are suggested by the table.

It is quite clear that only a few boys admitted to involvement in the various acts investigated and even fewer admitted to engaging in these acts frequently. Among the high school boys, the highest percentage of admissions (39 percent) was for the defiance of parental authority. Only 2 percent of the high school youths admitted to grand theft, and no more than 2 percent reported having been frequently involved in any one of the fifteen acts. In short, self-reported delinquency among high school boys in Tamil Nadu was infrequent and this was particularly true for serious offenses of the kind likely to be recorded in official statistics as crimes. The five most frequently

TABLE 4.1. **Percentage Distribution of Self-reported Delinquent Behavior among High School and Approved School Respondents**

Activity	High school	Approved school
Lied about self		
Never	64.0	47.1
Once or twice	28.1	31.4
Several times	6.0	14.4
Often	1.9	7.2
	(517)	(306)
Played truant		
Never	72.1	47.1
Once or twice	26.1	33.7
Several times	1.0	11.1
Often	0.8	8.2
	(517)	(306)
Defied parents		
Never	60.9	43.1
Once or twice	35.1	32.7
Several times	2.1	14.7
Often	1.9	9.5
	(516)	(306)
Ran away from home		
Never	91.9	39.5
Once or twice	7.4	29.3
Several times	0.6	18.4
Often	0.2	12.8
	(516)	(304)
Drank alcohol		
Never	93.6	81.4
Once or twice	5.6	11.4
Several times	0.2	4.2
Often	0.6	2.9
	(517)	(306)
Smoked marihuana		
Never	96.7	85.6
Once or twice	2.3	7.8
Several times	0.2	3.6
Often	0.8	2.9
	(517)	(306)

TABLE 4.1. Continued

Activity	High school	Approved school
Committed vandalism		
Never	88.8	80.7
Once or twice	9.9	12.7
Several times	0.6	4.6
Often	0.8	2.0
	(516)	(306)
Trespassed		
Never	91.7	80.9
Once or twice	4.6	9.5
Several times	1.7	5.6
Often	1.9	3.9
	(517)	(304)
Went joyriding		
Never	95.9	97.7
Once or twice	2.7	0.7
Several times	1.0	0.7
Often	0.4	1.0
	(517)	(306)
Committed petty theft (Rs.2/-)		
Never	82.6	60.5
Once or twice	15.9	25.8
Several times	0.4	6.9
Often	1.2	6.9
	(517)	(306)
Committed moderate theft (Rs.2-50/-)		
Never	96.1	80.4
Once or twice	3.1	14.1
Several times	0.4	3.3
Often	0.4	2.3
	(516)	(306)
Committed grand theft (over Rs.50/-)		
Never	97.9	83.0
Once or twice	1.7	9.2
Several times	0.2	4.6
Often	0.2	3.3
	(515)	(305)

TABLE 4.1. Continued

Activity	High school	Approved school
Committed extortion		
Never	96.9	86.9
Once or twice	1.9	9.8
Several times	0.6	1.3
Often	0.6	2.0
	(517)	(306)
Assaulted parent		
Never	97.1	84.6
Once or twice	1.5	9.2
Several times	0.6	3.9
Often	0.8	2.3
	(517)	(305)
Took part in gangfight		
Never	86.8	74.8
Once or twice	10.9	13.7
Several times	0.8	6.5
Often	1.6	4.9
	(516)	(306)

Note: Number in parentheses = total number of respondents.

admitted acts involved predominantly status offenses (e.g., defiance of parents, lying about self, and truancy) and two crimes (e.g., petty theft and "gang" or group fighting). The number of youths admitting to these offenses ranged from a high of 39 percent to a low of 13 percent. The five least frequently admitted offenses consisted of a variety of crimes (e.g., moderate theft, using marihuana, extortion, assaulting a parent, and grand theft). Fewer admissions to these acts (ranging from a high of 4 to a low of 2 percent) indicate that high school boys in Tamil Nadu rarely engage in serious illegality.

In contrast to high school boys, boys incarcerated in approved schools had engaged in more delinquent behavior; but even here the rate of admissions for most serious offenses was quite low. Sixty percent of the boys reported running away from home, while more than one-half of the respondents admitted to the other status offenses. Indeed, with the exception of petty theft, the type of behavior usually admitted to was status offenses. The range of admitted involvement in these acts extended from a high of 60 percent to a low of 40 percent. The least frequently reported offense (joyriding) was

62   Delinquency in India

committed by only 2.4 percent of the institutionalized boys (in contrast to the 4.1 percent of the high school boys admitting to this offense).* But, as with the high school boys, the five least frequently admitted offenses were criminal acts, although these offenses (e.g., grand theft, assault of parent, use of marihuana, extortion, and joyriding) differed somewhat from those committed by high school boys. The percentages admitting to these acts ranged from a high of 17 percent to a low of 2 percent.

On the whole, the official delinquents reported more frequent involvement in a greater number of delinquent acts. The percentages of high school and institutionalized boys admitting to running away from home and truancy varied substantially. And, for all other offenses (except vandalism and joyriding), differences between incarcerated and high school boys were greater than 10 percent. On the average, approved school boys' admitted involvement in delinquent behavior was 16 percent greater than that of high school boys. In other words, approved school boys, in general, were more delinquent than high school boys, although the difference was not substantial. Generally also, smaller percentages of the institutionalized boys denied involvement in any of the fifteen acts.

Overall 20.3 percent ($N = 167$) of all respondents reported that they had never engaged in any of the fifteen acts listed in the questionnaire. Undoubtedly had more offenses been listed, this percentage would be somewhat lower (Elliott and Ageton, 1980). However, the percentage varied considerably from school to school. A low of 3.3 percent of the boys in the public junior approved school and a high of 54.7 percent of the boys in one private aided high school stated that they had not committed any of the acts in question. Over 38 percent of the boys in the other private aided high school said they had never committed any of the acts, whereas 21.2 and 17.1 percent of the boys in the two private high schools respectively made the same claim. Similar percentages (i.e., 27.8 and 18.0) of the boys in the two Madras city corporation schools said they had never engaged in any of the acts, but only 6.5 percent of the village (public) school boys made the same statement. Interestingly, while 9.6 percent of the public senior approved school boys claimed never to have engaged in any of the fifteen acts, 19.6 and 11.5 percent of the boys in the two private approved schools respectively indicated no involvement. On

---

*In most instances, this behavior concerned a boy who "borrowed" his father's car without the father's permission. While not "joyriding" in the typical sense, this behavior could result in the youngster being brought before legal authorities.

the average, 26.9 percent and 9.2 percent of the high school and approved school boys respectively said they had not committed any of the fifteen acts included in the questionnaire.

The 823 respondents reported involvement in the fifteen offenses on one or more occasions a total of 2,270 times (out of a possible 12,345 admissions). On the average, then, each of the respondents admitted involvement in 2.7 offenses. The admissions to status offenses were about twice the number for property crimes (e.g., petty theft, moderate theft, grand theft, joyriding, extortion, vandalism, and trespassing). Admissions to these seven offenses were, respectively, six to eight times more frequent than admissions to either of the two personal offenses (e.g., gangfighting and assaulting a parent) or the two substance-related offenses (e.g., alcohol and drug use).

Also, admissions per offense indicate that status offenses were more frequently admitted, with an average of 314 admissions for each of the four acts. While infrequent, involvement in personal offenses was reported on the average of 104.0 times per offense. Thus, while each offense was admitted to by the 823 boys on the average of 0.18 times, each status offense was admitted to by each boy on an average of 0.38 times. In contrast, admissions to property, personal, and substance offenses were comparatively infrequent. These figures are summarized in Table 4.2.

The 517 high school and 306 approved school boys differed considerably in terms of relative admissions. In every instance, average admissions were higher for approved school than for high school boys, with each institutionalized boy admitting to an average of 4.30 delinquent acts compared to the high school boys' average of 1.90 offenses. The mean number of admissions per offense for high school boys was only 0.12 while the comparable figure for institutionalized boys was 0.28—more than twice as frequent. These differences persisted for each offense category with the greatest discrepancy in personal and substance-related offenses.

While institutionalized boys did indeed report more frequently that they had committed delinquent acts, the rank ordering of the percentages of each group admitting to these offenses was almost identical. To determine whether or not the proportions of high school and approved school boys admitting involvement in each of the fifteen offenses were similar, the offenses were ranked in terms of the proportions of boys in each sample admitting to each offense—from most frequently to least frequently admitted—and a Spearman Rank Order Correlation Coefficient was computed. The coefficient of .83 indicates that the two groups did not differ. Thus, the boys incarcer-

TABLE 4.2. *Total and Average ($\bar{X}$) Admissions of High School and Approved School Boys by Offense Type*

Admissions	Total offenses	Status	Property	Personal	Substance
Total sample					
No. admissions	2,270.00	1,256.00	656.00	207.00	151.00
$\bar{X}$ per respondent	2.70	1.50	0.80	0.25	0.18
$\bar{X}$ per offense	151.00	314.00	94.00	104.00	76.00
$\bar{X}$ per respondent/off.	0.18	0.38	0.11	0.12	0.09
High school sample					
No. admissions	966.00	574.00	259.00	83.00	50.00
$\bar{X}$ per respondent	1.90	1.10	0.50	0.20	0.10
$\bar{X}$ per offense	64.00	144.00	37.00	42.00	25.00
$\bar{X}$ per respondent/off.	0.12	0.28	0.07	0.08	0.05
Approved school sample					
No. admissions	1,304.00	682.00	397.00	124.00	101.00
$\bar{X}$ per respondent	4.30	2.20	1.30	0.40	0.30
$\bar{X}$ per offense	87.00	170.00	57.00	62.00	50.00
$\bar{X}$ per respondent/off.	0.28	0.56	0.18	0.20	0.16

ated for delinquent behavior, were similar to high school boys in terms of the relative type of conduct in which they engaged with greater or lesser frequency. It was probably the overall volume of delinquency involvement, and the frequency with which boys were involved in certain types of conduct, that resulted in some boys remaining free of judicial control while others found themselves in correctional institutions. These points will be pursued further in a following chapter.

Although, they are not directly comparable to official statistics, these findings confirm the impression one might gain from such reports regarding the incidence of delinquent conduct in India. Regardless of the official or nonofficial status of offenders, it is clear that serious delinquent behavior of any kind is rare among Indian boys. The bulk of the offenses that do occur are rather petty. To the extent that the youngsters we surveyed are representative of Indian youth in general, it would appear that delinquent behavior in India is hardly a matter to warrant serious concern.

When the findings of this study are compared to similar research conducted on samples of American and other Western youngsters, it appears that our respondents differ from Western youth in the overall frequency of their involvement. However, the patterns of conduct are similar as far as the type of activity is concerned, although involvement with drugs and alcohol is dramatically lower among Indian youth. This suggests that the major differences in delinquency to be found through cross-national comparisons are in its frequency, rather than in the type of behavior. If this is so, then delinquent behavior is probably "normal" for young people in the sense that it is essentially universal. Thus, attention should be directed not to delinquent behavior as such but to the *differences* in the relative rates of its occurrence in varying sociocultural environments.

Patterns of Involvement

Regardless of the country, it is possible that different segments of the juvenile population are disproportionately involved in various types of illegality. That is, various categories of young people may differ in their overall delinquency (i.e., the frequency of the involvement in a spectrum of delinquent acts) or their relative involvement in specific types of offense behavior (i.e., personal, theft, or status). To test this possibility and to assess the distribution of delinquency, it would be useful to measure the relative involvement of young people in delinquency as such or the various forms of delinquent behavior throughout the juvenile population—in terms of the number of offenses to which juveniles admit and the frequency of admissions to such behavior. One could then compare these "rates" of admitted delinquency in terms of some dimension such as social class or residence. To do so, the admissions of our respondents to the fifteen offenses were factor-analyzed. The responses to several offenses form two distinct dimensions or meaningful scales and were thus used to construct two offense-type scales (see Appendix C). The first of these consists of six items (i.e., truancy, defiance of parents, running away, lying about self, petty theft, and use of alcohol). With the exception of petty theft and alcohol use, these offenses are all status offenses. Thus we decided to call this a "status-offense" scale.* The second, a "theft-offense" scale, is composed of several property crimes (i.e., trespassing, vandalism, moderate theft, and grand theft).† When unweighted, scores for the status-offense scale could range from a low of 0 (never) to a high of 18 (frequently involved in all six offenses) and for the theft scale from 0 to 12.

To construct a measure of "overall" delinquency, a third scale was created by combining each boy's responses to all of the fifteen items. Although our data are, of course, ordinal-level measurements of delinquency, this procedure is justified both on the basis of face validity and the fact that analysis of ordinal data derived from a large, randomly selected sample provides results that are similar to, and can be treated as, interval-level measurements (see Labovitz, 1967, 1970; Greenberg, 1979).†† Unweighted scale scores on the "delinquency" scale could range from 0 (never) to 45 (frequently engaged in the fifteen acts).

A fourth scale, SES, based on factor analysis of the income and occupational rank of the respondents' parents, was also constructed

---

*While technically "crimes," petty theft and alcohol use are not typically treated by juvenile authorities as serious offenses. Thus including them under the designation "status" is not unreasonable in this context and more clearly suggests the nature of the offense behavior comprising this scale than would some designation like "minor" crime.

†Although only two of the offenses included in this scale are "theft" offenses, they are the more serious of the four. Moreover "trespass" may involve theft. Thus it was decided that "theft" was the most appropriate designation here.

††Correlation and other analyses of these data based on both ordinal- and interval-level measurements produced almost identical results. Since statistics used for interval-level data provide more powerful and sensitive results, we feel that the possible errors that may occur from such a treatment of these data are offset by the gains that are achieved in their analysis as interval-level measurements.

to measure the association between socioeconomic status and delinquency. Since factor weights were almost identical for the component items of this scale (indicating their equal impact on the composite dimension), raw, unweighted scores were used to assign scale values to each respondent. The scores on this scale could range from a low of 2 to a high of 12.

Table 4.3 presents the mean (unweighted) scores of these four scales of the total sample and of the respondents sampled in each of the various high schools and approved schools. The category "combined" refers to the combined scores of all the respondents in the two types of schools.

Analysis of Table 4.3 suggests the following conclusions. The overall SES score ($\bar{X} = 6.99$) for the total sample of respondents is about midway in the possible range of scores on this scale. However, the combined high school sample has a substantially higher SES score than the combined approved school sample ($\bar{X} = 7.77$ compared to 5.32), and the slightly higher standard deviation (2.25 compared to 1.87) suggests that there is slightly greater variation in SES for high school youngsters than for approved school boys. However each type of high school is essentially homogeneous as far as socioeconomic status is concerned, so each type can be treated as a distinct group (e.g., corporation, private aided, private) in terms of SES. Also, on the basis of this SES measure, it appears that the youngsters in the various schools can be classified into a rough hierarchy of social rank, with approved school boys at the lowest end of the spectrum and children in private high schools at the top.

The total sample's mean score of 3.96 on the delinquency scale score indicates that overall self-admitted delinquency was extremely low. The combined approved school mean delinquency score, however, is almost three times higher than that of the combined high school score. With the exception of the village boys, high school youngsters generally received lower scores than approved school boys on this scale. Indeed, the respondents in the state-run approved schools received comparatively high scores. Nevertheless, they were rather low in delinquency with a mean score in the lower quarter of the scale's possible range. In short, given the possible range of involvement in illegality measured by the scale, even "delinquent" boys in Tamil Nadu were infrequently involved in delinquent behavior.

A similar pattern occurs for the status-offense scale, with both high school and approved school boys scoring well below the median possible value for the scale. Compared to overall delinquency, admis-

TABLE 4.3. **SES, Delinquency, Status-offense, and Theft-offense Scale Scores (Unweighted) by Schools**

Schools	SES $\bar{X}$	SES s.d.	SES N	Delinquency $\bar{X}$	Delinquency s.d.	Delinquency N	Status offense $\bar{X}$	Status offense s.d.	Status offense N	Theft offense $\bar{X}$	Theft offense s.d.	Theft offense N
Total sample	6.99	2.42	742	3.96	4.95	809	2.65	2.92	818	0.64	1.52	816
High schools												
Combined	7.77	2.25	505	2.33	2.77	509	1.59	1.70	514	0.35	0.92	513
Village	5.36	2.14	31	3.94	2.67	31	2.48	1.73	31	0.55	0.81	31
Corporation #1	6.41	1.60	81	2.39	3.65	87	1.47	1.91	89	0.43	1.08	89
Corporation #2	6.97	1.53	60	2.43	2.86	60	1.49	1.51	61	0.50	1.03	60
Private aided #1	6.91	1.64	64	1.34	2.31	64	0.83	1.22	64	0.20	0.65	64
Private aided #2	6.73	1.58	75	2.09	2.91	75	1.28	1.76	75	0.44	1.35	75
Private #1	8.70	1.67	84	2.27	2.06	84	1.79	1.51	85	0.26	0.70	84
Private #2	10.41	1.18	110	2.56	2.32	108	1.98	1.76	109	0.26	0.58	110
Approved schools												
Combined	5.32	1.87	237	6.72	6.40	300	4.47	3.59	304	1.13	2.11	303
Public #1 (senior)	5.33	1.93	91	6.39	6.55	103	4.16	3.21	104	1.25	2.41	104
Public #2 (junior)	5.44	1.99	109	9.12	6.19	117	6.33	3.73	118	1.41	2.04	119
Private #1 (senior)	4.92	1.21	37	3.48	5.58	56	1.91	2.23	56	0.54	1.79	56
Private #2 (junior)	—*	—*	0	4.04	3.53	24	2.77	1.86	26	0.62	1.24	24

Note: For ease of interpretation, unweighted, raw scale means are presented in this table for the status- and theft-offense scales. However the correlation and other analyses presented later in this chapter which use these scales are based on factor-weighted values.
*SES not computed because of missing data.

sions to the six status offenses were relatively more frequent among approved school boys who appear to have been somewhat more serious offenders than high school respondents. Admissions to theft behavior are negligible since respondents from all schools received scores near the possible minimum on this scale. However, the generally greater involvement in delinquency of the approved school boys continues along this scale.

In short, admitted delinquency, either overall or for specific types, was low among the boys responding to this survey. As would be expected, status offenses were somewhat more frequently reported than criminal (theft) behavior. Institutionalized boys tended to be somewhat more "delinquent" on all measures than high school boys, although some variability did exist within the individual school categories.

Correlation coefficients between the (weighted) status- and theft-offense scales were computed to determine whether involvement in one form of delinquency (e.g., status behavior) was related to involvement in other types of illegality.* In almost every instance, significant, high, positive correlations were found (see Table 4.4). That is, youngsters who admitted to status offenses were also likely to admit to theft behavior and vice versa. The strength of these correlations do, however, vary somewhat from school to school, and in one of the private aided schools a significant correlation was not found. Almost no changes in these correlations occur when SES is controlled. In other words, boys of higher socioeconomic status who admitted to delinquency were as likely as boys of lower status to admit to a spectrum of various types of illegality. Thus, it appears that Tamil Nadu youths may be more, rather than less, generally delinquent instead of "specialized" in the kinds of illegality in which they engage. This corresponds to the findings of research on Western youngsters that young people tend to engage in a wide spectrum of delinquent conduct rather than limit their involvement to certain specific forms of delinquent behavior (see Gibbons, 1981).

Most criminological inquiry based on official sources of data has found that offenders disproportionately represent lower socioeconomic status groups. As a consequence, many theories of criminal behavior directly or implicity attempt to attribute such conduct to poverty or to one or another contingency related to lower-class status (see Cohen, 1955; Miller, 1958; Cloward and Ohlin, 1960; Merton,

*It might be noted that Spearman's Rho and the Pearson Correlation Coefficients computed for these scales (weighted or unweighted) are almost the same in magnitude.

1956). In recent years, however, a number of self-reported delinquency studies have questioned the class-delinquency link and labeling arguments have contended that official statistics actually reflect a class bias in law enforcement rather than a greater criminogenic tendency on the part of poor people. By implication, theories of delinquency based on official data may be misleading, if not totally wrong. That this is by no means a settled issue at present is suggested by a number of studies which attempt to more accurately assess the relationship between social class and delinquency. Some of this research indicates that early self-report research may have glossed over the relationship between social class and delinquency or that some writers may have been overly enthusiastic in discounting the relationship. And this research implies that labeling theory is wrong in asserting that lower-class juveniles are discriminated against by the criminal justice system. Some scholars, however, persist in arguing that lower-class youths are not more delinquent than juveniles from higher classes (see, for example, Tittle et al., 1978; Hindelang et al., 1979; Clelland and Carter, 1980; Elliott and Ageton, 1980; Krohn et al., 1980; Braithwaite, 1981).

It is not our purpose here to attempt to resolve this controversy or to even seriously address the debate. However, given the greater

TABLE 4.4. **Pearson Product Moment Correlations between the Status-offense and Theft-offense Scale Scores by School**

Schools	Correlations	
	r^2	N
Total sample	.57	811
Village school	.46	31
Corporation school #1	.80	88
Corporation school #2	.51	60
Private aided school #1	.50	64
Private aided school #2	.15†	75
Private school #1	.35	84
Private school #2	.37	108
Public approved school #1	.70	104
Public approved school #2	.45	117
Private approved school #1	.52	56
Private approved school #2	.38*	24

Note: Asterisk indicates significance at .05 level; dagger indicates entry is not significant; all other entries significant at .01 level.

extent of poverty and the conversely low rates of crime and delinquency found in developing countries relative to developed ones, it would be informative to explore in this context the extent to which self-reported delinquency and social class are related among our respondents.

Correlations between the boys' scores on the SES scale and the three offense scales were computed for the total sample and the high school and approved school samples respectively. For the total sample, low, negative (approximately $-.20$) Pearson Product Moment correlations were found. However, among the high school and approved school samples, negligible (approximately .06), nonsignificant relationships occurred. Moreover, regardless of the sample or offense scale in question, the value of *eta* is uniformaly higher than the Pearson *r*. This suggests that the relationship between SES and delinquent behavior may in fact be a curvilinear one, rather than linear. But such summary statistics do not reveal the pattern of this relationship. Thus, to determine further if the difference in SES and involvement in the various measures of delinquency among the several schools are significant, *t*-tests of the mean SES and various offense-scale scores were computed for the several categories of schools. The results of this analysis are presented in Table 4.5.

As indicated by Table 4.5, the mean SES scores of high school and approved school youngsters differ significantly—the SES of high school students is higher than that of approved school boys. Similarly, significant differences exist in the delinquency, status-scale, and theft-scale scores of the two school types, but in an inverse direction. In other words, the (lower SES) approved school boys are significantly more delinquent than (higher SES) high school boys on all scales of offense behavior.

In comparing the various categories of high school respondents, it is clear that, in terms of SES, corporation school youngsters are significantly lower than private aided or private school boys, and private aided boys are lower than private school boys. That is, respondents in the three types of schools can be ranked from high (private) to low (corporation) in terms of SES scores. Their respective involvement in delinquency, however, does not parallel the SES ranking; nor do mean scores on these scales always differ significantly among the various high school categories. That is, when compared to private aided school boys, corporation school youths are significantly more delinquent overall and in terms of status offenses, but as far as theft behavior is concerned they do not differ significantly. Interestingly, respondents from the three high school categories are significantly different in mean theft scores only when private and corporation schools are compared. Thus, it appears that corporation school boys are somewhat more frequently involved in theft behavior than are private aided boys, who, in turn, are somewhat more frequently involved than private school boys. Interestingly also, while private school boys are significantly more delinquent in terms of the delinquency and status-offense scales, no significant differences were found on these scales between private and corporation school boys. Thus, with the exception of theft behavior, private aided school (what might be called middle rank) boys are essentially less delinquent than either corporation (lower-rank) or private school (upper-middle-rank) boys. In short, a curvilinear pattern of delinquency appears to

TABLE 4.5. **Differences in $\bar{X}$ SES, Delinquency, Status-offense, and Theft-offense Scale Scores of Pairs of Schools**

Schools	SES scale	Delinquency scale	Status scale	Theft scale
High schools/ approved schools				
Difference in $\bar{X}$s	2.46	−4.39	−2.88	−0.78
t-value	15.63	−11.27	−13.15	−6.11
D.f.	(549)	(366)	(385)	(370)
Private aided/ corporation				
Difference in $\bar{X}$s	0.74	−0.82	−0.51	−0.16
t-value	3.90	−2.46*	−2.80	−1.39†
D.f.	(309)	(315)	(317)	(316)
Private/ corporation				
Difference in $\bar{X}$s	3.40	−0.18	0.28	−0.22
t-value	19.38	−0.63†	−1.51†	−2.23*
D.f.	(366)	(308)	(374)	(273)
Private/ private aided				
Difference in $\bar{X}$s	2.66	0.63	0.78	−0.06
t-value	14.69	2.33*	4.73	−0.75†
D.f.	(329)	(264)	(322)	(241)

Note: Asterisk indicates significance at .05 level; dagger indicates entry is not significant; all other entries significant at .01 level. D.f. is degrees of freedom.

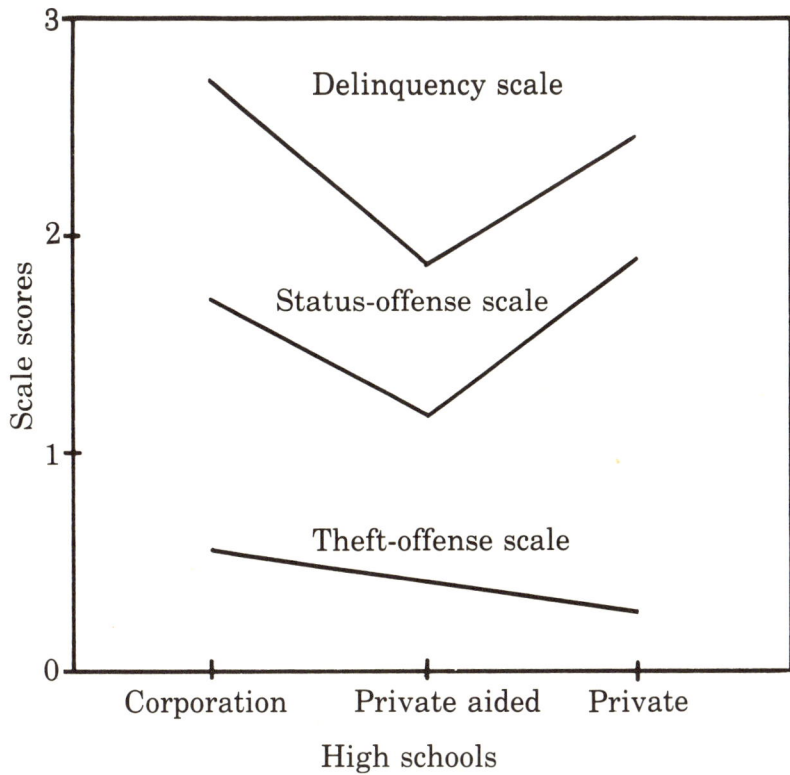

FIGURE 4.1. ***Offense-scale Scores of Corporation, Private Aided, and Private High School Respondents***

exist for high school boys of different SES backgrounds. This pattern is visually presented in Figure 4.1.

The findings of this analysis parallel some of the research conducted in the United States which suggests that while delinquency is more common among lower SES groups, it is not unique to them. With the exception of the more serious acts of theft, higher SES high school boys admit to delinquency with at least equal frequency as lower SES corporation school boys (see Short and Nye, 1958; Empey and Erikson, 1966; Hirschi, 1969; and Williams and Gold, 1972). Yet, we cannot discount the fact that the lowest SES approved school respondents do admit to delinquency, and delinquency of various types, significantly more frequently than high school boys.

In brief, involvement in delinquency among boys in Tamil Nadu is probably linked to SES in the sense that those who most frequently admit to such conduct (i.e., institutionalized boys) also tend to come from lower socioeconomic backgrounds. This does not, however, lessen the possibility that low SES may be related to the probability of incarceration as a delinquent. But since there does not appear to be a consistent relationship between SES and delinquency, except in the case of theft behavior, an unequivocal assertion that delinquency is related to socioeconomic status cannot be made from these data. As suggested by Carter and Clelland (1979), there is probably a much more complicated relationship between social class and delinquency than past theory and measurements have anticipated. At a minimum, it would appear that SES is related to involvement in specific types of conduct more than it is to the fact of delinquency itself. Insofar as lower SES boys are more often engaged in the types of delinquency legal officials deem worthy of official reaction, it is not surprising that we find greater numbers of them in correctional institutions. And the overwhelming number of very poor boys found in correctional institutions in India may bias SES values to such an extent that comparing these boys with high school youths is not as meaningful as it might appear to be. A better comparison would be between low SES, institutionalized boys and low SES, noninstitutionalized boys, youngsters who are not likely to be in high school but who may or may not be engaged in delinquent forms of conduct.

Delinquency and Economic Development: Some Observations

Official statistics and the findings of our self-reported delinquency survey in India correspond to the limited research on delinquency in other Third World countries. This research suggests that young people throughout the world are probably involved in similar patterns of delinquent behavior, although the rates of such conduct in developing nations are generally dramatically lower than in developed countries. These similarities and differences in delinquency rates, therefore, pose a major explanatory problem for criminology—one that may not be amenable to existing criminological theory.

DELINQUENCY IN POSTINDUSTRIAL SOCIETIES

In addition to noting that delinquency rates are not only higher in the more urbanized and industrialized nations of North America and Western Europe, a number of writers also point out that rates of delinquency are increasing within those countries that are modernizing at a rapid rate (e.g., Clinard and Abbott, 1973; Toby, 1979). Not all developed countries exhibit equally high rates of delinquency. Both Japan (Clifford, 1976) and Switzerland (Clinard, 1978) have low crime and delinquency rates. Also, although there is considerable variation in the dimensions and character of the "youth problem" among different developed societies, the fact that high delinquency rates are correlated with modernization or economic development seems inescapable (Shelley, 1981a).

Alienation and Youth: Given that variations in the gross rates of delinquency do seem to correspond to differences in the political economy of countries, it is possible that these variations might be accounted for in terms of certain features of economic development and the social arrangements they produce. A number of writers (Ritchie and Koller, 1964; Demos and Demos, 1973; Tucker, 1974; Rosenberg, 1975; Scott and Tilly, 1975; Stone, 1977) have analyzed societies' views of youth and treatment of young persons throughout history. It appears that high rates of delinquency in Western or postindustrial nations are a consequence of the social creation of adolescence as a life stage, and the resultant exclusion of young people from dominant social and economic activity, namely participation in the labor force, and the consequent alienation of young people this exclusion produced.

For example, Friday (1980) and Friday and Hage (1976) have argued that certain features of postindustrial societies lead to an extended period of adolescence and a consequent exclusion of young people from the labor market. The major economic condition generating this phenomenon is the elimination of the need for a large pool of unskilled labor. When they are no longer needed in the labor force, young people are forced to delay their entry into adult work roles. Being thus excluded, the commitment of young people to the dominant social norms of adult society is weakened. Moreover, the isolation of young people results in the growth of an adolescent subculture different from, and often antagonistic to, the world of adults. The social isolation generated by the economic irrelevance of young people does not, of course, affect all youths in the same way or to the same extent. But, in the aggregate, it increases the probability that large numbers of adolescents will engage in law-violating activity.

Greenberg (1978) also describes the consequences of the exclusion of young people from the labor force in advanced capitalist societies. According to Greenberg, young people in such societies have been transformed into an adolescent "leisure class" separate and distinct from the dominant (working) adult population. This separation has affected their patterns of interpersonal relationships, social status, economic independence, and orientations to the dominant norms of the society. As a result, the probability that they will engage in a variety of deviant or delinquent forms of behavior increases.

Role Relationships: According to Friday and Hage (1976), other economic requirements of postindustrial societies have important implications for the patterns of role relationships that integrate the individual into the larger society and its dominant norms (also see Toby, 1963). For the young, while role relationships involving kin, school, community and work have become impaired, relationships with peers have become more salient. As a consequence, while young people associate and identify more closely with peers than with adults, they also adhere to the values and emulate the behavior of an adolescent subculture. And as Friday (1980) contends, the peer group associations of young people generated by their exclusion and consequent alienation from the adult (work) world impede their integration with family and their commitment to the conformity-inducing requirements of school.

Perhaps it is not ipso facto their lack of contribution to the productive well-being of society that generates deviant and delinquent behavior. Rather, as with other disenfranchised groups (i.e., the poor, minorities), it is the powerlessness caused by this exclusion that acts as a stimulant for deviance. It should not be surprising that, lacking the opportunity to have much of a say in what is to be done with their own lives, the young (and others) would act in ways that flaunt the standards, values, and morality of those they consider responsible for their predicament. Indeed, in his study of dispute settlement by the police in the United States, Black (1980: 155) nicely summarizes the position of youth in modern Western society:

> The police readily use their authority against a juvenile who is criticized by a parent, but when the situation is reversed . . . they show no sympathy at all, and usually treat the complaint itself as an offense. Patterns of this kind should be expected wherever one person or group is far below another in social status, as is true of slaves and women in many societies. . . . In modern America, however, hardly anyone is lower than juveniles.

In a sense, living in, but not being a meaningful part of, a world over which they have little control liberates young people from the necessity to conform to the norms of that world, but not without consequence.

In short, the socioeconomic requirements of developed societies seem to promote the separation and alienation of youth, thereby increasing the likelihood of their being involved in acts considered inappropriate or illegal. Where the characteristics of post industrial development are absent or not yet active, the social consequences of such development should also be absent. India appears to be a case in point.

DELINQUENCY IN AN AGRARIAN SOCIETY

According to Greenburg (1978: 78), in peasant and tribal societies, and in the Western world prior to industrialization, children were not excluded from serious work activities and juvenile crime rates were low (see also: Robertson, 1974; Tucker, 1974; Stone, 1977). This is probably also true of premodern societies throughout the world today. For example, the absence of a delinquency problem in India might be explained in terms of the socioeconomic features of the country which operate to integrate young people into the dominant social system and which, as a result, inhibit tendencies on their part to challenge or deviate from the dominant social order.

Role Relationships: While the economic and production characteristics of industrialized societies lead to the segregation of role relationships and the exclusion of some segments of the population from meaningful productive activity, Third World economies (particularly under conditions of scarcity such as those found in the agrarian economy of India) appear to have the opposite effect. That is, in peasant or agrarian societies the integration of young people into the dominant socioeconomic order is enhanced. In India, this integration is partly a result of the network of role relationships involving a variety of obligations to family, *jati* (or subcaste), and community in which Indians in general are immersed (see Beteille, 1974; and Mandelbaum, 1970). Social relations are organized on the basis of these interpersonal ties and the loyalties and interdependencies they require. It is expected that one would care for others, including distant relatives and even employees. Marriage, dietary patterns, social contacts, and economic opportunities are often dependent upon one's *jati* membership. And an attack on a member of one's community or village is a matter for the entire group to deal with (Gough, 1955; Srinivas, 1955; Beals, 1980).

The social ties, mutual obligations, and interdependencies of Indian society extend beyond kin and village. For example, an agricultural laborer is not simply the employee of a landowner. Rather, because of his or her employment, the two are welded together in a social bond of interdependency. This dictates the mutual obligations and patterns of authority, deference, and respect that are beyond the requirements of the contractual work role relationship. The employer becomes almost a surrogate parent to the worker and is obliged to look after the employee's (and the employee's family's) welfare. The worker, in turn, has obligations to the employer (or provider) that are not due simply to economic dependence, but are defined by the work role itself.

One's location in the class structure is largely determined by the ownership, control, or use of land or other means of production.* Access to these "means of livelihood," of course, is important to one's life chances. And one's position in the labor force is by no means inconsequential in India, as elsewhere in the world. But, while work role relationships are significant in themselves, they are intertwined with those of family, *jati*, and community. In many respects, interpersonal relationships are determined more by family, *jati*, and community membership than by one's occupation or participation in the labor force. Indeed, even class membership, insofar as it involves land ownership or occupational status, is influenced by family or *jati* membership and the position the family or *jati* has in the community. A low-caste individual may acquire enough capital to purchase a small plot of land (and thereby move up the class structure somewhat), but other members of the village may block the person's efforts to purchase land, or too much of it, by a variety of coercive tactics. One's place in the social structure, in short, is more a function of family and *jati* than occupation or monetary earnings. Thus the essence of one's existence is dictated by ascriptive rather than achieved attributes. Individuals define themselves and are defined by others primarily in terms of these characteristics. In effect, regardless of one's place or participation in the economy, a set of ready-made role relationships and their corresponding obligations and ties exist for the individual. While these are in part determined by one's work

---

*The rural population in India can be grouped roughly into five major classes based upon ownership and use of land. These are: (1) landowners (those who own but do not cultivate land); (2) owner-cultivator (those who own and cultivate land); (3) tenants (those who rent land from landowners and farm it themselves or employ someone else to do so); (4) sharecroppers (people who do not own but cultivate the land for a portion of the harvest); and (5) agricultural laborers (nonowners who work for wages). See Beteille (1974) and Beals (1980).

role, they also determine the economic or work relationships the individual is likely to achieve. This is as true, although to a somewhat more limited extent, of urban Indians as it is of rural Indians. Family, *jati*, and community ties remain strong for the urban Indian. Kinship terms may be employed by urban migrants from the same village (Beteille, 1974; Wiebe, 1976) and extended family ties and obligations are not forgotten or replaced. Similarly, *jati* membership remains a major factor in social and marital relationships as well as occupational opportunities.

In short, regardless of rural or urban residence, individuals in India are (to greater or lesser degrees) immersed in networks of role relationships apart from and defined in terms other than their participation in the labor force. While such participation (at least by some members of the family) is, of course, essential for survival, it is not the essense of their existence nor the major criterion for self and social identification. This, and the implications of scarcity generated by a preindustrial economy, may explain why a youth subculture has not emerged in India and why, as a consquence, Indian society has not yet produced a delinquency problem in a behavioral sense.

Youth and Work: In contrast to postindustrial economies where unskilled labor is economically irrelevant, the agrarian economies of countries such as India demand the utilization of large numbers of unskilled labor in all spheres of activity. Children and young people are a ready source of such labor. Laws in India prohibit or limit the use of children in industry or commerce. However, one finds children working in some capacity or another in nearly every realm of the nation's economy. The sight of rag- or paper-picking boys throughout Madras, for instance, is a common one. Almost every factory or business employs young boys (and sometimes girls) to work as "apprentices" or day laborers. Indeed, there are probably more than 16 million children working in the mining, brick-making, construction, and match-making industries alone.

The typical economic activity in India is small-scale or cottage industry (both agricultural and nonagricultural). Such businesses are normally family enterprises in which the children of the household are expected to participate. Particularly among the more deprived families in the countryside, children are essential to the family's economic survival. The one or two rupees or bowl of rice a child might earn each day for helping in the fields, herding cattle, or carrying firewood may be all that keeps the family from starvation.

In these family businesses, the senior male member of the

household in effect acts in the dual capacity of head of household and employer. At an early age the children of the family are inducted into the business or craft. At first they carry out simple tasks, but as they grow older they engage in more difficult or important activities.

As a complementary source of income, child labor is not only expected, but is largely accepted throughout the community. Indeed, as the school officials in the village we studied suggested, they were reluctant to enforce mandatory education laws because forcing a child to attend school when he or she was needed at home or in the fields could mean a financial hardship for the child's family who might retaliate by refusing to let the child attend school.

Besides helping on the farm or in the family business, boys clean windshields, fill tires with air, or engage in similar tasks at every "petrol bunk" (gas station). Construction and highway work are often family enterprises; the older males engage in digging and bricklaying while women and children carry dirt or bring building supplies to the men. But even when this kind of employment is not available, the child's financial potential cannot be ignored. Sometimes this may involve the child in illegal activity such as begging or carrying contraband liquor. Indeed, a large number of the children who come to the attention of legal authorities (at least in Tamil Nadu) are those involved in such "criminal" behavior or those who, for some reason or another, have lost family relationships and are thus severed from economic support. Begging, petty theft, scalping train or movie tickets, etc. become their only means of livelihood. And it is this kind of activity which seems to get them into trouble with the law.

Except in the more affluent families, even if children are employed outside the household, their labor at home is essential to the daily life of the household. In an economy that lacks the capacity to produce or purchase the so-called labor-saving devices found in post-industrial societies, household members must perform a number of tasks simply to put food on the table (or more correctly, on the floor). Thus, activities like cleaning rice, collecting the wood or cow dung for the cooking fire, grinding grain, watching younger siblings, tending the garden, and fetching water are among those that children throughout India perform routinely. In this way, besides contributing to the operation of the household, the child becomes an essential part of it (Beals, 1980).

Social Integration: Because they are part of the economic structure, Indian children are also included in almost all forms of social activity. The "adolescent hangouts" commonly found in the United States and Europe are practically nonexistent in India. Age-segregated parties or social events are rare. Children and adults are found together almost everywhere. In short, as in economic life, adults and children in India intermingle in all spheres of social life.

Indian youth therefore have little opportunity to deviate from general social norms and little reason to establish the kind of subcultural structures of values and behavior found among adolescents in postindustrial societies. Being a part of the social and economic systems, Indian youth develop a stake in the status quo. Thus, if it is true that features of developed societies serve to alienate young people (or other segments of the population) from the dominant society and, consequently, promote a delinquency and crime problem, the economic and social requirements of predeveloped or developing societies may explain why an adolescent subculture, separate and distinct from adult society, simply has no room or necessity to develop. As a result, the delinquency-promoting effects that may emanate from such a subculture are absent.

Moreover, in India the traditional role relationships of family, *jati*, and community have remained largely intact. In addition to their economic impact, these traditional role relationships provide an alternative integrative mechanism apart from labor force participation. Thus, regardless of one's position in the economic structure, one still belongs in the larger social system in terms of family, *jati*, and community membership. A person may be low on the membership hierarchy, but in any case he or she is a member. Since the social sphere of family, *jati*, and community interconnects with the economic sphere of labor force participation, the essence of one's being is not defined solely by labor force participation. Rather, one's place in the economic sphere is in part determined by one's position in the social sphere. In other words, *who one is*, rather than *what one does*, is important for one's place in the social order.

It would seem, therefore, that the delinquency problem in India differs, both in its intensity and character, from that found in the West because either the cultural definition of youth or the place young people have within these societies differs. If this is true, as India modernizes and comes to more closely resemble the West, it is likely that a gradual erosion of the integrative forces of the society will occur and, as a consequence, there will be a growth in delinquency and the ultimate emergence of a delinquency problem.

Conclusion

This chapter has presented findings from the self-reported delinquency study we carried out in Tamil Nadu. The implications of these findings were discussed in conjunction with the impressions about delinquency one gains from official records. Both self-reported and official sources of information suggest that delinquent forms of behavior are comparatively infrequent among Indian youth. However, such conduct does appear to occur, with greater or lesser frequency, among all socioeconomic groups. The delinquent behavior which occurs most often consists of status-type and petty property-related forms of illegality. Serious criminality and personal violence are rare. In this respect, delinquency in India resembles delinquency in other parts of the world. But, in contrast to delinquency in developed nations, delinquency in India appears to be considerably less pervasive and certainly less serious.

As has been suggested by a number of criminologists, it is argued here that, in part, the relatively low rates of delinquency in India (and apparently in other developing countries as well) are probably a function of the social and economic integration of young people into the dominant social system. This integration appears to be characteristic of the economic requirements of preindustrial economies. In contrast to young people in developed societies, juveniles in developing nations such as India are a part of the system and, therefore, have little reason or opportunity to rebel against or deviate from dominant social norms. This argument will be extended and elaborated on in the chapters to follow when we consider official and societal reactions to delinquent youth.

PART THREE

Official Control: Arrest, Judicial, and Correctional Processing

CHAPTER 5

Official Reaction

In the United States and other Western countries the behavior of young people has been a matter of public concern for at least the past quarter-century. Whether that concern is justified or what in fact may have occasioned it are questions beyond the scope of the present inquiry. However, that the young have been subjected to special and extensive attention by legal authorities in most developed nations is well known. Salvaging young people by means of formal, legal mechanisms of social control may simply be one inevitable feature of an industrialized and bureaucratized social system that lacks other conceivable alternatives. It could also be a function of the degree to which youth in these nations are, or at least are perceived by their elders to be, troublesome and in need of control (Schur, 1973; Krisberg and Austin, 1978).

But what about the social control of youth in societies that do not as yet evidence a "delinquency" problem? What are the characteristics of the young people subjected to legal control in these societies? What are their relative numbers? How are they and their behavior viewed and treated by legal authorities? Is it inevitable that the formalization and bureaucratization of social control must proceed at a pace with industrial development (see Quinney, 1975)? That delinquent behavior is not widespread in Tamil Nadu, and probably the rest of India as well, has been established by the data presented in the preceding chapters. But are delinquent youth treated differently in India as a consequence?

We cannot, of course, answer all these and related questions here, but data collected from diverse sources on the operation of Tamil Nadu's system of juvenile justice may provide some clues as to what the answers might be. In this chapter we shall examine these

86 Delinquency in India

data and, where possible, attempt to compare juvenile justice in India with the system operating in the United States—i.e., we shall compare the operation of law, justice, and corrections in two localities which have quite different views toward, and incidences of, delinquent behavior. In Chapter 6 we shall look at dispositional data and information regarding correctional programs as well as the implications that might be drawn from that analysis and the data presented in the present chapter.

Arrests

One measure of societal reaction is the rate of arrests. Official arrest statistics for the United States, India, and localities within Tamil Nadu are described and compared below.

INDIA AND THE UNITED STATES

As indicated in Table 5.1, a total of 141,000 juveniles were arrested throughout India in 1974 (the most recent year for which such data were available). As with recorded crime, the bulk of the I.P.C. arrests (excluding the "other" category) are accounted for by theft-type offenses, with a sizable portion, approximately 20 percent, of the total involving arrests for riots. Similarly, many of the youngsters apprehended under special and local laws were arrested for violations of the Prohibition Act or the Gambling Act, with these two offenses together accounting for over 46 percent of all juvenile arrests in this category.

For most offense categories, 3 percent or less of the total arrests involve arrests of juveniles, and for some offenses almost no arrests of juveniles occur. However, for a variety of crimes the relative proportions are two or more times higher than the overall percentages. Basically, these crimes consist of the two sex offenses (rape and violation of the Suppression of Immoral Traffic in Women and Children Act) and two property crimes of burglary and theft. But, given that about one-half of the Indian population is below age twenty-one, these percentages are still dramatically low.

Although direct comparisons are not possible, it appears that the number of juveniles arrested in India is probably no more than 4 percent of the number arrested in the United States during any given year. Since there are about 300 million Indians below age twenty-one and only about 30 million Americans below that age, the relative rates of arrests are dramatically different; the total number of juveniles arrested in India, relative to their portion of the population, is minuscule compared to the United States. Whereas juvenile arrests make up only 3.3 percent of all arrests in India, in the United States about 40.0 percent of the persons arrested are below age twenty-one. And the percentage of juvenile arrests in the United States, compared to India, is dramatically higher for almost every offense category. Indeed, even for specific crime categories American juveniles are arrested much more frequently than are Indian juveniles. The one exception to this appears to be gambling. Arrests of juveniles for this offense in the United States are about one-fourth of the number arrested for this activity in India. In short, compared to Indian adults, Indian youths are arrested infrequently. When compared to American youths in terms of the actual number of arrests, the percentage of total arrests, or their proportion in the total population, this is even more striking.

The total number of arrests in India (approximately 4 million) is about one-half the number of arrests for all age groups in the United States. Since India's population is more than three times larger than the population of the United States, this number is relatively low. Where reasonable comparisons can be made in terms of specific offense types, the number of arrests in India average about 15 percent of those in the United States.* The frequency of arrests is higher in India only for murder and embezzlement. It is about double the American number, but still small given the differences in population sizes. Thus, it appears that the low number of juvenile arrests in India reflects not only the relatively infrequent occurrence of delinquency among Indian youth, but also the overall tendency of the Indian police not to make or record juvenile arrests of any kind.

Although the police systems in India (see Bayley, 1969) and the United States differ in many ways, a part of the variation in arrest rates may stem from differences in the relative size of the police forces of the two countries. The total number of police (civilian and armed) in India in 1974 was 766,859—about 1.3 police personnel per 1,000 population (Bureau of Police Research and Development, 1977). There are about 500,000 police (officer and civilian employees) totaling about 2.7 police personnel per 1,000 in the United States—about twice the relative rate for India (*Uniform Crime Reports* data for 1974). Thus, the lower arrest rate in India could partially reflect

---

*Based on *Uniform Crime Reports* data for 1974. These comparisons can be reasonably made for offenses such as murder, theft, burglary, and the like. Other offenses are not uniformly reported in these documents.

TABLE 5.1. **Arrests of Juveniles for Violations of the Indian Penal Code and Special and Local Laws in India, Tamil Nadu, and Madras, 1974**

Offense	India		Tamil Nadu		Madras	
	N	% juvenile	N	% juvenile	N	% juvenile
I.P.C.						
Murder	1,428	2.9	24	0.3	5	8.2
Rape	284	7.2	—	—	—	—
Kidnapping and abduction	605	4.6	2	0.6	2	18.2
Dacoity	1,472	2.7	—	—	—	—
Robbery	854	3.7	7	3.4	7	17.5
Burglary	10,017	8.4	587	9.8	86	21.4
Thefts	20,872	8.1	1,999	10.1	725	22.1
Riots	12,616	3.0	277	1.1	246	19.5
Criminal breach of trust	298	2.0	9	1.7	6	3.0
Cheating (fraud)	326	2.7	9	1.4	9	2.5
Counterfeiting	1	0.2	—	—	—	—
Other	14,872	2.9	165	0.5	90	1.3
Total I.P.C.	63,645	4.3	3,079	3.3	1,176	9.3

	India		Tamil Nadu		Madras	
Offense	N	% juvenile	N	% juvenile	N	% juvenile
Special and local laws						
Arms act	491	1.2	—	—	—	—
Opium Act	220	1.8	—	—	—	—
Gambling Act	21,527	6.4	1,362	2.2	1,320	18.0
Excise Act	3,739	2.3	1,569	2.5	408	8.4
Prohibition Act	14,838	4.7	2,009	1.5	1,114	6.5
Explosives Act	7	0.4	2	1.3	—	—
Suppression of Immoral Traffic	2,150	13.7	596	6.8	303	18.7
Motor Vehicles Act	495	0.0	—	—	—	—
Customs Act	—	—	—	—	—	—
Prevention of Corruption Act	1	0.0	—	—	—	—
Railways Act	1,415	4.7	—	—	—	—
Other	32,111	2.6	15,999	4.5	13,355	11.3
Total special and local	76,994	2.8	21,537	2.8	16,500	9.0
Total all offenses	140,639	3.3	24,616	2.8	17,676	9.0

Source: Based on Bureau of Police Research and Development, *Crime in India, 1974* (New Delhi: Ministry of Home Affairs, Government of India, 1977).

the inability of India to support a large law enforcement apparatus or the lack of a desire on the part of Indians to commit their resources to that task. But it is also possible that Indians possess a more tolerant, if not fatalistic, view of juvenile offenders and are thus less likely to report delinquents. And even when they do report them, law enforcement agencies are not likely to deal with them in any formal manner.

While the present research cannot attest to the extent these factors influence arrest rates in India, it is possible that low rates of arrests in that country are a function of more than low rates of delinquent conduct. That is to say, while delinquent behavior does indeed appear to be relatively infrequent in India, official reaction to that behavior (as measured by arrest statistics) is also infrequent. Such reaction may be influenced by a variety of factors, such as the perceptions of delinquents or delinquent conduct held by authorities (see Black, 1980) and the organizational structure of the police department (see Wilson, 1968; Littrell, 1979; Bittner, 1980). Moreover, since a good deal of police activity is citizen initiated, arrest rates are, to some extent, a product of "public reaction." As suggested by Bayley (1969), the relatively low rates of arrest found in India may be partly the result of citizen mistrust of, and antagonism toward, the police. Indeed we found this to be the case in the public attitude survey carried out in Tamil Nadu (also see Shane, 1980; 77–100).

TAMIL NADU AND MADRAS

While the total population of Tamil Nadu (43 million) is only 7 percent of the total Indian population (over 600 million), 23 percent of all crimes and 12 percent of all juvenile crimes recorded in India are listed as having occurred in Tamil Nadu. Assuming that these figures reflect the actual occurrence of illegal behavior, it appears that crime takes place much more frequently in Tamil Nadu than in India as a whole. A part of this discrepancy is accounted for by the much higher "crime" rate for violations of special and local laws in Tamil Nadu. And this higher rate is largely a result of prohibition offenses—a function of Tamil Nadu's "dry law" which in other states either did not exist or was not considered a matter worthy of serious legal attention.

Eighteen percent of all arrests and 17 percent of all the juvenile arrests recorded for India take place in Tamil Nadu. Compared to recorded crimes, fewer adults and more juveniles are arrested in Tamil Nadu; thus arrest rates in Tamil Nadu clearly reflect the activities of law enforcement personnel as much as the relative incidence of crime. Assuming that juveniles constitute about the same proportion (approximately one-half) of the total population in Tamil Nadu as they do in the rest of India, it appears that law enforcement personnel in Tamil Nadu are somewhat more prone to arresting juveniles even though the percentage of juvenile arrests of all arrests in Tamil Nadu is somewhat lower than in all of India. Since only 6 percent of the total Indian police force is located in Tamil Nadu (with a rate of 9.8 police per 10,000 population compared to 13.1 per 10,000 in India), these comparatively high arrest rates, especially of juveniles, in relation to "crime" rates probably reflect more rigorous police activity in Tamil Nadu than elsewhere in India. This can be partly accounted for by the sociohistorical developments that took place in Tamil Nadu. For example, Tamil Nadu was the first state in India to enact a Children Act, to establish a separate judicial and correctional system for juveniles, and to create a specialized juvenile squad in its police force. And since many states in India have given only nominal special attention to youthful offenders, it is possible that the higher (overall or in contrast to crime rates) arrest rates for juveniles in Tamil Nadu are a product of more profesionally sophisticated and organized police activity regarding juveniles (Wilson, 1968). If this is true, we can expect that juvenile arrest rates in other Indian states will increase as the states develop more sophisticated juvenile justice systems.

Returning to the arrest statistics presented in Table 5.1, it is clear that most of the juvenile arrests in Tamil Nadu (approximately 72 percent) take place in the principal city of Madras. Since the population of Madras is only about 8 percent of the total population of Tamil Nadu, it appears that police attention regarding juveniles is concentrated in the city rather than throughout the state. Indeed, all, or many, of the juvenile arrests for specific crimes occur in Madras. Almost all of the juvenile arrests for gambling and over one-half of those for violations of the Prohibition Act take place in Madras, while over 80 percent of the arrests for violations of "other" special and local laws occur in Madras.

Although self-reported delinquency is no greater in Madras than in Thamaraikulam village, it is conceivable that delinquency (or serious offense behavior) is comparatively more frequent in the city than elswhere in the state. Indeed, the arrest percentages here are strikingly similar to the percentages of reported crime discussed in Chapter 3. To what extent crimes are only recorded as "reported" after an arrest has been made is not known, so it is impossible to determine if the two rates are actually different measures. Yet it is clear that it is in the city that youngsters come to the attention of authorities and are subjected to arrest. For instance, the 246 juveniles arrested for rioting in Madras is a consequence of the fact that riots are largely an urban phenomenon; since it is the city that is the seat of government, demonstrations and similar activities are more likely to take place there than elsewhere. Thus, arrest rates for this activity are likely to be disproportionately large for the city. Also, many of the arrests for "other" offenses involve things like "ticketless travel" for which youngsters (many of whom have come from rural areas) are apprehended in the Madras train stations. Other youngsters, having migrated to the city for excitement, jobs, or whatever, may be apprehended for "wayward wandering."

Still, the pattern of arrests for delinquency in Tamil Nadu and Madras mirrors the general pattern for all of India (and the world) in that it consists of arrests for theft behavior, substance abuse, or other technical violations—those acts which tend to occur most frequently and which are most visible and readily detected by authorities.

In any case, the fact that the police give greater attention to juvenile offenders in Madras than they do in the rest of the state is evidenced by the higher percentages of juveniles arrested for specific offenses in Madras. Although information allowing for a comparison of the relative numbers of police personnel situated in Madras and the rest of Tamil Nadu is not available, over 16 percent of the civil and district armed police in Tamil Nadu are located in Madras. Thus in part, the differences in arrest rates reflect the disproportionate allocation of police personnel in urban areas.

The overall proportion of total arrests accounted for by juveniles is about three times greater in the city than in the state as a whole, and for every offense category juveniles are more often arrested in Madras than they are in Tamil Nadu. In most cases this corresponds to the proportion of juvenile crime recorded for Tamil Nadu versus Madras. Madras youth, in other words, are not only more frequently arrested for illegal activity than are their peers in the rest of the state, but such activity is more often attributed to juveniles in the city than for the state as a whole. As elsewhere, delinquency in Tamil Nadu, as well as official reaction to delinquent youth, are largely urban phenomena. Given this, what are the characteristics of the youngsters arrested?

Characteristics of the Offenders

Table 5.2 summarizes the social and economic characteristics of the juveniles arrested in India, Tamil Nadu, and Madras. Most of

TABLE 5.2. **Characteristics of Juveniles Apprehended in India, Tamil Nadu, and Madras, 1974**

Characteristic	India		Tamil Nadu		Madras	
	N	%	N	%	N	%
Age						
7–16	28,516	21	9,689	39	4,661	26
16–21	112,123	79	14,927	63	13,015	74
Sex						
Boys	132,135	94	22,724	92	16,559	94
Girls	8,514	6	1,892	8	1,117	6
Religion						
Hindu	86,753	62	16,234	66	11,876	67
Non-Hindu	53,886	38	8,382	34	5,800	33
Community						
Scheduled caste/tribe	54,510	39	10,949	44	6,634	38
Nonscheduled	86,129	91	13,667	56	11,042	62
Education						
Below primary	114,239	81	20,405	83	15,898	90
Primary or above	26,400	19	4,211	17	1,778	10
Family						
With parent/guardian	128,593	91	22,762	92	17,092	97
Homeless	12,046	9	1,854	8	584	3
Income						
Below Rs.150 p.m.	102,796	76	19,978	81	14,012	79
Rs.150–Rs.500	27,583	20	4,516	18	3,612	20
Rs.500–Rs.1000	3,742	3	113	—	52	—
Rs.1000 +	928	—	9	—	—	—
Recidivism						
No record	112,048	87	22,704	92	16,145	91
Record	18,591	13	1,912	8	1,531	9

Source: Based on Bureau of Police Research and Development, *Crime in India, 1974* (New Delhi: Ministry of Home Affairs, Government of India, 1977), pp. 88–91.

those arrested are between ages sixteen and twenty-one, predominantly male, and Hindu (although non-Hindus are somewhat over-represented relative to their proportion—approximately 20 percent—of the population). Although about 20 percent of the Indian population is classified as belonging to what are called "scheduled" castes or tribes, about 40 percent of those arrested in the various localities belong to one or another of these groups. And while about 80 percent of the total Indian population is illiterate, approximately the same proportion of juveniles arrested are illiterate. The vast majority of the juveniles arrested come from "intact" homes, but the families of most are impoverished. Although it is to be expected that many of the persons arrested will be poor, the dramatically large number of impoverished juveniles arrested (those from families having annual incomes below Rs.150) suggests that law enforcement is heavily directed toward the poor (for income data, see Sarma, 1980). Remarkably few of the juveniles arrested have any prior record; most apparently are first offenders.

In summary, the typical youngster arrested in India, Tamil Nadu, or Madras, is in the upper age brackets of the juvenile population, male, likely to be from a minority background, poorly educated, and poor, although from an "intact" home, and a first offender. In these respects the juveniles arrested in India resemble those arrested in Western countries; the outstanding fact is, of course, that far fewer of the youth in India experience this kind of attention from legal authorities.

Self-reported Delinquency and Legal Contact

Research conducted in Western countries suggests that youngsters from lower socioeconomic or minority backgrounds are overrepresented among those juveniles who get into trouble with legal authorities. Our self-report survey also indicates that the offenders processed by legal authorities tended to engage more frequently in delinquent conduct and serious offense behavior. In India as elsewhere, legal control of delinquency tends to be focused on lower-status and serious offenders.

The self-reported delinquency survey administered to the 823 high school and approved school boys in Tamil Nadu included four questions regarding the contact respondents had with the criminal (juvenile) justice system. These were whether they had ever been arrested, whether they had appeared before a juvenile court judge, whether they had received a sentence from a court, and whether they had been placed on probation. Table 5.3 shows the percentages of those who admitted to each of these measures of judicial contact on one or more occasions.

As suggested by the percentages, the legal machinery in India acts in a manner similar to that of Western law enforcement agencies in that relatively few youngsters come to the attention of legal authorities. However, distinct differences do exist between the proportions of the high school and approved school boys who experienced encounters with the police or other judicial authorities. Although delinquency is common among high school boys in Tamil Nadu, extremely small numbers of these boys reported that they had ever been arrested or processed by a juvenile court for their misconduct. A substantial majority of the institutionalized respondents did state that they had appeared before a judge and had been sentenced by the court, but a surprisingly small number stated that they had been arrested. This apparent anomaly might be explained by several things. First, a number of youngsters who had actually been apprehended by the police may have been unaware that this action constituted an "arrest." In this respect, the percentage is probably an underreport. Second, a large portion of the boys incarcerated in the approved schools were housed in these facilities as dependent or neglected children so that even though they were incarcerated, they had not necessarily been arrested. Third, certification to an approved school generally requires judicial action and the imposition of some "sentence"; however, the police are not the only ones who can bring a youngster to the attention of the court. As in the United States, a host

TABLE 5.3. *Percentage of Total Sample, High School, and Approved School Boys Admitting to Contact with Legal Authorities*

Contact	Total sample	High school sample	Approved school sample
Arrest	13.4	4.3	29.1
Court	35.8	4.5	88.9
Sentence	38.3	5.1	94.4
Probation	9.4	1.6	22.2

96 *Delinquency in India*

of persons (school officials, relatives, and social workers) may refer a juvenile to judicial authorities without the direct involvement of the police. Since Indians indicate a general reluctance to deal with the police, it is possible that this percentage (although probably an underreport) is accurate.

In Chapter 4 we reported that approved school boys were generally lower in socioeconomic status than the high school sample and also that they had higher mean scores on the delinquency, status-offense, and theft-offense scales. Moreover, although corporation, private aided, and private high school boys differed significantly in terms of SES, with the exception of theft behavior, there appeared to be a curvilinear relationship between SES, overall delinquency, and status-offense behavior. And there were considerable differences in the proportions of approved school compared to high school respondents who admitted to all four measures of judicial contact. But, are these differences a function of the lower socioeconomic status of approved school boys or of their greater involvement in delinquency? In other words, is legal control of delinquency in Tamil Nadu (and India generally) a product of the offender's socioeconomic status, delinquency involvement, or some combination of the two?

To assess these possibilities, it would be useful to analyze the relationship among SES, delinquency involvement, and the extent to which young people become embroiled (both in terms of frequency and extent) with juvenile justice agencies. Preferably, we would construct a scale of judicial contact which would allow us to explore the relative degree of contact young people of different characteristics have with the judicial system. Zero-order correlation coefficients among the various measures of judicial contact suggest that arrest, court appearance, sentence, and probation are all strongly related to one another. Moreover, Guttman-scale analysis indicates that at least three of these measures (sentence, court, and arrest) do form a reasonable scale. Consequently, these three measures were combined by adding the responses to each to form a contact scale. Zero-order and partial correlations were computed between scores on this scale and the scales of SES, delinquency, status-offense, and theft-offense behavior.* The results of this analysis are presented in Table 5.4.

As might be expected, when the total sample of high school and

---

*While it would probably be preferable to employ regression and partial regression analysis in this context, since we were not predicting any explicit impact of independent variables, we felt that such a procedure would be unwarranted at this time.

Official Reaction 97

approved school students is combined, judicial contact is significantly related to both SES and the three offense scales. Indeed, SES is negatively related to contact, suggesting that the frequency of judicial contact increases as SES decreases. Contact is positively related to the various dimensions of delinquency so that as delinquency (either overall or of specific types) increases, encounters with juvenile

TABLE 5.4. *Zero-order and Partial Correlations among the Judicial-contact, SES, Delinquency, Status-offense, and Theft-offense Scales*

Relationship between:	Zero-order	Controlling		
		SES	Status-offense	Theft-offense
Total sample:				
Contact/SES	−.37	—	−.31	−.33
Contact/delinquency	.62	.60	.08*	.47
Contact/status-offense	.66	.64	—	.54
Contact/theft-offense	.46	.44	.13	—
SES/delinquency	−.20	—	NS	−.13
SES/status-offense	−.22	—	—	−.15
SES/theft-offense	−.16	—	NS	**
High school sample:				
Contact/SES	NS	—	NS	NS
Contact/delinquency	.42	.42	.20	.37
Contact/status-offense	.38	.38	—	.32
Contact/theft-offense	.23	.23	.10*	—
SES/delinquency	NS	—	−.10*	.08
SES/status-offense	NS	—	—	.10
SES/theft-offense	−.07*	—	−.11	—
Approved school sample:				
Contact/SES	NS	—	NS	NS
Contact/delinquency	.49	.49	.19	.23
Contact/status-offense	.46	.46	—	.27
Contact/theft-offense	.46	.46	.28	—
SES/delinquency	NS	—	NS	NS
SES/status-offense	NS	—	—	NS
SES/theft-offense	NS	—	NS	—

Note: NS = Not significant; asterisk indicates significance at .05 level; all others significant at .01 level.

authorities similarly increase. The weak correlations, although negative and significant (probably because of the large sample size), between SES and delinquency suggest that the two phenomena, while somewhat interrelated, may in fact be independent of one another. That is, boys of lower SES are somewhat more delinquent than boys of higher SES, but not greatly so. However, delinquency, in general, is much more strongly related to contact than is SES. It appears then that it is delinquency more than SES that explains official reaction to young offenders. In fact, the relationship between SES and contact changes very little when status-offense and theft-offense scores are partialled out. While a slight reduction occurs, the relationships remain negative and moderate. Similarly, when SES is controlled, the relationship between contact and delinquency is only slightly reduced. But when other categories of offense behavior are controlled, substantial reduction occur.

More than any other variable, status-offense behavior appears to have a greater impact on judicial contact as indicated by the sizable reductions in the correlations when it is controlled. That is, much of the high-to-moderate correlations between delinquency and contact may be an artifact of status-offense behavior for which youngsters are labeled delinquent. This may be true because it is the most frequently occurring form of delinquent behavior and it (or some form of it) relates to social life situations (e.g., begging) which lead to young people of lower SES being either detected by or brought before judicial authorities.

The weak correlation between SES and contact and the moderate-to-high correlations between delinquency and contact may, in part, result from the fact that institutionalized boys tend to be more delinquent than high school boys and from lower SES groups. However they may also be due to the fact that institutionalized boys register higher contact scores. Thus, the relationship between delinquency and contact may be a spurious one, influenced by the association of SES with both delinquency and institutionalization. If this is true, we can expect a reduction in the strength of the relationships between contact and each of the various measures of delinquency when the high school and approved school samples are analyzed separately. To some extent this appears to be the case. That is, within both the high school and approved school samples, the correlations between SES and contact and SES and delinquency are not significant and the relationships between contact and delinquency (while significant, moderate, and positive) are reduced for both groups of respondents.

While there appears to be a curvilinear relationship between overall delinquency, status-offense behavior, and SES when the three categories of high school respondents are compared (see Chapter 4), no significant differences exist in the contact scores of corporation, private aided, and private school respondents in spite of variances in SES and the differences or similarities in their delinquency involvement.* That is, regardless of SES or involvement with delinquency, youngsters from different high schools are not likely to experience greater or lesser judicial contact. However, those institutionalized boys with lower SES scores who are more delinquent are also more likely to register comparatively higher contact scores.

These findings and the official statistics reported in the earlier sections of this chapter indicate that although delinquent behavior is infrequent in India compared to developed countries, judicial authorities respond to it in much the same way in the two types of societies. That is, relatively few youngsters come to legal attention, and still fewer are processed through the judicial machinery. Those who do find their way to a correctional institution tend to be the most serious offenders (in terms of frequency and seriousness of conduct) from the more-deprived socioeconomic backgrounds. In short, poor Indian youth find themselves in the same situation as poor Western children. They (at least the poorest of them) seem to more frequently violate the dominant societal norms and are less immune to being treated as violators than are higher-status youth, who may actually have violated some of the same norms.

Conclusion

The comparatively low incidence of delinquent conduct among Indian youth compared to Western youth is revealed in the numbers of those arrested for such behavior. In this respect, official reaction to delinquency in India is a reflection, at least in part, of the magnitude of the problem with which officials are confronted. Few juveniles experience legal control in India because few of them act in ways that are deemed threatening enough to warrant such action by legal authorities. However, aside from the frequency of judicial response, official reaction to delinquency in India probably parallels that of developed countries in several ways. First, although status and

---

*T-tests comparing the judicial contact of corporation, private aided, and private school respondents are all nonsignificant and, for that reason, are not shown here.

minor technical violations are the most frequent forms of delinquent behavior, the bulk of juveniles arrested for crimes are property offenders or those who flaunt the standards of dominant morality through their gambling activity, violation of prohibition laws, or similar conduct. The type of offense behavior which receives official notice, in short, is not dramatically different in India and the developed countries of Europe and North America, although some specific variations do, of course, exist.

Second, those youngsters who incur official reaction in India are similar to those who do so in the West. That is, enforcement efforts are disproportionately focused on the members of the most deprived segments of the population. We cannot say whether this represents discriminatory law enforcement; however, it does appear that these individuals may be among the more "serious" offenders.

Third, the incidence of official reaction does not, apparently, depend totally on the occurrence of delinquent behavior. At least in part, arrests (and other forms of reaction) correspond to the extent to which law enforcement agencies are organized and mobilized to deal with juvenile offenders. Of course the degree of preparedness may be a reaction to the frequency, or perceptions of the frequency, of delinquent behavior. Whatever the case, part of the "official delinquency" problem is a function of the resources and energy devoted to governmental control of young persons. The extent of this effort appears to be somewhat lower in India than in the more developed nations.

The severity of a social problem—as measured by the extent and intensity of reaction—can vary depending upon: (1) the objective seriousness of the condition (its scope, magnitude, extent, prevalence, and frequency); and (2) the extent to which groups are willing or able to devote resources and energy to "deal" with the condition. While the second factor could, of course, be influenced by the first, there is no necessary direct causal relationship between the severity of a condition and the severity of the reaction to it (Becker, 1966; Hartjen, 1977). However, the lack of a serious delinquency problem in India is, to some extent, a consequence of the fact that authorities either do not choose to perceive the behavior of Indian youth as particularly troublesome and warranting formal control or see no need to take official action (e.g., arrest) to deal with the situation, or both.

Since the specific acts, and the individuals responsible for them, receiving official attention in India are similar to those that come under legal control in the United States and other developed countries, it is apparent that authorities (and possibly citizens) in these countries view the same kinds of acts and individuals as warranting formal control. Thus, it would appear quite reasonable to argue that the lower frequency of official reaction in India is a direct result of the low frequency with which delinquent behavior occurs. Undoubtedly this would explain much, if not most, of the variance in arrest rates between India and Western nations. However, since any condition can be perceived as a threatening social problem, any form of behavior could also be construed as warranting formal social control. That is, what is considered "delinquent" in one society *may* not be considered delinquent in another, and vice versa. Thus while a logical correlation may appear to exist between conditions and reactions, it is not a necessary correlation. And, of course, something besides the severity of the condition could account for the character and extent of reaction to it. In addition to the low frequency of "illegal" conduct on the part of juveniles, two other factors appear to influence the manner in which delinquent behavior is treated in India. These factors which will be discussed more fully in the chapters that follow center on: (1) the differences in the problem of social control faced by authorities in developed versus developing countries, and (2) the relationships between age generations in developing and developed countries and the perceptions these generational groups have of one another. Both of these factors are related to the socioeconomic conditions that stimulate the formulation of a youth subculture and the consequent increase in youthful misconduct such a subculture appears to produce in developed countries.

CHAPTER 6

Judicial and Correctional Processing

Formal social control normally begins with the act of arrest, but the official designation of "delinquent" requires the actions of judicial authorities and the actual exercise of penal control requires the participation of correctional authorities. In this chapter we shall extend the preceding analysis to include dispositional and correctional data and discuss, in some depth, the implications these data have for understanding social control in developed and developing nations.

Dispositions

It is quite possible that many juveniles who come to the attention of the police in India are treated informally so that no official record of their encounters with legal authorities is made. However, once an arrest is made, it appears that most offenders are referred to judicial authorities for further processing. A description of how these young people are treated by judicial and correctional officials can provide further insight into the nature of the delinquency problem in India.

Table 6.1 presents the number of young people (below age twenty-one) referred to a court (either juvenile or adult) in India, Tamil Nadu, and Madras and details of the dispositions received by these persons during 1974 (the most recent year for which data were available). As these figures suggest, young offenders are treated rather leniently by Indian courts; for the country as a whole, only about 27 percent of the juveniles dealt with in that year were incarcerated, while the majority were either acquitted or otherwise disposed of (usually by means of a fine or dismissal). Probation (in contrast to its frequent use in the United States) is seldom used as a means of handling young offenders.

Although disproportionately greater numbers of youngsters are apprehended for illegal behavior in Tamil Nadu and Madras than in India in general, those who come before the court in Tamil Nadu, and especially in Madras, are typically treated quite leniently, since very few of them are incarcerated or placed on probation. This tendency may reflect official policy or simply the fact that a large portion of those arrested or picked up for trivial offenses are considered by the courts not to warrant more than token punishment.

At present, Tamil Nadu has sightly over fifty juvenile court magistrates presiding over nine courts throughout the state. Typically juvenile court judges are young and inexperienced magistrates just beginning their judicial service. For most of them, juvenile court is basically a stepping stone to higher office. In Madras, the court is housed in a dilapidated building once occupied by the humane society (new quarters were being prepared for the court). In spite of laws to

TABLE 6.1. *Dispositions of Juveniles Sent to Courts in India, Tamil Nadu, and Madras, 1974*

Disposition	India	Tamil Nadu	Madras
Number sent to court	114,839	19,996	13,165
Restored to guardian	5,745	2,810	459
On probation	2,235	708	64
Remanded to reformatory or Borstal school	975	259	29
Remanded to school or institution	1,231	223	66
Remanded to adult institution	396	59	19
Imprisoned	15,935	239	123
Acquitted or otherwise disposed of	41,398	14,590	11,780
Pending disposition	46,741	1,708	625

Sources: Based on Bureau of Police Research and Development, *Crime in India, 1974* (New Delhi: Ministry of Home Affairs, Government of India, 1977), p. 85.

the contrary, the court has the appearance and atmosphere of a regular criminal court. Cases are presented in a formal manner by a prosecuting attorney and some offenders are represented by a defense counsel dressed in traditional robes. While the police are supposed to be out of uniform when appearing in juvenile court, and the proceedings of the court are supposed to be confidential, we observed that these regulations were not strictly followed.

Basically, Tamil Nadu juvenile courts are authorized to hear four types of cases involving delinquent, destitute, neglected, or victimized children. Available data indicate that in 1971 (the most recent year for which this information was available) over 6,000 cases were brought to trial before the various juvenile court magistrates in Tamil Nadu.* Of these, 56 percent involved delinquent, about 10 percent destitute, 33 percent neglected, and less than 1 percent victimized children. Table 6.2 presents the dispositions received by youngsters whose cases were heard under these four categories. Of the 4,159 juveniles tried, only about 12 percent were placed in an approved school or children's home. Most were either discharged, released to parents, or placed in the care of some other guardian. Similarly, and ironically, all the victimized and most of the destitute and neglected children were restored to their parents or guardians. Of the 6,688 juveniles dealt with by the court in that year, only 874 (or 13 percent) were institutionalized. This, of course, is similar to the proportion of juveniles in the United States receiving some form of institutional placement (see Jensen and Rojek, 1980). While relatively few of the destitute children received institutionalization as the disposition, 17 percent of neglected children, a somewhat higher percentage than delinquent children, were institutionalized.

Unfortunately, no information is available to determine the dispositions received by youngsters (in delinquency cases) who were accused of different types of offenses or who came from different backgrounds. However, our interviews with various judicial and correctional officials suggest that impoverished, homeless, and minority children are probably more likely to be institutionalized than those from more favorable social backgrounds. Also, those accused of serious crimes are probably more likely to be placed in an

*The discrepancy in the number of persons tried in Tamil Nadu reported in this reference and the figures given in *Crime in India* is partially accounted for by the difference in the years covered (1971 vs. 1974) as well as by the fact that the 1971 report covers children seventeen years of age or younger while the 1974 report includes juveniles up to age twenty-one and provides statistics for both adult and juvenile courts.

TABLE 6.2. **Dispositions of Delinquent and Nondelinquent Cases by Tamil Nadu Juvenile Courts, 1971**

Disposition	Delinquent		Destitute		Neglected		Victimized	
	N	%	N	%	N	%	N	%
Number brought to trial	4,159		513		2,533		57	
Discharged	246	6	—	—	49	2	—	—
Restored to guardian	802	19	494	96	1,637	65	57	—
Released with admonition	898	22	—	—	30	1	—	—
Released on supervision	417	10	—	—	—	—	—	—
Remanded to children's home	65	2	9	2	161	6	—	—
Remanded to approved school	418	10	10	2	211	8	—	—
Entrusted to fit person	199	5	—	—	—	—	—	—
Other	856	21	—	—	—	—	—	—
Number disposed of	3,901	94	513	100	2,217	88	57	100

Source: Based on Central Bureau of Correctional Services, *Social Defense: A Statistical Handbook* (New Delhi: Department of Social Welfare, Government of India, 1976), p. 142.

approved school. But since only a small number of these children are actually brought before Tamil Nadu courts, the majority of the youngsters who are incarcerated have probably committed minor or trivial offenses, or their delinquency is coupled with impoverishment. Thus, for the bulk of the institutionalized offenders, it is their life situation as much as the seriousness of their delinquency that determines their placement in a correctional facility.

In short, in their handling of juvenile offenders, the police and juvenile courts in Tamil Nadu are quite similar to law enforcement and judicial agencies in the United States. Relatively few youngsters coming to the attention of these authorities receive formal or severe reaction so that, as in the United States, youthful offenders in Tamil Nadu (and probably throughout India) are generally not subjected to the full impact of legal control. Thus, relatively few of the youngsters who could be remanded to correctional programs actually experience this treatment in either country. Those who do find their way into institutions are likely to be serious offenders or youngsters whom the authorities deem in need of care. This, in part, is due to a lack of alternative ways of dealing with them. However, given that the incidence of serious delinquency is low while the proportion of destitute, homeless, or needy children is higher in India than in the United States, it is likely that the populations housed in correctional facilities will differ somewhat in the two countries. With the absence of foster homes, adoption services, orphanages, and the embryonic state of probation services in India, it appears that those youngsters who are not released directly to parents or guardians are likely to be institutionalized in Tamil Nadu, even though the severity of their "delinquent" conduct may not warrant such treatment. In this respect juvenile justice in India resembles that in the United States; in most instances the issue faced by judicial officials is not so much a question of what to do *for* the youngsters as what to do *with* them. Since Indian officials are either less inclined or less able to intervene in the affairs of India's young people or their families, in most instances the resolution of this question is that either nothing is done or the child is placed in some facility, with the former alternative being the more frequently selected.

*Correctional Facilities**

Like the United States and other Western nations, the several states and Union Territories of India maintain a number of institu-

---

*Much of the material in this section is reported in Priyadarsini and Hartjen (1981).

tions of various types to house delinquent, dependent, neglected, victimized, or other children. In contrast to a number of other states which have few if any such facilities, Tamil Nadu has established a large number of diverse schools, homes, or shelters. These are either fully financed and operated by the state, or they are private, charitable institutions operating with some government subsidy and support. Based on a list provided by the Department of Correctional Administration, facilities in Tamil Nadu exclusively established for the care of delinquent and other children can be categorized as follows: (1) government and private approved schools; (2) government and private reception (detention) centers or homes; (3) government-run after-care facilities; (4) two government homes established for repatriates from Burma; (5) a private, special child welfare home; (6) government and private institutions for handling cases under the Suppression of Immoral Traffic in Women and Children Act; and (7) government and private rescue ("Muffassil," i.e., noncity) shelters.

While "delinquent" children may be housed in almost any of these institutions, approved schools and reception homes are the primary facilities for accommodating delinquents, although they may, of course, house other types of children as well. These institutions most closely resemble the training schools and detention centers found in the United States. The following discussion, therefore, focuses primarily on these facilities, with greater attention being devoted to several approved schools that were directly observed during the course of this inquiry.

RECEPTION HOMES

While they await trial or sentencing, youngsters not released to the custody of parents or guardians are placed in a reception center (otherwise known as remand or observation homes). In Tamil Nadu, eleven such homes are maintained (four government and seven private), housing about 600 youngsters (predominantly boys) on any given day, with about 7,000 children passing through these facilities each year. The majority of the persons placed in these homes are housed for six weeks or less pending disposition, with a few remaining up to six months or more. Following disposition of the case, children are likely to remain in the home for another six weeks to six months, but none are retained for a period longer than six months. No systematic program of therapy, rehabilitation, or the like is carried out in these facilities, although the staff consists of a diverse number of administrative personnel, teachers, case workers, medical personnel, and others who look after the needs of the various wards. Basically, however, reception homes are congregate jails for children (and some women) and serve much the same function that jails or detention centers do in the United States.

Most of the nondelinquent youngsters placed in reception homes are under fourteen years of age, while the delinquents tend to be slightly older. Of the nondelinquents admitted, most (approximately 60 percent) are destitute. About 15 percent are incarcerated because parents are unable or unfit to care for them. Another 14 percent have been designated uncontrollable and about 10 percent are beggars. Among the "delinquent" children, about one-third are incarcerated for theft and about 10 percent for prohibition offenses. Smaller numbers of delinquents are placed in these facilities for other kinds of behavior, including such things as "offenses affecting life," "mischief," and gambling. The vast majority of the youngsters (over 60 percent) leaving these facilities in any given year are restored to parents or guardians or are acquitted (about 25 percent); only about 11 percent of those discharged are placed in prisons or approved schools. Some children are placed on probation, either directly by the court or upon release from a home.

PROBATION

Probation programs and the use of probation as a correctional measure are infrequent in India, although in Tamil Nadu a good deal of effort is apparently being devoted to expanding this service. According to available information, in Tamil Nadu approximately 6,000 persons are placed on probation each year; about 5 percent of these are children below the age of sixteen. The vast majority of the juvenile and adult probationers are male, from rural backgrounds, with less than primary school education, unskilled, employed in agricultural occupations, and earn less than Rs.500 per month. The majority of these individuals were convicted for theft-related or prohibition offenses. All the juveniles (and most of the adults) placed on probation are retained under supervision for one year or less. Those placed in correctional facilities, however, receive considerably longer sentences.

APPROVED SCHOOLS

Throughout Tamil Nadu, twenty-two approved schools housing delinquent and other youngsters are maintained. Seven of these schools are run directly by the state government and fifteen are managed by private organizations which receive per-head stipends for accommodating "approved school" children. Of the government schools, six (two of which are designated as "senior" and four as "junior") are boys' approved schools. The single facility for girls is a combined senior and junior school. Six of the private institutions are for boys, while the others are either girls' schools or house younger children of both sexes. Three of these institutions are designed to house "mentally defective" or "mentally handicapped" children. Most are "junior" schools, so they tend to house children younger than those found in the government facilities. Generally, the private institutions house orphaned and other nondelinquent children, while the government facilities have a greater proportion of delinquent youth.

According to law, youngsters are placed in either junior or senior schools depending upon their ages. On the average, children are incarcerated for three years, and the law stipulates that no one can be sentenced to an approved school for less than two or more than five years. Since the persons placed in approved schools are on an average fourteen years of age, it appears that most of them remain incarcerated until they reach legal majority. In both government and private schools, wards can elect to remain at the facility beyond their sentence as "club boys" to complete their education or craft training, and we were informed that this is not an unusual occurrence. In private schools, many youngsters choose to stay at the institution until the age of twenty-one at which time they are required by law to leave.

Correctional Programs

During the course of our research, three (two junior and one senior) government approved schools, two private approved schools, a reception center, and a private children's home in Tamil Nadu were observed and in-depth, unstructured interviews were conducted with their staff members. In addition, visits were made to several other facilities throughout Tamil Nadu and the neighboring state of Andhra Pradesh. Since we were primarily interested in the correctional programs for delinquent boys, the following discussion is limited to describing the programs of and our observations at the five approved schools.

110   *Delinquency in India*

GOVERNMENT SCHOOLS

Since they are managed by a centralized state authority, the three government schools located in the towns of Chengalpattu, Ranipet, and Tanjore resemble each other in their programs, management, and populations. At the time of our observations, the senior facility at Chengalpattu housed about 800 boys and the two junior facilities at Ranipet and Tanjore housed about 600 and 300 boys respectively. At Changalpattu the inmates were between twelve and eighteen years old and in both junior facilities they were between seven and seventeen. In all schools several boys had chosen to remain as "club boys." All the boys in Chengalpattu and Ranipet had been sentenced to the facilities under one or another "delinquency" or Children Act statute. Since Tanjore is both a correctional facility and a reception center, a number of the boys in this institution were awaiting trial or disposition and wore different uniforms and were housed in separate cottages to distinguish them from the "approved school" boys.

By Western standards, these facilities appear bleak and uncomfortable. Furniture is sparse, the brick and concrete buildings (some quite old) are colorless and stark in appearance, with barred windows, poor lighting, and few amenities.* However, within the Indian context, these facilities are comparable to Western training schools and provide considerably better accommodations than many of the boys are probably accustomed to. Indeed, for a large number of the wards, the schools offer a reprieve from deprivation.

Chengalpattu: The senior approved school is located in a centuries-old decaying fort. The school occupies twenty-three acres of land and the staff of 119 consists of teachers, administrators, groundskeepers, cooks, and others. The boys sentenced to Chengalpattu remain incarcerated for an average of 3.5 years. Grouped according to physical size, 120 of the boys are housed in each of six "cottages." A group leader (usually one of the older boys) has the responsibility of overseeing each cottage. Some teachers are given the additional job of housemaster and remain with the boys until 8:00 A.M. when school begins. There are no guards or other security personnel on the premises and boys could easily leave the institution by

*It should be noted that this description of approved schools is generally applicable to Indian homes. Particularly in the south, houses are normally brick and concrete dwellings, with barred windows (for air circulation) and sparse furniture. And since paint is expensive, few homeowners are able to afford this luxury.

simply climbing the sloping, crumbling walls of the fort or walking through the front gate. According to the staff, few boys do. Thus, the chronic runaway problem faced by many Western training schools does not occur.

Wards are required to attend the high school located on the premises and can be educated through the tenth standard (grade). In addition, each child is provided training in one or another vocational skill, such as carpentry, mechanized or handloom weaving, tailoring, and welding. As part of their vocational training, the boys manufacture products sold by the institution to other government agencies or on the open market. A share of the money received from these sales is returned to the state, some to be used for the operation of the school and part to be paid as wages to the boys manufacturing the products. The cloth used for the uniforms worn by the wards is woven (as are towels, bedsheets, and mats) and tailored by the boys in the school.

A farm and small dairy herd are located on the premises and provide all the dairy products and most of the vegetables and grain used by the staff and wards of the school. On the whole, the boys appeared to be well fed, adequately educated, and busy. None seemed to have been abused. However, the faces of the boys wore a general look of despondency, and for many the physical signs of their past impoverishment were clearly visible.

According to the staff, discipline is not a problem in the school. They did indicate, however, that some homosexuality and exploitation of younger boys by older ones do occur.

At the termination of their sentences, boys leave the institution or, if the maximum age is reached, transfer to a Borstal school. Orphaned and destitute youngsters are released at age eighteen. Children are typically released to the custody of their parents under the supervision of a probation officer; otherwise they are sent to an after-care facility. Typically, a "probation" officer provides follow-up for three years. According to the school superintendent's estimates, 50 percent of those discharged are "well settled," 25 percent are "not traceable," and 10 percent are "returned to custody."

Ranipet and Tanjore: Except for physical plants and the younger ages of the wards housed within them, the two junior approved schools are quite similar to Chengalpattu in operation, programs, and the like. The Tanjore school is located in an old British prison used to incarcerate activists during the independence movement so the school does have a prisonlike atmosphere. However, boys are not housed in the old cells, many of which are used as play areas and some as storage areas. Physical restraints such as walls and gates pose no hindrance to anyone who wants to abscond. Housed in a forty-acre compound, the 300 residents are cared for by 100 staff members.

Besides the old cell blocks, the facility consists of five dormitory-cottages, three of which are in regular use. Quarters for senior staff and a variety of other buildings (e.g., kitchen, classrooms, workshops) are located on the premises.

According to the superintendent's rough estimate, only about 20 percent of the boys in the school are "delinquent" in the sense that they committed crimes. Most are orphaned, destitute, or unwanted children. Schooling is provided up to the ninth standard and craft training up to grade six.

In comparison to Tanjore, the Ranipet facility is a completely open institution, with no walls around its forty-five acres. Approximately 100 staff members supervise the 619 inmates. This school provides education from the first to the eighth standard, along with vocational training.

As in the senior school, boys in the two junior facilities are housed in cottages according to their physical size. The children in these two schools also manufacture products for sale, receive a small wage for their labor, take care of the premises, and grow part of their own food.

If boys reach the age of seventeen before their sentences have been served, they are transferred to the Chengalpattu school. Upon discharge from the school, boys are released to parents under probation supervision or sent to an after-care facility.

PRIVATE SCHOOLS

The two private schools we observed are markedly better than the government facilities in terms of physical appearance. Both schools rely heavily on donations for their maintenance. The staff of both schools were adamant in their claims that their boys are not "delinquents," although a number of their residents are incarcerated under one or another Children Act statute. Most of the boys in these schools, however, are orphans and/or destitute children. The schools differ from one another in terms of their orientation and program.

Shaligramam: The larger of the two private facilities is located on the outskirts of Madras city. The school was opened in 1966 as one of several institutions run by Seva Samajam (a voluntary agency) for the care and rehabilitation of destitute and orphaned children. Situated on 3.5 acres of land, 365 boys are supervised by a staff of 13 (plus teachers from the affiliated "day school" located just within the school compound). Of the residents, 15 are handicapped and 110 are "approved school" boys. The rest are "sponsored" boys supported by various individuals through charitable (some international) organizations. Most of the approved school boys come to the institution via the court under section 29 (the omnibus clause) of the Children Act. The others are usually brought to the school by parents or relatives who are too poor or otherwise unable to care for them.

Children here attend classes with other (noninstitutionalized) children in the school affiliated with the institution. Vocational training is available in carpentry, box-making, auto mechanics, and tailoring. Since 90 percent of the boys are unable to pass the eighth standard, they are usually diverted to vocational training on a full-time basis. The boys are housed in four cottages that accommodate about eighty boys each. Compared to the government schools, this institution is colorful and otherwise more physically attractive. An administration building, kitchen, school, and other structures, as well as a large furniture- and box-making factory, are located on the grounds.

The distinctive feature of this institution is the furniture factory. It affords training for the wards and provides goods for the school and external sale. Proceeds from this enterprise provide a substantial portion of the school's income. According to staff, boys (apparently the majority) who do not perform well academically are "put to work" in the factory as unpaid apprentices. Wards are given pocket money and extra funds only as rewards for exceptional performance. They are not paid for their work as is the practice in the government schools. Indeed, this facility gave the impression of being a factory that uses cheap, child labor under the guise of vocational training.

Since many of the boys in the school are orphaned or destitute and have been in one of the Seva Samajam homes since childhood, they tend to remain affiliated with the institution until they are eighteen and only leave the school when they reach legal majority, and many graduates are employed in the factory.

Nekkunram: Classified as a junior approved school operated by Daya Sadan, this school is an offshoot of the Daya Sedan Beggar Home and Shelter in north Madras. Started in 1946 with the objective of housing orphaned and destitute boys separately from beggars suffering from communicable diseases, the school now houses boys almost all of whom are orphans.

The school has a staff of nine who care for forty-nine boys ranging in age from six to nineteen. Children are divided into different age groups, but within the cottages they are mixed so that younger boys can be cared for by older ones. A variety of buildings, including the six cottages where the boys sleep, an administration building, superintendent's quarters, kitchen, and dininghall, are scattered throughout the school's seven-acre premises. The school is financed largely by donations and a monthly per-head stipend from the state for housing approved school boys. Much of the financing comes from a leading local industrial family.

By Indian standards the buildings are modern, attractive, and relatively comfortable, and trees and gardens are located throughout the grounds. With a sizable temple situated in the center of the compound, there is a distinctly "religious" air about this school. No classroom or craft-training facilities are located on the grounds; the wards are sent to nearby schools. The superintendent, who maintained that craft training only gives boys an excuse to avoid academic education, was opposed to starting any such activity.

Like the other schools, this institution is largely inmate-run, but here the organization of wards into "ministries" appeared to be more for educational than simple maintenance purposes. Perhaps because of its small size and the philosophy of its superintendent, the school closely resembles a large extended family, with the superintendent playing the role of the *pater familias* as well as the school's administrator. Acting in this surrogate parental role, the superintendent actively sees that his wards become employed, learn to manage money, and have adequate resources upon discharge to establish a separate household.

At the time of admission, most boys are between five and ten years of age; the average age of the boys in the institution is twelve. The wards are free to leave the school upon reaching nineteen and they cannot be retained beyond the age of twenty-one. Most of them, apparently, do decide to remain with the school until that age. Upon leaving the school, wards are required to deposit their income in a joint account held by the superintendent. Each boy is given an allowance and is required to save the rest of his earnings so that he will have a "nest egg" for establishing his own household upon marriage. The superintendent claimed to arrange proper marriages for the boys and help them establish themselves.

This institution is unique in that the children seemed happy, relaxed, and playful when compared to those observed in the other schools. The youngsters seemed to have free run of the school grounds, and were described by the superintendent as "his children"; indeed, they were treated as such.

IDEOLOGICAL ORIENTATION OF STAFF

Although limited, our observations and interviews of staff in these facilities suggest that there are several important differences between correctional programs for juveniles in Tamil Nadu and those typically found in the United States. Of the several dozen staff members we talked with, all expressed a tolerant, positive attitude toward the children under their charge. A characteristic statement in reference to the past delinquency of the boys was "What is past is past." What the child had done before coming to the school did not seem important and the staff tended generally not to discuss the past behavior of the boys. What seemed to matter was that each boy should receive the training and education necessary to live a decent life upon discharge. The wards were not characterized by staff as bad, sick, or otherwise aberrant. Rather, they were viewed as poor youngsters who had had some nasty breaks in life. As far as the staff were concerned, the children were not in the school for punishment and, indeed, we observed a more blatant use, or threatened use of corporal punishment in some of the high schools we visited than in these correctional facilities.

The therapeutic orientation of many Western correctional programs for juveniles was simply not in evidence. Perhaps this is partly the result of the fact that the concept has not caught on yet in India. What staff members called "rehabilitation" was simply education and job training. That is, correctional institutions in India appear to differ from those of the West both in philosophical orientations and programs. While a mixture of punitive/therapeutic goals characterize most American institutions, Indian facilities appear to be more oriented toward the physical maintenance and education and vocational training of inmates. Indeed, these schools more closely resemble boarding schools for poor children than correctional institutions.

Of course, the distinctive orientations may be partly explained by the different populations housed in correctional facilities in the two countries. While American institutions are largely reserved for repeaters and confirmed delinquents, the bulk of the populations in Tamil Nadu approved schools are either mild (petty) offenders or simply homeless, destitute children. And if one considers the differences in the magnitude of the delinquent behavior occurring in the two localities, correctional institutions in India are probably not faced with as serious a problem as their Western counterparts.

Social Control and Economic Development

As in developed countries, the juvenile justice system in India operates as a large people-processing apparatus that screens out substantial portions of those who come to its attention. Thus, those who receive judicial processing and correctional treatment are only a small portion of the numbers who might be considered eligible for such programs. The two major differences between the Indian and Western systems appear to be: (1) the relative frequency with which various dispositions are given out; and (2) the orientation toward and treatment of those who experience incarceration.

Concerning the former, in India the situation seems to be one of a choice between two alternatives, release or incarceration—a decision that is not necessarily based on the offense behavior of the youngster; indeed, the propensity to choose one or the other of these alternatives varies greatly from state to state in India. While this also tends to be true for many of the jurisdictions in the United States, the range of alternative services available to American juvenile court judges is often much greater. Perhaps more important, however, is the apparent difference in correctional philosophy and programs discussed in the preceding pages.

What might occasion the seemingly less reactive and nonpunitive posture authorities in India take toward delinquent youth? In part, it probably reflects the underdeveloped state of juvenile justice and juvenile corrections in India. Surely also, since there are relatively fewer and less serious delinquents in India, part of the answer lies in the fact that authorities have little with which to be concerned. But this does not explain why those who do receive formal reaction are not treated more harshly than they are. Perhaps, then, we should examine the forces that created the delinquency problem in developed countries while none has emerged in developing nations like India.

SOCIAL CONTROL IN DEVELOPED SOCIETIES

In developed societies the same socioeconomic forces that create an alienated subculture populated by young people and increase their involvement in delinquent conduct serve to generate a "problem" of social control in those societies in which adolescent subcultures have emerged (see Platt, 1969). As Christie (1978: 221) observes, youth in postindustrial societies

> can be regarded as a segregated group. Segregated groups are, however, particularly difficult to control. They do not have as much to lose, they tend to create cohesive subsystems, and they are handicapped in finding role-models outside their own categories. Together, these tendencies create a situation with greatly increased risk for conflicts with the formal system of control.

According to Christie (1978: 226–227), three major factors generic to economically developed societies hamper the social control of young people. First, being excluded from the work force, young people are "outside the most easily applicable system of rewards and punishments." Since young people are not monetarily rewarded for their labor (largely achievement in school), the threat of withholding such rewards for deviance loses its force. In a world where "money counts," grades are a poor substitute, and for a fifteen-year-old schoolboy, the promise of future monetary reward for "good grades" has little immediate relevance.

Second, Christie argues that "members of segregated units could become difficult to control because they create a subsystem of equals," one in which members are thrown into daily contact with one another through their forced attendance in schools. When children are united by age and exclusion and are massed together in schools, the negative sanctions of adults are likely to be less meaningful than they otherwise would be and, indeed, may even be regarded as rewards. Their impact as devices of control is consequently weakened (Larkin, 1979).

Third, the separation (both social and physical) of the young from adults makes their actions (deviant or otherwise) more difficult to detect and less subject to immediate control. Indeed, as self-report research indicates, the delinquent conduct which does come to light is only a small fraction of that which apparently occurs. Difficult to detect, such behavior is also difficult to prevent. It becomes subject, instead, to ex post facto repression.

But beyond the "problem" of control, the very forces which necessitate that young people be subjected to control increase the likelihood that such control will become more formal and judicial as societies advance from pre- to postindustrial economies. That is, the creation of an alienated youth subculture increases the probability that young people and their behavior will be seen as and reacted to as a problem. In the first place, because they are a marginal, if not a fully outcast, group in modern societies, young people are more likely to be perceived by adults as different, threatening, and, therefore, worthy of repressive reaction. As criminological (and other) research indicates, it is the marginal members of a society who are most subject to, and most frequently subjected to, repressive reaction. Having been cast into the ranks of the outsider—being seen by, and in turn seeing, adults in terms of "them" rather than "us"—the young in modern society experience the same fate that similar groups have traditionally been required to suffer.

Second, since they lack a place in the production/social system, young people also lack the economic and other power to ward off official control or to alter the conditions of their exclusion which produced and necessitated that control in the first place. As Martin (1973: 353) suggests, "the power of a group determines its ability to keep its people out of trouble with the law, even in instances where they have actually violated it." While Martin's analysis clearly concerns the differential labeling of the more impoverished segments of the juvenile population (something which apparently occurs universally), it has implications for understanding the high rates of labeling experienced by young people in general in modern society. While different segments of the juvenile population may be more or less immune to judicial intervention (because of their parents' relative positions in the stratification-power structure) in comparison to adults, young people in general are a powerless group and, like other powerless groups in society, they have little clout in blocking the efforts of adults to subject them to control.

Finally, postindustrial economy requires the delineation of distinct work roles that are separate from and antithetical to the role relationships of family and community. In such societies, one "is" what one "does" and doing nothing (i.e., not working) means that one is a "nobody" worth nothing. But the affluence generated from postindustrial economy allows that a large segment of the population need not directly participate in the actual activity of production. Instead, such individuals keep busy by engaging in a variety of tasks oriented to caring for and managing other members of the society. In addition, the affluence of postindustrial economic activity provides the resources necessary for employing an army of service workers whose business it is to control others on behalf of their employers. It should be no surprise, therefore, to find in developed societies an increasing portion of the work force engaging in so-called "service" occupations many of which have become professional organizations whose primary business is that of managing the affairs of others. In this respect, postindustrial economy relies upon and expands the operational scope of formal (as opposed to informal) agents of social control. The police and the courts, rather than the family and community, become the agencies to contend with youthful misbehavior and, as such, they serve to transform that behavior into a legal issue—a matter of official social control.

SOCIAL CONTROL IN AN AGRARIAN SOCIETY

If it is true that the economic conditions leading to the exclusion of young people from meaningful participation in adult society are responsible for producing a social-control problem in developing societies and, parenthetically, a delinquency problem as a matter of formal, governmental action, then it is possible that the agrarian economy of preindustrial or developing nations may serve to prevent the development of a youth subculture and also allow for alternative mechanisms of social control. This does indeed appear to be the case in India.

In light of Christie's analysis, it appears that Indian youth have reward systems other than direct monetary payment (i.e., family and *jati* status) available to them. Also, much of one's labor in agrarian society is not directly rewarded in monetary terms. Thus, being outside the labor force in India does not have the same effect that exclusion from the major reward system has in developed nations. Behaving appropriately now so that one can gain that intangible something later is not as powerful an inducement for conformity in India as it is among potential wage earners in the West. Thus, the continual denial of that future reward does not have the same meaning in India that it does in Western nations.

Also, since Indian youth are not members of a separate subgroup of equals, they are not likely to develop alternative definitions of rewards and punishments. While they may, of course, be members of a subgroup which adheres to values at variance with the general society (e.g., the so-called criminal tribes that for centuries earned their livelihood through criminal activity, or the present gypsies found throughout India), young people as a group have not united in the way they have in countries like the United States. Instead, children and youth are located within the status-power hierarchy of their family, *jati*, and community and, as such, are subject and responsive to the controls of the elders, superiors, and authority figures within these systems.

Equally important, it is rare for children and young people to engage in social activities or interaction with others outside the home or family. One's "peers" are likely to be siblings or relatives, not "kids on the block." Thus children are constantly within view of some adult (usually a relative) who takes active responsibility for their actions. Consequently, potentially delinquent behavior can often be stopped in the bud so that it is not likely to become a matter necessitating subsequent formal control or intervention by "outsiders" (e.g., legal authorities).

Further, while the economic affluence and delineation of work roles found in developed nations allow for and necessitate the employment of a large number of formal agents of social control, the agrarian economies of developing nations not only make it difficult to support such persons, but tend to promote a multiwork-role society. Thus, social-control activities may be just as prevalent as they are in developed societies, but they are more likely to be of an informal kind. Family elders, uncles, village leaders, owners of businesses, the school's headmaster, and others—not the police or the courts—are called upon to sanction the wayward and delinquent (see Chapter 9). Thus, much sanctionable conduct is, in effect, diverted from the agents of formal control. As a result, the frequency with which such conduct is recorded in statistics measuring the severity of a "delinquency" problem and justifying the actions taken by officials is reduced.

Finally, since they are not outside the dominant society, young people in India are not as likely to be perceived as threatening and therefore requiring repressive reaction as they are in Western nations. And, while the children of the relatively powerless segments of the society are more often subject to legal control in India (as they are in developed nations), as a class children are not the powerless group they are in developed nations. Although they may have little to say with regard to their lives or activities, they do have some clout (if only in the form of potential) in blocking efforts to subject them to control. A parent will likely think twice before locking up a child who provides a needed addition to family income or the only source of support in old age.

In short, the socioeconomic conditions of developing and underdeveloped countries prevent the emergence of an adolescent subculture. At the same time, they neutralize the problem of subjecting large numbers of young people to formal social control. Moreover, these conditions are conducive to insuring that people within these societies will be reluctant to perceive misconduct as needing formal control or to call upon agents of such control even when it is felt that they have an appropriate role to play.

Conclusion

In light of the information presented in this and the preceding chapter regarding arrests in India, it would appear that relatively few juveniles are subjected to legal control, but that those who are so subjected are generally treated in a tolerant, nonpunitive manner. In this respect, not only is delinquent behavior in India infrequent and mild, but official reaction to such behavior is also infrequent and lacking in severity. Of course, it is impossible to determine the relative rates of reaction *vis-à-vis* the occurrence of delinquent acts in India compared to some country like the United States. However, there does appear to be a distinct tendency in India not to treat youthful misconduct as a matter for formal social control. As a result, delinquency does not materialize as a "social problem" in India; or, at least, it is one with considerably smaller dimensions than are found in Western or developed nations.

Given the rather substantial differences in the frequency of delinquent behavior and the extent of official reaction to it in developed versus developing countries, it seems plausible that social arrangements relating to the economic conditions generic to these kinds of countries might help to explain why (1) young people engage in illegal conduct with different rates of frequency; and (2) why the agencies of formal social control react to such behavior with different frequencies and in different ways. This chapter, therefore, expands on the arguments presented in Chapter 4 and focuses on the differential impact of economic development on the utilization of formal control. The basic argument is that since youth in India are integrated into the dominant socioeconomic system, they are not likely to require, or to be perceived as requiring, legal repression by police, courts, or correctional agencies.

PART FOUR

Societal Perceptions and Reactions

CHAPTER 7

Shaping Reactions: Crime and Delinquency News

The successful generation of public concern regarding some form of behavior is a necessary condition for the creation of a social problem. The generation of such concern on a wide scale requires access to the mass media (Hubbard et al., 1975; Tuchman, 1978). Thus, whether something will be perceived, and possibly reacted to, as a social problem depends, in part, upon whether or not, to what extent, and the manner in which it is portrayed in the mass media. Indeed, any condition, regardless of its "seriousness," (in terms of some objective measure of its frequency, extent, or distribution) could become a public issue if those who shape the contents of media presentation are willing and able to portray it as a topic worthy of concern and action (Schwartz and Leitko, 1977).

Only a small segment of any society experiences (either as witnesses or victims) crime and delinquency directly. Thus, public awareness of "crime" as a social problem is a consequence of the vicarious experiences provided by the media and "consumed" by members of the public (Higgins and Ray, 1978; Chung, 1980). Available research in Western countries indicates that there is no necessary correlation between real instances of law violations and the images of crime presented by the media (Davis, 1952; Gerbner and Gross, 1976; Higgins and Ray, 1978; Sherizen, 1978). Moreover, media portrayal fails to depict the reality of crime in terms of its incidence or distribution. Indeed, as Sherizen (1978: 205) suggests, the "reality" of crime, as portrayed by its coverage in the media as news, is a "constructed reality"—one emanating from a process of selective presentation of crime news as well as the extent of the coverage given to crime by the media.

In the United States, crime is an integral part of the mass media (both as news and entertainment), ranking near the top of those items routinely presented by the media. According to Sherizen (1978) and Hubbard et al. (1975), crime provides the media with a continuous news and entertainment source. It also serves as an alternative (i.e., "filler") when media are short of other news. Thus the media-consuming public is constantly made aware that crime is a problem deserving ongoing concern. For example, Stinchcombe et al. (1980: 122–135) found that instances of personal crime victimization are highly concentrated within certain geographical areas and social groups. Hence, different segments of the population have greater or lesser probabilities of being victimized. However, fear of crime, perceptions of it as a problem, and the attitudes people hold regarding its control are almost uniformly distributed throughout the population. Moreover, the selective portrayal of crime, either as entertainment or news, serves to construct an unreal ideology of crime that may not reflect reality: i.e., crime is pictured as consisting largely of personal violence engaged in by lower-class individuals (see Quinney, 1970: 281–285; Epstein, 1973; Higgins and Ray, 1978). Other types of "crime" are less accessible to crime reporters and, since they are unexciting or uninteresting, are not considered to be newsworthy.

In addition, stories may be actively suppressed either by those who work for the media, control it, or provide the media with information (Barrett, 1973; Epstein, 1973; Altheide, 1974; Roshco, 1975; Sherizen, 1978). Indeed, government officials such as the police provide much of the staple for crime news. What is portrayed as crime, therefore, in large part depends upon the self-interests of these agencies and upon what they consider worthy of public dissemination. Other vested interests also have an impact on crime news. The periodic release of statistics regarding crime or its control, political campaigns for "law and order," or proposals by "experts" to reform the system to more effectively deal with "the epidemic of crime" give legitimacy to the media portrayal and help to shape awareness of the "problem's" extent, nature, and solution.

Studies have sought to account for the typical media characterization of crime (Molotch and Lester, 1974; Lester, 1980). While we might assume that the same or similar forces are at work universally, our interest here is not so much to explain the amount and content of crime news in Indian newspapers as to understand the orientations that Indians hold regarding delinquency and its control. Although delinquent behavior in India is similar to that which occurs in the West in type and distribution, it differs in its relative frequency. But regardless of its frequency or form, the manner in which members of a society react to delinquency can be affected by the extent and type of coverage given to it by the press.* Thus, even though one would be hard pressed to argue that India is faced with a delinquency problem similar to that which exists in the West, the public perception of delinquency as a social problem in India could be heightened if there were extensive media attention to even the limited amounts of delinquency that do occur. Conversely the systematic exclusion of youthful misconduct from media news could reduce public concern and thus serve to condition the nature and extent of societal reaction to it.

Relative Coverage

As indicated in Table 7.1, crime news (including all stories relating to reports of crimes, law, criminal justice, accusations of political crime, and riots) is routinely found in the Indian newspapers we studied. Six to nine crime-related news items appeared in the three newspapers each day, with an average of about fifty-five lines (six column inches) devoted to each item. Although the total newspaper space given to crime is not substantial (ranging from 1.5 to 3.3 percent of total space), it is comparable to the lower limits of the amount of space given to crime by Western newspapers (Sherizen, 1978: 208).

The three dailies differed in amount of coverage devoted to crime. *The Hindu* (known as a "respectable" conservative newspaper) contained about 500 fewer crime-related stories than the other two papers, although the number of lines per story was about the same. *Dina Tanthi* and *The Indian Express* gave about equal coverage to crime news, both in terms of number of stories and the average

---

*The selection of these resources was described in Chapter 2. It might be noted here that while weekly news magazines are available in India, they are quite expensive and are not likely to be widely disseminated. Although both are state-run, radio is widespread but television is a luxury enjoyed by few Indians. In Madras, television stations operate only for a limited period each day (i.e., 6–10 P.M.) and largely provide brief news broadcasts (about 15 minutes) and then lengthy movies, few of which have crime as central themes. The most common source of crime entertainment provided by the visual media is the "western" film widely enjoyed throughout India.

length of these stories. As suggested in Figure 7.1, not only did all three papers devote a fair amount of coverage to crime news, but the relative amount of coverage was similar over the six-month period studied. An increase in crime news occurred in the second three-month period for all three newspapers. This was probably due to the increased space given to nonpolitical crime-related stories plus the already extensive coverage of the legal proceedings relating to Indira Gandhi's emergency rule.

During the first three-month period a small number of rather lengthy articles concerning Gandhi's alleged crimes appeared in all newspapers. As a result, there was little space for the inclusion of other crime news. Between September and October the amount of crime news increased for the *Dina Tanthi* but decreased for both *The Hindu* and *The Indian Express*. *Dina Tanthi* devoted more attention to riots and demonstrations during this period but maintained its relatively high coverage of other crime news. On the other hand, while increased space was given to public disorder issues, other crime-related news coverage declined in *The Hindu* and *The Indian Express*. Hence, variations among the three newspapers' crime-news coverage were the consequence of increased or decreased attention to riots, demonstrations, and political crime.

When we focus on the location of crime news in these three papers, it is clear that with the exception of "political crime" and an occasional sensational crime story, few items received front-page coverage or banner headlines. Most typically, crime-related news was scattered throughout the publications and the normal crime

TABLE 7.1. **Six-month Summary of Crime News in Three Indian Newspapers**

Amount of crime news	The Hindu	The Indian Express	Dina Tanthi
Total no. of stories	1,006.0	1,491.0	1,587.0
Total no. of lines	56,738.0	83,963.0	82,417.0
Lines per story	56.4	56.1	51.9
$\bar{X}$ stories per day	5.6	8.5	8.7
$\bar{X}$ stories per page	0.4	0.7	0.9
$\bar{X}$ lines per day	319.0	480.0	450.0
% space to crime news	1.5	2.2	3.3

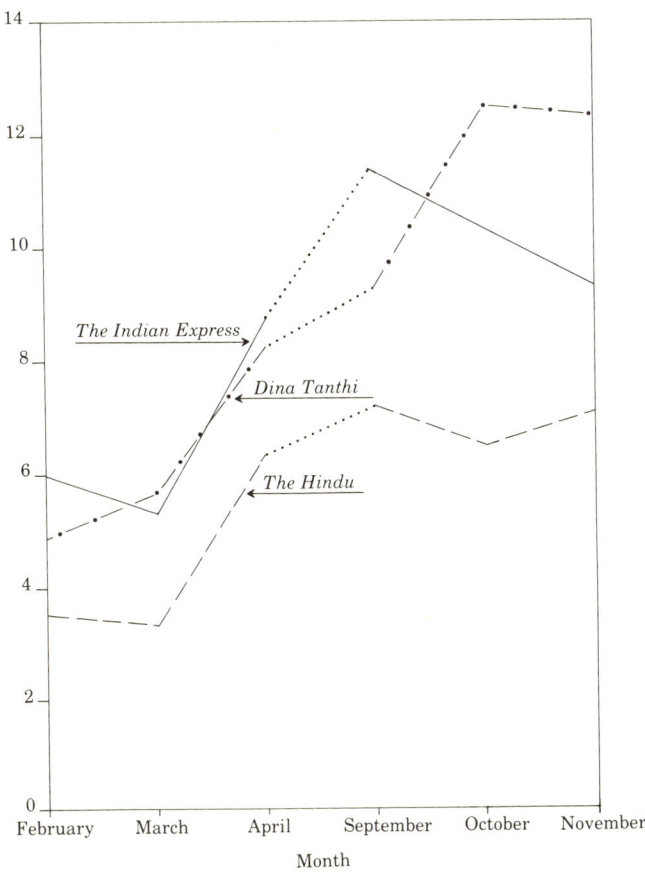

FIGURE 7.1. **Average Number of Crime Stories per Month in Three Indian Newspapers**

story depicting some criminal act, such as a theft or an assault, was a relatively brief, dispassionate description of the event in question.

Still, the three papers differed in the type of coverage given to crime. *Dina Tanthi*, for example, devoted more space to crime (about twice that of *The Hindu*), but the amount of space given each story was somewhat less. Basically, *Dina Tanthi* offered its readers more numerous, but relatively short, highly graphic, sensational portrayals of crimes. *The Indian Express* and *The Hindu* devoted more space to each item, but covered a more limited number of stories.

Moreover, while *Dina Tanthi* gave considerably more attention to descriptions of the victims and (where known) the characteristics of the offenders, the other newspapers were more inclined to depict the details of an event and the statements and actions of officials (usually the police) regarding it. For example, on Thursday, March 9, 1978, all three newspapers included crime news on the front page. On that day, *The Indian Express* ran a sixteen-line (front-page) story of the Central Bureau of Investigation's charges that a former minister was involved in an illegal land deal. This same story was printed in *The Hindu*, which devoted seventeen lines. In contrast, the *Dina Tanthi* had a forty-seven-line story about a woman robbed of her gold chain at knife point. Similarly, on Wednesday, November 15, 1978, *Dina Tanthi* carried a front-page, twenty-five-line story reporting how Prime Minister Desai was confronted by demonstrators in Goa regarding his moves to enact national prohibition against alcohol. On the same day *The Indian Express* ran a front-page story on the riot situation in Madras, describing how the city was returning to normal following the latest disturbance. *The Hindu*, on that day, carried no front-page crime news at all. In short, depending upon which paper one reads, the image of crime gained from these papers differs.

The Content of Crime News

The relative attention the three newspapers devoted to different kinds of crime-related stories is depicted in Table 7.2 and Figure 7.2. Clearly, regardless of newspaper, the bulk of the crime news, amounting to about 26 percent of total coverage, concerned riots and demonstrations.* Stories included in this category reported a wide spectrum of news items, several of which may have touched upon the same issue. For example, a political demonstration that resulted in police action and arrests (which was typical), the riot of fishermen against motorized competitors, a strike at a factory that led to violence and police intervention, or the mass march of disgruntled farmers on Madras (leading to mass arrests) might have occasioned news coverage—not only of the event itself, but also of the actions of officials and the invariable speeches of politicians that followed.

Running a close second were stories regarding political crime, totaling about 23 percent of total crime-news coverage. These typi-

---

*This percentage refers to average combined coverage for all newspapers. The relative percent of coverage per topic for individual newspapers is shown in Figure 7.2.

TABLE 7.2. **Crime-news Coverage by Type of Story in Three Indian Newspapers**

Type of Story	The Hindu		The Indian Express		Dina Tanthi		Total	
	No. of stories	Lines per story	No. of stories	Lines per story	No. of stories	Lines per story	No. of stories	Lines per story
Riots and demonstrations	319	58	437	53	303	51	1059	54
Political crimes	209	87	326	89	393	68	928	80
Personal crimes	122	41	221	39	402	50	745	45
Property crimes	127	31	190	28	211	41	528	35
Prohibition	88	37	73	48	127	37	288	40
Criminal justice	34	58	59	60	56	42	149	53
Law	33	85	56	88	14	60	103	83
Other	74	44	129	45	81	42	284	44

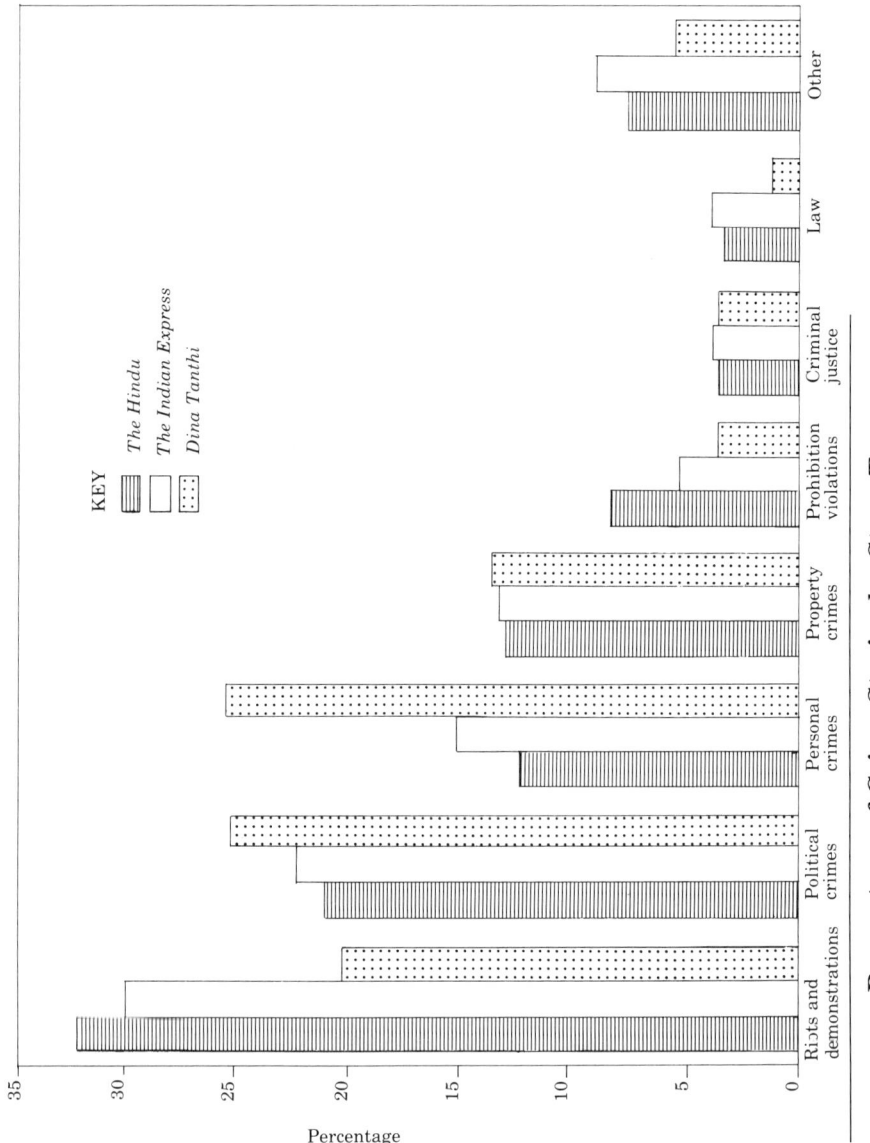

FIGURE 7.2. *Percentage of Crime Stories by Story Type*

cally included statements (both pro and con) by political spokespersons regarding the behavior of Indira Gandhi, her son Sanjay, or others accused of misconduct during her reign as prime minister. In addition, voluminous attention was given to the efforts to prosecute these persons and all papers printed lengthy editorials about political corruption.

Comprising about one-fifth of total coverage, personal offenses were the third most frequently covered crimes. These consisted of murders, assaults, and other personal victimizations. Much of this news focused on one particular event—the kidnapping and murder of a high-ranking army officer's two children. This crime became national news and was extensively covered by the media over several months. The "story" included lengthy descriptions of the crime and the victims, the arrest of two suspects (which was itself described as suspicious since the suspects were apprehended by soldiers while trying to board a train illegally), and the pretrial activities.

Comparatively little attention was given to property crime. This coverage generally focused on such things as chain snatchings, thefts, dacoity, and burglaries. Although it was a major political issue for Tamil Nadu and for the central government at the time, prohibition received relatively little coverage. Often this news consisted of speeches regarding the evils of alcohol and the desirability of national prohibition. Most typically, prohibition-related stories reported the arrests (usually mass arrests) of bootleggers or of those persons involved in the use of illegal alcohol.

The operations of the criminal justice system and the law received fewer, but longer, stories. The coverage consisted of various official announcements, the proposal or passage of new laws, and frequent editorials on police brutality, corruption, and inefficiency. The last category of crime news ("other") includes a variety of offense behaviors which did not fit into one of the other categories. Included are victimless crimes (prostitution), adulteration of food, and the smuggling (usually) of drugs.

Property offenses make up the large portion of crime actually occurring and prohibition violations a large portion of the work carried out by law enforcement agencies; however, analysis of the contents of newspapers' coverage of crime-related news indicates that the picture of crime presented in the mass media is one of public unrest, political corruption, and personal violence. Indeed, when reading these papers, one gains the impression that India is a violent, politically corrupt society on the brink of anarchy. Much of the commentary calling for "law and order" was directed not at street crime, but at the numerous riots and (often violent) demonstrations that were occurring throughout India over political and economic issues.* While such demonstrations were indeed frequent, as is indicated by official crime statistics, the disproportionate amount of coverage devoted to these events and to political corruption suggests that political and economic issues are of greater concern to the Indian print media than are routine or undramatic forms of criminality.

Thus, although crime is a major topic for newspaper coverage in India, the content of coverage differs a good deal from what one finds in Western newspapers. Indian newspapers report less street crime and personal violence. Although instances of victimization are considered newsworthy in India, the constant threat of personal victimization is not as evident in Indian news coverage. Much more striking, however, is the almost total omission of instances of youth crime.

Indeed, at no time was criminality on the part of juveniles reported in any of the three newspapers. Although this could be attributed to the legal requirement, also in effect in the West, that a youth's identity be protected, there was still a definite lack of editorial or other commentary regarding juvenile crime. On the few occasions where an offense was attributed to a "youth," the offender in question was invariably reported to be over twenty-one years of age.

In brief, juvenile delinquency in India is not only infrequent, it is apparently not considered by the media to be a topic of major significance. Indeed the limited media coverage may be one of the reasons why juvenile delinquency is not thought of as a matter requiring serious attention either on the part of the public or judicial officials. But what kind of press coverage is given to juveniles or delinquency in India? This is the topic we address below.

Delinquency News

In addition to the three newspapers described above, other publications were collected on an ad hoc basis for any articles concerning children, juvenile delinquency, or juvenile justice and corrections. All in all, fewer than two dozen articles, stories, and news reports dealing with youth and related matters were encountered by us during the year of research. And of these, only a handful concerned

---

*This is not unlike the situation in the United States during the 1960s and early 1970s. It is possible, therefore, that the period in which this research was conducted is not typical. Thus the relative amount of "political" crime and civil unrest reported here would be lower were another time frame to be studied.

Shaping Reactions 135

delinquency per se. However, one can ascertain the orientation of the media toward youth and youth crime by a brief review of these few publications.

Since 1978 was proclaimed the International Year of the Child by the United Nations, a half-dozen or so articles appeared in various publications concerning the status of children in developing countries around the world. Typically rather lengthy editorials or conference reports, these stories centered on issues of poverty, child labor, childcare, health, and similar matters throughout the world, with special emphasis given to India. None of them discussed youth crime or delinquency either directly or indirectly.

In the "weekly magazine" of one newspaper, one lengthy article apeared on orphanages run by a temple organization in Tamil Nadu. The focus of the article was on the inadequate funds of the orphanages and the struggle they were having in caring for the children. Another brief story reported the death penalty sentence of a schoolboy for the murder of a classmate. And one of the newspapers and a weekly news magazine printed stories on the homosexual exploitation of boys by adults.

Of the handful of articles directly related to delinquency, juvenile justice, and juvenile corrections, all presented rather sympathetic accounts of delinquent children or described the workings or shortcomings of the juvenile justice and correctional systems in Tamil Nadu or India generally. One rather sophisticated article appeared on delinquency laws and the inadequacies of official statistics regarding delinquency rates. This article stated that "crosscultural comparison of juvenile delinquency . . . projects indisputably the preponderance of juvenile and youth criminality in developed societies as against the refreshingly low official rates of delinquency in developing countries like India" (Rao, 1978). The author criticized the "deplorable lack" of uniformity in the Children Acts of the various states and discussed some aspects of delinquency based on official statistics.

Another article appearing in the same newspaper some time later argued that the "seeds of crime" are found in the inadequate care and neglect of children. Moralizing about the need to "produce a new kind of Indian hardworking, self-reliant, moral and nationalistic," the article depicted the problem of crime as being a product of the "total lack of concern" and "heartless indifference" of parents and society in general toward children (Baig, 1978).

A brief story appeared in another newspaper calling for the nationwide implementation of the Children Acts in order to develop "preventive action to control delinquency." Reporting on the meeting of the Central Advisory Board on Social Defense, the article described the Board's recommendations regarding judicial and correctional reforms (i.e., easing the overcrowding of jails, separating adults and children in institutions), loopholes in the laws concerning prostitution, and the problem of beggary. In the same edition of this newspaper, a story appeared headlined "'Court' That Dispenses Sympathy." It described the reporter's observations of a New Delhi juvenile court. Quoting the comments of Child Welfare Board members that the "root cause" of the problem faced by the children they handle "is generally poverty," the story provides several sympathetic "human interest" accounts of typical cases heard by the court (Chauhan, 1978):

> There was the young lad who stole and sold a bicycle to get the Rs.80 required for medical treatment of his tubercular father. He got a sympathetic and understanding hearing instead of being branded a thief.
>
> A girl who was repeatedly and badly beaten and burnt by a stepmother was brought in by a concerned neighbour. The father insisted that the girl should be returned to him. But the girl who showed Board members her scarred body decided she would prefer to stay in the Children's Home. Her wishes were upheld.

The usual cases heard by the court are described as involving lost children, village boys lured by the glamour of the city, exploited children, and only occasionally criminal and uncontrollable children. Briefly lamenting the lack of funds, services, and facilities of the court and auxiliary agencies, the story reports observations not unlike those we gathered from our study of the Madras city court.

Finally, there was an article on correctional programs for children in India. Stating that the objective of sending a juvenile to an approved school was to "make him economically, socially, and emotionally independent" (Shukla, 1978), the author of the article argued that the social stigma attached to children who are discharged from these facilities impedes their full integration into society and the realization of the benefits received from the vocational and other training given them by the schools. The focus of the article suggests that specialized vocational training, "while not the answer to every problem," would help to make the individual more acceptable to the outside world. Thus, youth, and to a limited extent matters concerning delinquency, are recognized as newsworthy topics by the Indian press.

Probably of equal importance, however, are the elements missing from these publications: reports of assaults by young people on others, security in the schools, widespread drug or alcohol abuse, roving gangs of young hoodlums, and similar crime and youth problems. These are conspicuously absent from the media's coverage. Perhaps—as suggested by the preceding chapters of this book—there is little of this kind of "news" to be reported. But there is also an almost systematic effort to depict delinquency as a problem of poverty, childcare, and the need to improve facilities. Youthful crime is played down; emphasis is placed on helping children rather than punishing those who go astray. Thus the problems of delinquency portrayed in the Indian press is one of *need* rather than one of *unruly* and *vicious* children; this is quite unlike the picture presented in the Western press.

Conclusion

As indicated above, crime is frequently a topic in the Indian newspapers we studied, but the bulk of such coverage centered on public unrest and political corruption. While personal violence also found frequent coverage, other forms of crime—the kinds that, according to official statistics, occur more often—are reported less often. While property crimes, violations of prohibition laws, and gambling comprise the bulk of the crime reported in official records, only a small portion of crime news is devoted to these kinds of activities. Youth crime, delinquency, and related matters are also conspicuously absent from the media. And where such matters are covered, the reports most often emphasize the plight, rather than the criminality, of young people.

It is conceivable that delinquency is not a topic of importance in India because delinquent behavior (or, at least, its most violent and predatory forms) is itself uncommon in most of India. Also, it is possible that the media may not devote much attention to the subject because it is not one of significant interest to the media-consuming public. On the other hand, delinquency may not be an issue for either the public in general or governmental officials *because* it is of little interest to the press.

The lack of attention devoted to youthful misbehavior could change if various interest groups were to increase their public relations activities or levels of activism, thereby making delinquency an issue that could not be readily ignored by the press. In fact, there are a number of organizations (e.g., Children's Aid societies) throughout India that could, if they chose to do so, increase the attention given to delinquency by the press. At this time, however, they have chosen not to attempt this or they still lack enough power to influence the media. More likely than not, other matters of more pressing concern to Indians or to the government effectively preempt the resources and thereby divert media attention away from delinquency as a major issue.

Sociologists still have a long way to go before being able to establish any relationship between agency behavior, public orientations, and the prevalence and seriousness of social conditions. And it is not yet clear just what role the media play in contributing to this relationship. Besides being a "window on the world" (Tuchman, 1978), the news may also provide a frame for categorizing that world in the form of events (Lester, 1980). To the extent that newsmaking (reporting) is not a free-agent activity, but rather is shaped by a variety of forces, the world one sees when looking through the window of the news is indeed a constructed or fabricated reality (Phillips, 1977, discusses some of the conditions for news "fabrication").

In the coverage it receives in Indian newspapers, delinquency is a part of that constructed reality. But, at present, it is, at best, an inconsequential part. It could very well be, therefore, that delinquency in contemporary India is at a preemergent stage of development as a social problem, since it is not extensively covered by the press or reacted to as such by the public. It is to the latter issue that we now turn.

CHAPTER 8

Public Reaction

There is no necessary correlation between the dimensions of a social condition and the public's knowledge of, opinions regarding, or reactions to it. Usually, of course, conditions that are not (or at least not known to be) widespread or seriously harmful create little concern and generally occasion only mild reaction. Those that are (or are thought to be) widespread or seriously harmful can generate a good deal of concern and may result in concerted action to "do something" about rectifying the situation.

One way to measure the degree of concern people have regarding various social conditions is by surveys designed to solicit the reactions of samples of the public toward instances of the condition in question. Hence, if delinquent conduct is viewed as frequent or harmful, people are likely to recommend that severe action be taken to combat it, for example, by legal prohibition or the application of severe penalties. On the other hand, if it is not felt to be harmful or worthy of concern, people are likely to not react to it at all or to recommend that either no measures or only mild, informal ones be taken (see Newman, 1976; Stinchcombe et al., 1980). Thus, how the public "feels" about juvenile misconduct can ultimately influence the kind and extent of measures taken to deal with youthful offenders (Parker, 1970). It is the purpose of this and the following chapter to discuss some aspects of public perceptions of and reactions to delinquency in Tamil Nadu.

Dimensions of Perception

Perceptions of the world and, therefore, the opinions people have of and their reactions to social phenomena are, in part, shaped by the extent and kinds of knowledge they possess of the world (Berger and Luckmann, 1967: 42; Holzner, 1968: 23). A person's knowledge, in turn, is largely shaped by his or her interests and values and, therefore, influenced by the person's place in the larger social structure. A substantial body of research (e.g., Walsh, 1944; Lerner, 1958; Becker, 1963; Smith, 1967; Mishra, 1970) suggests the importance that information and knowledge have for an individual's attitudes and behavior. How a person perceives the world and, therefore, the likely way in which he or she will react to social phenomena are dependent upon the person's associations with others. As these associations vary, we can expect to observe variation in knowledge and, as a result, variation in the opinions members of divergent groups hold regarding any social phenomenon and in their attitudes as to how it should be dealt with and who should do so.

Social control (i.e., the mechanisms whereby members of a group are encouraged to conform to or discouraged from deviating from standards of behavior) invariably involves certain enforcers of negative or positive informal and formal sanctions (Erikson, 1964). The presence or absence of such sanctions and their severity can be interpreted as indicating: (1) the behavior people think should be a matter of concern and reaction: (2) who has the power and responsibility to enforce various norms; and (3) what specific means should be employed to deter further deviation. Social sanctions and their enforcers, of course, vary from one society to another, probably depending upon their degree of contractural, formal, bureaucratized structure (Durkheim, 1964; Pepinsky, 1976; Black, 1976). Moreover, research on deviance indicates that reactions to norm violations vary considerably depending upon the characteristics of the observer, the offense, and the offender (e.g., Hollingshead and Redlich, 1953; Schur, 1965; Rooney and Gibbons, 1966; Wiseman, 1970). Thus, as knowledge and opinions of delinquency and delinquency laws may vary, how or to what extent people feel various delinquent acts should be dealt with is also likely to vary. Thus, the "social problem" status of delinquency may differ from community to community quite apart from the objective frequency or severity of delinquent behavior.

Yet negative attitudes toward certain acts do not necessarily lead to such behavior being actually treated as a social problem. Even if people feel that certain acts warrant legal prohibition, they may still be reluctant to rely on formal agents of control to react to the offender. Instead, a variety of informal, or quasi-formal, persons may be called upon to take action. These could include family members, religious leaders, teachers, community leaders, or other such individuals who have social, but not necessarily legal, authority to deal with the situation. Given the possible range and variety of social-control agents, the extent of formal reaction to youthful misconduct can vary considerably, even though the actual behavior of young people in these societies is quite similar in form.

Similarly, the strategies social groups select for dealing with wayward youth can vary. Although the choice of control agent a group makes indicates how serious they feel the behavior is, knowing the choice of control agent does not fully reveal the attitudes and reactions of the public to delinquent behavior. For example, it does not tell us what action the public feels is needed to "correct" or control the behavior. Calling the police to intervene in a situation involving a misbehaving youth does not necessarily mean one wants the youngster arrested or placed in some correctional facility (Black, 1980). The police (as formal agents of control) may be relied upon to simply "put a good scare into the kid" (an informal sanction). The choice of agent of control and sanction, in short, need not always correspond.

Choice of sanction, of course, may vary depending upon one's beliefs, values, and other ideological orientations. Existing research suggests that a good deal of consensus exists in the way people rank-order crimes on the basis of the penalties they feel are appropriate for various acts (Rossi et al., 1974). Also, support for harsher penalties is related to the salience of crime in various communities (Stinchcombe et al., 1980), but the correspondence between the evaluation of seriousness and the choice of appropriate sanction has not been established. It is possible that in spite of similar evaluations of an offense, the chosen penalty (and/or control agent) may vary from one cultural-social group to another. That is, societal reactions to deviant or delinquent behavior may differ in form, frequency, and severity quite independently of peoples' feelings about the behavior in question. As Newman's (1976) research suggests, the members of two societies may agree that a specific act or type of conduct should (or should not) be legally prohibited and responded to with some kind of reaction and control. However, they may disagree as to who should be responsible for reaction or what form that reaction should take. Insofar as social problems are the consequence of reactions to social conditions, the character of delinquency as a social problem could differ considerably from one society to another simply because the members of these societies have developed different ways of reacting to delinquent youth.

In order to gain some understanding of how delinquency is

viewed and reacted to by the Indian public, the public opinion survey described in Chapter 2 was implemented as a part of this research. That survey presented respondents with twenty-five projective scenarios describing sixteen delinquent acts committed by persons of different sex, socioeconomic status, or age. For each scenario, four dimensions of public perception were measured. These were the respondents' (1) *knowledge* of the law; (2) *opinion* regarding the legal status of each act; (3) *choice of appropriate agent* or person to whom to report the offender; and (4) the *type of action* to be taken or sanction to be imposed.

Law, Knowledge, and Opinion

Responses to the knowledge and opinion questions for the twenty-five offense/offender cases described in the survey instrument are presented in Table 8.1. Even a cursory examination of the percentages of respondents who knew that the twenty-five acts were legally proscribed and those who felt that they "should" be allows us to draw several conclusions.

First of all it is clear that proportionately small percentages of the respondents were knowledgeable of or in agreement with the laws regarding juvenile-status offenses (e.g., truancy, defying parents, running away, smoking) and some of the criminal offenses (e.g., assault of parent, petty theft, trespass by a female offender, and vandalism). Compared to those who believed status offenses were illegal, the percentage of respondents who felt such acts *should be* prohibited by law was considerably larger (although this percentage rarely exceeded 50 percent). That is, some of the respondents did not realize that such behavior was illegal; however they were in favor of its prohibition.

If we compare the responses of rural and urban residents, it becomes clear that on most of the offenses, proportionately more urbanites were knowledgeable about the law. For two serious offenses—joyriding (by a higher-status youth) and grand theft— there was virtually no difference between the urban and rural respondents.* For all the other offenses (except marihuana use) rural respondents tended to say less frequently that the behavior in ques-

---

*If no offender characteristic is indicated, either none was mentioned in the particular scenario or we are referring to both instances of an offense committed by two persons of different characteristics.

TABLE 8.1. **Percentage of Respondents Saying Act Should Be or Is Illegal by Offense/Offender**

Offense/offender*	Total sample (N = 803)		Rural (N = 200)		Urban (N = 603)	
	Should be	Is	Should be	Is	Should be	Is
Truancy	26.9	10.0	19.0	3.5	25.5	12.1
Defiance of parents						
Boy	17.4	9.5	8.0	5.0	20.0	11.0
Girl	41.0	9.7	0.5	0.0	22.4	13.0
Runaway						
Boy	34.0	24.6	13.6	9.5	40.8	29.5
Girl	41.0	26.8	16.1	6.0	49.3	33.7
Smoking	50.2	13.4	35.5	7.5	55.1	15.4
Alcohol use						
Higher status	71.4	80.4	62.0	86.5	74.5	78.4
Lower status	78.0	85.5	64.3	88.4	82.6	84.6
Marihuana use	81.6	80.8	82.0	93.5	81.5	76.5
Ticketless travel						
Higher status	91.2	90.0	89.0	94.5	91.9	88.6
Lower status	82.9	87.7	84.5	91.5	82.4	86.5
Vandalism						
Older	64.6	57.1	42.5	52.5	71.9	58.7
Younger	43.7	40.1	7.0	20.0	55.9	46.8
Trespassing						
Boy	91.1	85.8	89.0	93.5	91.9	83.2
Girl	27.7	37.3	2.5	12.0	36.0	45.8
Joyriding						
Higher status	80.3	84.0	69.5	84.9	83.7	83.7
Lower status	91.4	86.3	88.5	91.5	92.4	84.6
Petty theft	52.1	51.3	21.1	31.7	62.3	57.8
Grand theft						
Higher status	78.2	83.7	61.0	83.0	83.9	83.9
Lower status	79.3	84.4	66.0	85.5	83.7	84.0
Weapons use	77.1	69.2	69.5	81.5	79.6	65.1
Assaulting parent	26.9	15.9	13.5	3.5	31.3	20.1
Fighting						
Older	54.5	45.8	39.0	42.0	59.6	47.2
Younger	29.9	20.3	4.5	2.5	38.4	26.3
Gangfight	80.4	72.8	68.0	67.5	84.5	74.6

*Unless otherwise indicated, all offenders are male.

tion should be illegal. This was not the case, however, with regard to the rural and urban respondents' relative knowledge of the legal status of such conduct.

The percentage of the respondents who felt that the acts were illegal varied from a low of less than 10 percent (defying parents) to a high of 90 percent (ticketless travel by a higher-status youth). Among the villagers, knowledge regarding laws prohibiting the defiance of parents was quite low (0 to 5 percent, depending upon the characteristics of the offender), whereas about 95 percent of the rural sample knew that ticketless travel (by a higher-status youth) was legally prohibited. Among the urban respondents, the smallest percentage (11 percent) were familiar with the fact that defiance of parents could be legally punished, and the largest percentage (almost 89 percent) knew that ticketless travel (by a higher-status youth) was illegal. That is, as far as their knowledge of some of the laws is concerned, the rural and urban samples had some similarity. But it is evident that more of the urban residents were familiar with various laws.

Except for a few anomalies (assault of parent, fighting, possession of a weapon, and petty theft), the proportions of the total sample (rural and urban combined) who were knowledgeable about the law and who expressed the opinion that the prohibitions should exist increase as the behavior in question becomes more serious. Indeed, the congruence between knowledge and opinion for the more serious offenses is quite striking and varies less than 10 percent for almost all such acts. Although few dramatic differences exist between the percentages of those who knew an act was illegal and those who felt it should be, for some offenses substantial differences did result. In all these cases, a higher percentage of the respondents wanted the act in question to be prohibited. Thus, it would appear that for the more serious offenses, Indian adults are not only aware that such conduct is prohibited by law, but generally concur with that fact, although there is by no means unanimity in this regard. However, for the less serious and status offenses, wider discrepancies exist between knowledge and opinion and these discrepancies are particularly pronounced among the urban respondents.

For the total sample, in seven of the twenty-five cases the percentage of respondents who knew that the acts were illegal was greater than the percentage who thought such conduct *should be* prohibited by law.* Among the rural respondents there were fourteen

---

*We did not consider any difference of less than 5 percent to be meaningful.

cases in which the percentage of respondents who said the various acts were illegal exceeded the percentage who thought they *should be*. Such disagreement only occurred in four instances for the urban sample.

Conversely, in thirteen cases proportionately more of the total sample felt that various acts should be illegal than thought that they actually were. Among the rural respondents, fewer people knew that running away from home and smoking were illegal than felt such acts should be. On the other hand, more of the urbanites knew that trespass by a girl was illegal, but fewer felt that it should be.

In summary, it is quite clear that a consistently higher proportion of the urban sample preferred that the twenty-five offense/offenders presented in the questionnaire be controlled by legal means (statutorily prohibited). This could indicate a greater concern with or a more conservative orientation toward juvenile misconduct on the part of urban dwellers. Or, what is more likely, it could represent a greater tendency on the urbanites' part to rely upon formal as opposed to informal mechanisms of social control. Indeed, this finding concurs with research carried out in the United States (Boggs, 1971). Regardless of their opinions, however, both rural and urban respondents evidenced a high level of knowledge about the laws governing juvenile misconduct and were generally supportive of the laws concerning the more serious misconduct.

Even if their responses do not actually reflect a greater tolerance of juvenile misconduct, it is clear that rural residents are more opposed to formal prohibition of behavior that violates norms, especially when such conduct is of a petty (or a *mala prohibita*) variety. Existing literature (e.g., Bayley, 1969) suggests that this could be a result of the local communities' ambivalence toward, if not outright opposition to, the representatives of government such as tax collectors and the police. Indeed, the contrasting development of rural and urban India is perhaps reflected in the differing reactions toward formal or governmental controls. Historically there has always been some distance between the urban centers of power and administration and the mass of Indians dwelling in relatively isolated rural communities. There was little contact between the rural Indian public and the British authorities, and the officials who drew up the original and still active Indian Penal Code evidenced little consideration for "Indian" opinion. While the present government is paying greater attention to public opinion, there is still little reason to assume that the hinterland, compared to the urban power elite, has an equal voice in public policy. Therefore, it is not surprising that some disparity would exist in the opinions of urban and rural respondents with regard to that policy.

VARIABILITY IN OPINION

A substantial body of research (e.g., Adorno et al., 1950; Rosen, 1956; Bernstein, 1958; Kohn, 1959; Bendix and Lipset, 1966) suggests that socioeconomic and other characteristics influence peoples' beliefs, attitudes, values, and life orientations. Such characteristics may not have cross-cultural significance partly because of the impact of cultural factors or the relative meaning of various personal characteristics in different social systems. But within any specific sociocultural context, it is likely that variability exists in the knowledge, opinions, and attitudes people have, depending upon socioeconomic attributes that are comparable within that context, with regard to specific social phenomena.

With respect to crime and delinquency, a number of studies have been conducted in Western societies regarding "public opinion" and its variability in terms of a variety of factors. The bulk of this research suggests that respondents exhibit a high degree of consensus with regard to the seriousness of various offenses and that they generally rank-order offenses in terms of perceived seriousness in similar ways (see Sellin and Wolfgang, 1964; Normandeau, 1966; Akman et al., 1967; Rossi et al., 1974). Moreover, this research indicates that factors such as race, sex, age, education, and the like are not highly influential in general perceptions of Westerners as to the seriousness of various crimes.

While informative, such research is limited in its theoretical significance. Even though respondents concur on seriousness, their perceptions of crime and delinquency may differ depending upon the circumstances of the offenses and the social or demographic characteristics of the offender and those of the respondent. While somewhat contradictory and hardly conclusive, a variety of studies imply that this might very well be the case (see Boggs, 1971; Conklin, 1971; Gibbons et al., 1972; Newman, 1974; Garofalo, 1977; Taylor et al., 1979).

As the percentages in Table 8.1 indicate, several of the nine scenarios in which the social or economic characteristics of the offender were reversed for the same offense produced differences in reactions depending upon the offender's age, sex, or status. Proportionately more respondents thought that fighting and vandalism should be legally prohibited if committed by an older youth compared to a younger one. Mixed results occurred, however, when the sex and socioeconomic status of the offender were varied. More people favored the prohibition of running away if a girl, instead of a boy, was involved, but comparatively fewer thought that trespass by a girl, in contrast to that by a boy, warranted legal prohibition. Joyriding by a lower-status youth was more often thought to deserve legal control than if the same act were committed by a higher-status youngster. But respondents were more frequently in favor of laws prohibiting ticketless travel if the offender was a higher-status compared to a lower-status person.

Similar patterns of response were found, although with some variations as to the magnitude of the differences in percentages, for the urban and rural samples. However, a higher percentage of rural respondents favored the legal prohibition of defying parents if the offender was a boy rather than a girl, whereas urbanites were more likely to want the consumption of alcohol to be legally forbidden lower-status rather than higher-status offenders. Thus, while it does indeed appear that opinions with regard to the legal restriction of various behaviors do vary in terms of the characteristics of the offender, the respondents' residence does not greatly influence the pattern of this variance—although, as noted above, urban residence does appear to be related to the overall proclivity to favor formal prohibition of juvenile misconduct.

Perhaps, however, other demographic characteristics of individual respondents with, or apart from, the characteristics of the offender have some influence on their opinions as to the desirability of legally forbidding specific activities. Chi-square analysis of the relationships between opinion and the respondents' sex, age, education, income, religion, and prior victimization experiences yielded nonpatterned and only a limited number of significant associations— a fact which suggests that these characteristics have little impact on opinions. In general respondents exhibited a high degree of unanimity in their opinions. Where variability did exist, it was not great nor did any discernible pattern result. So, to this extent, Indian adults appear to resemble the respondents surveyed during similar research conducted in the United States and elsewhere.

VARIABILITY IN KNOWLEDGE

Comparatively few variations in respondents' knowledge of delinquency laws occurred when the offense was portrayed as having been committed by youngsters of different social characteristics.

Indeed, there were substantial differences for only three offenses. That is, for the combined sample, a higher percentage of the respondents (57 percent compared to 40 percent) knew that vandalism involving an older youth is prohibited. Eighty-six percent of respondents felt that trespassing was illegal for a boy, but only 37 percent felt that the same act was illegal if committed by a girl. Similarly, when an older youth was involved, almost one-half (46 percent) of the total sample said that fighting was illegal, but only 20 percent gave the same response when the offender was described as a younger person. Although the percentages varied, the pattern of these differences in knowledge was identical for the rural and urban samples. This suggests that perceptions of the illegality of the behaviors described in the questionnaire as a function of the characteristics of the offender were not substantially influenced by residence.

Rural and urban respondents did differ, however, in their knowledge regarding the legal status of various offense types. In most instances, urbanites, more often than rural dwellers, felt that the acts in question were illegal. Rural people were more likely to say that smoking marihuana and carrying a concealed weapon were illegal, but for all other offenses, the percentage of respondents saying the act was illegal was higher for the urbanites.

The majority of both sample groups felt that the more serious offenses were illegal, whereas negligible numbers of respondents thought the various status offenses (truancy, defying parents, running away, or smoking) were illegal. Thus, knowledge of the law varies somewhat when different offenders are involved, tends to be greater among urban respondents, and is closely related to the severity of the offense.

As with opinions, relatively few significant differences in knowledge of the law were found among the various subgroups. Of all the possible 175 relationships between the 25 cases and the socioeconomic characteristics of respondents, only 38 were statistically significant for the entire sample of 803 respondents. Among the villagers, only 8 were significant, whereas 29 relationships were found among the urban sample. Most of the significant relationships that were found occurred for the socioeconomic status variables of education, occupation, and income. Thus, while there does appear to be some positive association between knowledge of delinquency laws and socioeconomic status, this relationship is not patterned and is overridden by the rather large and more systematic differences found between residence and this (and other) dimensions of reaction.

Sanctions and Agent of Control

Reactions to the hypothetical instances of delinquency were measured by asking respondents to indicate to *whom* they would report such conduct and *what* actions should be taken against the offender. Responses to these questions can be arranged in terms of the degree of seriousness or formality of the penalty suggested as appropriate. Thus, for each offense/offender case, respondents could suggest that it not be reported to anyone and/or that no action be taken against the offender. Similarly, they could stipulate that an "informal" agent be called upon and/or that some action ("informal") short of ("formal") arrest, adjudication, or imprisonment be taken. And, finally, respondents could suggest that some "formal" agent (e.g., police) be called upon and/or that some "formal" sanction be imposed.* The results of this inquiry are presented in Table 8.2.

RURAL RESPONDENTS' CHOICE OF AGENT AND SANCTION

Responses to the "criminal" acts described in the vignettes indicate that although only small proportions of respondents think most juvenile misconduct should be ignored, certain acts are considered more serious than others in that the respondents recommended that some agent of social control deal with the offender. Juvenile-status offenses, however, tend to evoke fairly mild reactions, especially among the rural respondents.

For example, over two-fifths of the rural sample stated that truancy should not be reported at all. This is the largest of all the percentages of rural respondents who feel that an act should be ignored. In contrast, the largest percentage of urban respondents who would ignore an offense was 15 percent (for trespass by a girl). Fewer than 5 percent of the rural respondents, however, would ignore grand theft, ticketless travel by a higher-status boy, fighting by a younger youth, and gangfighting. With the exception of the status offenses, most acts did seem to evoke a desire for intervention, but not necessarily by some official agent.

For most of the status offenses and minor crimes, a sizable portion of the rural sample (10 percent or more) said that the offender

---

*For purposes of conciseness, the original response categories to the "who" and "what" questions (agent and sanction) are collapsed and combined in this section.

TABLE 8.2. *Percentage of Respondents Recommending Different Social Control Agents and Sanctions by Locality and Offense/Offender Type*

Offense/offender	Total sample		Rural		Urban	
	Agent	Sanction	Agent	Sanction	Agent	Sanction
Truancy						
No one/nothing	13.0	10.0	43.0	23.0	3.0	6.0
Nonformal*	83.0	45.0	54.0	59.0	93.0	40.0
Formal	4.0	45.0	2.0	18.0	4.0	54.0
	(803)	(803)	(200)	(200)	(603)	(603)
Defiance of parents (boy)						
No one/nothing	12.0	19.0	14.0	17.0	11.0	20.0
Nonformal	82.0	47.0	79.0	62.0	83.0	42.0
Formal	6.0	34.0	7.0	21.0	6.0	38.0
	(800)	(801)	(200)	(200)	(600)	(601)
Defiance of parents (girl)						
No one/nothing	10.0	15.0	11.0	11.0	10.0	16.0
Nonformal	83.0	55.0	87.0	86.0	82.0	45.0
Formal	7.0	30.0	2.0	3.0	8.0	39.0
	(801)	(801)	(200)	(200)	(601)	(601)
Runaway (boy)						
No one/nothing	11.0	10.0	29.0	21.0	5.0	7.0
Nonformal	64.0	38.0	53.0	50.0	67.0	34.0
Formal	25.0	52.0	18.0	29.0	28.0	59.0
	(802)	(801)	(199)	(200)	(602)	(603)

Runaway (girl)						
No one/nothing	6.0	8.0	13.0	15.0	3.0	6.0
Nonformal	67.0	44.0	71.0	59.0	67.0	39.0
Formal	27.0	48.0	16.0	26.0	30.0	55.0
	(803)	(802)	(199)	(199)	(603)	(603)
Smoking						
No one/nothing	11.0	10.0	12.0	23.0	10.0	6.0
Nonformal	85.0	47.0	85.0	64.0	86.0	42.0
Formal	4.0	43.0	3.0	13.0	4.0	52.0
	(801)	(802)	(200)	(200)	(601)	(602)
Alcohol use (higher status)						
No one/nothing	4.0	2.0	3.0	2.0	5.0	3.0
Nonformal	62.0	34.0	68.0	52.0	60.0	27.0
Formal	34.0	64.0	29.0	46.0	35.0	70.0
	(803)	(802)	(200)	(200)	(603)	(602)
Alcohol use (lower status)						
No one/nothing	2.0	4.0	3.0	6.0	2.0	3.0
Nonformal	53.0	33.0	63.0	55.0	50.0	26.0
Formal	45.0	63.0	34.0	39.0	48.0	71.0
	(801)	(802)	(199)	(199)	(602)	(603)
Marihuana use						
No one/nothing	1.0	1.0	3.0	1.0	1.0	1.0
Nonformal	46.0	23.0	35.0	26.0	48.0	21.0
Formal	53.0	76.0	62.0	73.0	51.0	78.0
	(801)	(801)	(200)	(200)	(601)	(601)

(continued on next page)

TABLE 8.2. Continued

Offense/offender	Total sample		Rural		Urban	
	Agent	Sanction	Agent	Sanction	Agent	Sanction
Ticketless travel (higher status)						
No one/nothing	1.0	1.0	1.0	0.0	0.0	2.0
Nonformal	26.0	18.0	15.0	18.0	31.0	17.0
Formal	73.0	81.0	84.0	82.0	69.0	81.0
	(803)	(803)	(200)	(200)	(603)	(603)
Ticketless travel (lower status)						
No one/nothing	4.0	5.0	6.0	3.0	3.0	5.0
Nonformal	30.0	21.0	25.0	19.0	31.0	22.0
Formal	66.0	74.0	69.0	78.0	66.0	73.0
	(801)	(801)	(200)	(200)	(601)	(601)
Vandalism (older)						
No one/nothing	1.0	3.0	2.0	7.0	1.0	2.0
Nonformal	56.0	32.0	74.0	54.0	50.0	25.0
Formal	43.0	65.0	24.0	39.0	49.0	73.0
	(802)	(801)	(200)	(200)	(602)	(601)
Vandalism (younger)						
No one/nothing	2.0	8.0	5.0	11.0	1.0	7.0
Nonformal	75.0	44.0	92.0	72.0	69.0	35.0
Formal	23.0	48.0	3.0	17.0	30.0	58.0
	(801)	(803)	(200)	(200)	(601)	(603)

Trespassing (boy)						
No one/nothing	0.0	2.0	1.0	2.0	0.0	2.0
Nonformal	20.0	12.0	13.0	11.0	22.0	12.0
Formal	80.0	86.0	86.0	87.0	78.0	86.0
	(802)	(801)	(200)	(200)	(602)	(601)
Trespassing (girl)						
No one/nothing	14.0	33.0	11.0	31.0	15.0	34.0
Nonformal	79.0	43.0	88.0	67.0	76.0	35.0
Formal	7.0	24.0	1.0	12.0	9.0	31.0
	(801)	(799)	(200)	(200)	(601)	(599)
Joyriding (higher status)						
No one/nothing	1.0	3.0	3.0	6.0	1.0	3.0
Nonformal	42.0	25.0	52.0	42.0	38.0	18.0
Formal	57.0	72.0	45.0	52.0	61.0	79.0
	(801)	(802)	(199)	(199)	(602)	(603)
Joyriding (lower status)						
No one/nothing	1.0	2.0	1.0	1.0	0.0	0.0
Nonformal	18.0	14.0	27.0	22.0	16.0	12.0
Formal	81.0	84.0	72.0	77.0	84.0	86.0
	(803)	(803)	(200)	(200)	(603)	(603)
Petty theft						
No one/nothing	4.0	12.0	8.0	22.0	3.0	8.0
Nonformal	73.0	36.0	77.0	59.0	72.0	28.0
Formal	23.0	52.0	15.0	19.0	25.0	64.0
	(799)	(798)	(199)	(198)	(600)	(600)

(continued on next page)

TABLE 8.2. Continued

Offense/offender	Total sample		Rural		Urban	
	Agent	Sanction	Agent	Sanction	Agent	Sanction
Grand theft (higher status)						
No one/nothing	6.0	1.0	3.0	8.0	1.0	5.0
Nonformal	49.0	26.0	62.0	47.0	45.0	20.0
Formal	50.0	68.0	35.0	45.0	54.0	75.0
	(803)	(802)	(200)	(200)	(603)	(602)
Grand theft (lower status)						
No one/nothing	1.0	3.0	1.0	6.0	1.0	2.0
Nonformal	37.0	25.0	59.0	42.0	30.0	20.0
Formal	62.0	72.0	40.0	52.0	69.0	78.0
	(803)	(802)	(200)	(200)	(603)	(602)
Weapons use						
No one/nothing	6.0	7.0	6.0	10.0	6.0	6.0
Nonformal	43.0	20.0	42.0	33.0	43.0	16.0
Formal	51.0	73.0	52.0	57.0	51.0	78.0
	(802)	(799)	(200)	(198)	(602)	(601)
Assaulting parent						
No one/nothing	5.0	7.0	7.0	13.0	5.0	6.0
Nonformal	87.0	57.0	89.0	75.0	86.0	50.0
Formal	8.0	36.0	4.0	12.0	9.0	44.0
	(802)	(802)	(200)	(200)	(602)	(602)

Fighting (older)						
No one/nothing	1.0	3.0	1.0	2.0	1.0	3.0
Nonformal	69.0	31.0	76.0	50.0	66.0	24.0
Formal	30.0	66.0	23.0	48.0	33.0	73.0
	(802)	(802)	(200)	(200)	(602)	(602)
Fighting (younger)						
No one/nothing	2.0	7.0	5.0	11.0	1.0	5.0
Nonformal	92.0	47.0	93.0	69.0	92.0	41.0
Formal	6.0	46.0	2.0	20.0	7.0	54.0
	(802)	(801)	(200)	(200)	(601)	(602)
Gangfight						
No one/nothing	0.0	1.0	1.0	1.0	0.0	1.0
Nonformal	35.0	23.0	59.0	49.0	27.0	14.0
Formal	65.0	76.0	40.0	50.0	73.0	85.0
	(800)	(799)	(200)	(199)	(600)	(600)

Note: Number in parentheses = total number of respondents.
*Nonformal includes advice or punishment by family member, the act's observer, religious leader, doctor, teacher, or social worker; formal includes advice or punishment (e.g., fine, probation, incarceration) by the police or other government agent.

156   *Delinquency in India*

did not warrant a sanction; but over 90 percent of the respondents felt some sanction should be imposed on the offenders described in most of the other stories. With few exceptions, however, they rarely selected formal punishment, and some variability existed in the choice of sanction and sanctioning agent depending upon the characteristics of the offender. As one might expect, these responses indicate that rural Tamilians have varied degrees of tolerance for different acts and offenders.

Sanction: Although their responses were similar to those of the total sample, rural residents more frequently indicated a preference that nothing be done to the offender. Yet, for several offenses, almost all rural respondents felt that some punishment was warranted. A review of Table 8.2, however, suggests that there is no apparent pattern in the types of offenses or offenders rural respondents felt should receive no sanction, informal punishment, or formal sanction.

Agent of Control: The proportion of rural respondents who would not report an offense ranges from a low of 1 percent (for the diverse acts of ticketless travel by a higher-status youth, trespass by a boy, joyriding by a lower-status youth, grand theft by a lower-status youth, fighting by an older boy, and gangfighting) to a high of 43 percent for truancy. The highest percentage of the urban sample, in contrast, was the 15 percent who would not report trespass by a girl.

Most typically, rural respondents did not favor formal agents of control. The percentages of these respondents who would report delinquent acts to officials ranged from 1 percent (for trespass by a girl) to 86 percent (for trespass by a boy). Indeed, if an offense were to be reported to anyone at all, in the vast majority of cases the control agent preferred was a nonformal agent. In this respect, rural respondents indicated a distinct desire to avoid involving the "authorities" in cases of juvenile misconduct. Yet in some instances, formal agents were preferred by half or more of the respondents, although there is no clear relationship between type of offense and sanctioning agent preferred.

These findings suggest that certain property offenses may elicit more severe reactions among rural Indians, whereas juvenile-status offenses evoke rather mild reactions. This is quite understandable. The statutes forbidding these activities are an artifact of Western law "juvenilizing" young people. The apparent lack of concern Indians have for this kind of conduct is reflected in the nonchalant statements of the members of the public and various officials we interviewed. For example, they expressed the belief that runaways will not stray far and will return home once they get hungry. Similarly, truancy was not considered a serious problem. "Find something else for him (or her) to do!" was the usual comment regarding this behavior. On the other hand, there appears to be a pervasive paranoia regarding theft, particularly among middle-class Indians who take great care in locking valuables in safes and making sure that loose change and other goods are not available to servants who, they are convinced, would steal them if they had the opportunity. One is constantly reminded not to leave things unattended. Yet, when a theft does occur, it is not blamed on the offender, but on the victim who is careless enough not to take proper care.

Surprisingly, substance abuse, like alcohol consumption, did not elicit the harsh reactions we expected. Since Tamil Nadu was a "dry" state, we assumed that people would exhibit a sense of indignation at the violations of teetotalling norms and the Prohibition Act, particularly when the offender involved was young. But this was not the case. Thus, among rural Indians (where "toddy-tapping" has been a traditional cottage industry) concern over youthful drinking is perhaps not as extensive as one would assume it to be on the basis of anti-drinking laws.*

Congruence between Agent and Sanction: A comparison of respondents' choice of control agent with the sanction they feel is appropriate should reveal the extent of congruence between the dimensions of their attitudes. Respondents who chose similar types of social-control agents and sanctions can be said to exhibit congruence in their attitudes concerning the social control of young offenders. That is, if one's attitudes are congruent, one would say that no sanction should be imposed if one chose not to report questionable behavior. It is conceivable that one might want to report an infraction to a nonformal agent but not necessarily desire that any sanction be imposed. It is also possible for the obverse to occur. That is, a person who says an offense should not be reported to anyone or who states that it should be reported to a nonformal agent, could still want formal sanctions imposed on the offender; in this case these dimensions of a person's attitude could be said to be incongruent. Analysis of the percentage distributions presented in Table 8.2 suggests a number of things about the congruency in attitudes concerning reactions to delinquent conduct.

*Tapping the sap of palm trees, used in making fermented drinks.

There are considerable differences (10 percent or more) in the proportions of rural respondents who would not report several acts (truancy, smoking, and trespass by a girl) and those who recommend that no sanctions be imposed on these offenders. Similarly, there are noticeable differences in the proportions of rural residents who suggest reporting a boy's defiance of parents to some nonformal agent and those who say that nonformal sanctions should be levied against the offender. Although the percentage differences vary in magnitude, there is a similar lack of congruence between the choice of agent and sanction for alcohol use by a higher-status offender, vandalism, trespass by a girl, joyriding by a higher-status offender, petty and grand theft, and all types of fighting.

For a diverse number of offenses (i.e., truancy, defiance of parents by a boy, running away from home, smoking, alcohol use by a higher-status offender, marihuana use, vandalism by a younger offender, grand theft, and all instances of fighting), if we compare the proportions of the rural sample who said that an offense should be reported to formal agents with the percentage who recommended formal sanctions, it is clear that the number of respondents (10 percent or more) who would recommend formal sanctions is greater than the number who would recommend formal agents of control. For all the offenses listed above, respondents preferred nonformal agents of control but, at the same time, formal sanctions.

A variety of literature on human cognitive systems suggests that people strive for cognitive congruency among their attitudes and behavior. Other evidence indicates that people attempt to reduce cognitive dissonance in various ways (see Heider, 1946; Osgood and Tannenbaum, 1955; Festinger et al., 1956; Festinger, 1957). The respondents may not perceive the apparent incongruency in the dimensions of attitude found in this study in these terms; nor do they necessarily have any desire for balance in their attitudes (see Myrdal, 1944). Indians have lived with contradictions for centuries. Moreover, since the "nonformal" and "formal" response categories are actually collapsed from a combination of several response choices and include elaborations contained in the response to the "other" category, there may actually be more overlap in responses than the categorization system used here would reveal. It is more likely, however, that their responses to each of the two questions in fact indicate two unrelated aspects of *their* cognitive system. Our conversations with the public and correctional personnel suggest that seemingly formal sanctions may not carry the negative connotation and stigma that they do in countries like the United States. Indeed, most of the people we talked with expressed the view that approved schools were not places of punishment but rather facilities designed to help the youngster "shape-up" by means of discipline and regulation. In short, there is no reason to assume that type of sanction should necessarily correspond to type of scantioner in the Indian scheme of things.

URBAN RESPONDENTS' CHOICE OF AGENT AND SANCTION

Crime in India, as elsewhere, is largely an urban phenomenon. Although the respondents to this survey generally did not seem inclined to resort to formal social control in cases of juvenile misconduct, within India the factor of rural versus urban residence may influence perceptions of delinquency and therefore the attitudes a person has toward youthful offenders. If the severity of a social condition determines the probability that it will be viewed as in need of correction and thus the likelihood that a social problem will be created, we would expect that where delinquency is most prevalent (e.g., in urban areas) people would hold more severe attitudes toward youthful offenders and would be more likely to prefer that formal, organized action be taken to control delinquent youth. That this is at least partly true in India is indicated by the responses of the urban residents surveyed in this study.

It appears that in many cases a higher percentage of the urban respondents preferred a formal agent of control and in almost every instance, considerably more of the urban respondents suggested that a formal sanction be imposed on the offender. In short, in comparison to rural Indians, urban dwellers tend to be somewhat more severe in their reactions to juvenile misconduct and more willing to leave the task of controlling aberrant youth to formal agents—a finding that parallels research conducted in the United States (e.g., Boggs, 1971; Conklin, 1971). As with the rural respondents, the attitudes expressed by the urban residents differed depending upon the specific offense/offender in question.

Agent of Control: Very small percentages of the urban respondents would ignore any of the twenty-five offenses/offenders portrayed in the scenarios by suggesting that the offense not be reported. But this does not mean that they have a distinct preference for intervention by formal agents. Indeed, 50 percent or more of the urban respondents stated that some nonformal agent should deal with all the juvenile-status offenses and many of the criminal acts.

Formal agents were most frequently preferred for three of the property offenses (i.e., ticketless travel, joyriding, and grand theft) regardless of the offender's socioeconomic status. Carrying a concealed weapon and gangfighting were also thought to warrant action by a formal agent of control by over 50 percent of the respondents.

Sanction: Similarly, few urbanites felt that the offenses/offenders should go unsanctioned, except for defiance of parents by a boy (20 percent) and trespass by a girl (34 percent). With these exceptions, and the exceptions of assaulting a parent and defiance of parents by a girl, 50 percent or more of the urban respondents stated that they thought a formal sanction should be imposed on the offender. And for most of the serious property and several of the personal offenses, the percentages favoring formal sanctions were substantial (70 percent or more).

Congruence between Agent and Sanction: Unlike the rural respondents, urbanites exhibit little congruence in their attitudes regarding sanctioning agent and choice of sanction. In general, for status offenses more of the respondents preferred nonformal agents of control to nonformal sanctions, while substantial percentages of them suggested that formal sanctions would be appropriate. However, for almost all crimes (except several of the more nebulous acts), a higher proportion of the respondents stated that formal sanctions were preferable to formal control agents.

Few differences of any magnitude were found between the percentages of these who would ignore the offense and those who said that no sanctions be imposed. In almost all cases, substantially more respondents preferred formal sanctions to the intervention of a formal agent. In other words, among those who would actually report the incident or who stated that the offender should receive some sanction, it is quite clear that urban Tamilians were comparatively more willing to formally punish an offender than they were to call upon formal agents.

VARIABILITY IN REACTION

Chi-square analysis between respondent characteristics and these dimensions of reaction suggest that the social and economic characteristics of rural respondents have little impact in their attitudes, since only a small number of significant relationships were found between them and their choice of reaction. Although a consistent pattern in terms of the offense or offender type is not clearly visible, there is frequent significant variation in the attitudes of urbanites particularly when social-status variables are considered. Generally, lower-status groups prefer formal agents of control while higher-status respondents favor informal agents (a pattern not dissimilar to that which exists in the United States; see Black, 1980). A similar pattern emerges regarding choice of sanction. However, the more numerous significant relationships found among these variables when rural and urban samples are combined indicate that residence may be a more important variable than social status per se in shaping how people would respond to delinquent conduct. This is an issue we address in more depth in the chapter to follow.

SUMMARY

Although relatively few of the rural and urban adults surveyed felt that most of the conduct described in the scenarios should go unreacted to or unpunished, the pattern of their responses to the "to whom would you report" and "what do you think should be done" questions suggests a number of things regarding their attitudes toward youthful offenders. Generally, status offense/offenders were viewed with considerable tolerance; on the average about 10 percent of the respondents stated that no action should be taken against these offenders. For most offenses, a substantial number of the respondents (often a considerable majority) felt that "nonformal" (nongovernmental) agents should deal with the offender. However, in many cases, especially serious crimes, formal sanctions were preferred. Indeed, even when a high proportion of the respondents felt that intervention by formal agents was not warranted, they still preferred formal sanctions.

Compared to urban respondents, rural respondents exhibit a greater tolerance for most offense/offenders. They are less willing than urbanites to deal formally with cases of law breaking. And, at least among those who would report or want the offense/offender sanctioned, they are somewhat more congruent in their attitudes than urban dwellers. Urbanites, on the other hand, tend to agree with their rural compatriots about the desirability of avoiding governmental intervention (although they are somewhat more oriented to involving these individuals), but their attitudes regarding the kind of action to be taken against young offenders are decidedly harsher.

Conclusion

The nature of a social problem is determined by the type and amount of action people take regarding some social condition. In this respect, the behavior of the young people within any society can become a "public" issue and thereby be transformed into a problem to the extent that people feel that such behavior should be legally prohibited and are oriented to dealing with youthful offenders by formal mechanisms of control and the use of formal (penal) sanctions. While the creation of a delinquency problem (in the sense that delinquency is normally understood as a problem in the West) presupposes official action by agencies of the state, the fact that the same behavior could be viewed as warranting, and subsequently being dealt with by, "nonpublic" or extralegal action does not preclude its being a problem. It simply makes it a different kind of problem (e.g., a private family matter versus a public legal issue). As a social problem, delinquency is more than a phenomenon of youthful misconduct. Such conduct becomes a "delinquency problem" when, and to the extent that, it is the subject of organized action directed toward its prevention or control. In modern Western societies that action has largely been the province of judicial or related agencies of the state, but this need not be the case universally. What form a delinquency problem will take, in other words, depends upon how it is characterized. Empirically, this means what type of reaction it elicits and what action is taken against the behavior of society's young. The survey data reported in this chapter are suggestive of how adult Indians characterize youthful misconduct and the types of reaction they feel are appropriate when it occurs.

Until a similar study is conducted on a comparable sample of respondents in other countries, it is impossible to say to what extent our respondents' attitudes toward the control of young people parallel or differ from those of other people. We might speculate, however, that in some respects they will be similar while in others they will differ. Indeed it is not surprising that rural residents differ from urban respondents regarding some of the dimensions tapped in this survey (see Mandelbaum, 1970; Beteille, 1974; Wiebe, 1976). Moreover, research on American samples suggests that people are highly similar in the way they rank-order offenses on the basis of seriousness (e.g., Rossi et al., 1974; Berk and Rossi, 1977). But general agreement that one act is more or less serious than another does not presuppose that various categories of people will agree on what action should be taken against the offender or who should be responsible for taking that action.

In accordance with previous opinion research in criminology and deviance, our respondents exhibited a rather distinct ordering as far as their opinions regarding various delinquent acts are concerned. As might be expected, comparatively few respondents favored the legal prohibition of status offenses, whereas larger proportions did favor legal prohibition of more serious criminal-type conduct. Similarly, a majority of respondents realized that the more serious offenses were actually illegal, but smaller percentages were aware of the legal status of less serious crimes and most status offenses. Also, as might be predicted from existing research, our respondents appeared to be quite certain as to whom they would call upon to react to delinquent conduct and the type (or severity) of the sanctions they would impose on offenders.

Interestingly, however, with few exceptions respondents preferred that an "informal" agent of control be relied upon, even in several cases of serious crimes. And generally respondents indicated that something other than a formal (legal) sanction should be imposed on the offender. Thus, even though respondents knew the various acts were illegal and concurred with that designation, many of them did not want the offense/offender to be dealt with by formal authorities or to be formally sanctioned for the act (although in the case of serious crimes large proportions did opt for formal sanctions). In spite of their knowledge and opinions regarding delinquency laws, our respondents generally exhibited a rather tolerant, nonreactive attitude toward instances of conduct prohibited by these laws. The reasons for this cannot be directly discerned from our data. Perhaps Indians do not view such behavior as "serious" enough to warrant formal intervention, or perhaps they are opposed to such action for other reasons.

However, given the low congruence between choice of agent and sanction (especially among urban respondents), the rather numerous and distinct differences in attitudes (as opposed to knowledge and opinion) between rural and urban respondents, and the general lack of patterned relationships between these dimensions of perception and other socioeconomic characteristics of respondents, it appears that how Indians "feel" about and choose to react to delinquent conduct are related to the sociocultural milieu in which they reside. That is, the similarities and differences between the urban and rural environments of respondents may be conducive to shaping similarities and differences in, if not the structure of perceptions, the form or severity of reactions to delinquent conduct. In other words, social location, action, ideology, and the dimensions of knowledge, opinion, and attitudes investigated in this study form a complex web that influences how people perceive and react to the world in which they live. Therefore, before we speculate about the specific socioeconomic forces that condition the seemingly tolerant, nonreactive stance of Indian adults toward delinquent conduct, it may be useful to explore some of these relationships in more depth.

CHAPTER 9

The Structure of Public Reaction

The components of ideology—attitudes, beliefs, opinions, and values—provide the frame of reference for one's perceptions of and reactions to the world (see Fishbein, 1967; Liska, 1974). Since ideology is embedded in the social context of institutions, groups, and interrelationships, one's social location (e.g., residence and status position) may influence one's reactions to various social phenomena. That is, societal reaction to delinquent behavior can vary depending upon the reactor's social location and the meaning this behavior has for various individuals and groups.

As suggested in the previous chapter, it appears that in spite of familiarity and agreement with delinquency laws, rural and urban respondents differed in their attitudes toward particular offenses/offenders. A substantial body of research comparing rural and urban residents suggests that independent of socioeconomic status, one's residence (or cultural milieu) influences psychological dispositions, perceptions, opinions, and attitudes (see Wirth, 1938; Simmel, 1957; Lipset, 1959; Maccoby et al., 1958; Dewey, 1960; Inkeles, 1968; Boggs, 1971; Hackler et al., 1974).

Also, there is reason to believe that societal reaction is directed toward crimes in terms of general forms or types of conduct (e.g., Newman, 1957; Rooney and Gibbons, 1966). Indeed, Rossie et al. (1974) found that, as perceived by the respondents, various offenses could be grouped into types and these types of offenses could be ranked in terms of their relative seriousness. The frequency distributions presented in Chapter 8 suggest that our respondents viewed certain offenses in this manner. Thus, it appears that people may perceive crime and delinquency as classes of behavior rather than isolated, individual events or general phenomena.

The limited information available on public perceptions of and reactions to delinquency (especially in developing countries) precludes the testing of theoretically relevant hypotheses in this regard. However, we can gain a more complete understanding of the reactions of adult Indians to juvenile delinquency by exploring how various components of reaction vary on the basis of factors (such as residence and offense type) that may affect reactions.

For this purpose, composite scales of "knowledge," "opinion," choice of "agent," and choice of "sanction" were created to measure specific reactions to delinquency in general and to various types of delinquency. In addition, an SES scale was created on the basis of factor analysis of responses to the education, occupation, and income questions (see Appendix D for a description of these scales). Residence was dichotomized into rural or urban locality. Also, on the bases of offense categories typically found in the literature and analysis of frequency distributions, the twenty-five offense/offender scenarios depicted in the survey were categorized into five *types* of offense behavior: status offenses, minor (or petty) property offenses, major (or grand) property offenses, personal offenses, and substance-related offenses.

Six of the scenarios (four offenses) were categorized as *status* offenses: truancy, smoking cigarettes, defiance of parents (by both a boy and a girl), and running away from home (by both a boy and a girl). *Minor property* offenses consist of five items (three offenses): petty theft, vandalism (by both an older and a younger offender), and trespass (by both a boy and a girl). *Major property* offenses consist of six items (three offenses): grand theft, joyriding, and ticketless travel (each by an upper- and lower-status offender). The category of *personal* offenses is made up of five scenarios (four offenses): gangfighting, carrying a concealed weapon, fighting, and assault of a parent (by a younger and an older offender). And three scenarios (two offenses) comprise the *substance-related* category: drug use and alcohol consumption (by a higher- and a lower-status youth).

To measure the direction and magnitude of the relationships among the various dimensions of knowledge, opinions, and attitudes of rural and urban respondents in general or for specific offense types, correlation and regression analyses were used and path diagrams were constructed.*

*Normally path analysis is used to test hypotheses concerning the causal pattern among several factors, but path analysis is by no means limited to this use.

Interaction among Dimensions

Review of the coefficients presented in Table 9.1 suggests that in general the various dimensions of reaction are at least moderately correlated. The correlations, however, vary considerably depending upon the particular variables being considered, the type of offense behavior in question, and the specific group of respondents. Specifically, regardless of sample or offense type, it is quite clear that the most important single variable is the opinion respondents expressed regarding delinquency laws, for this factor is consistently highly correlated with the others.† Knowledge of the law, on the other hand, appears to have only a weak and sometimes (in spite of the large sample size) statistically insignificant correlation with other dimensions, while the correlations between choice of control agent and sanction are, for the total sample, weak to moderate. In most cases, the pattern of relationships among these factors is similar when the rural and urban samples are treated separately (i.e., controlled for locality of residence). However, for all offense types, the strength of the relationships between choice of agent and sanctions among the rural sample is moderately high, and this persists when other factors are controlled. On the other hand, among urbanites these relationships are, at best, weak. While opinion appears to have about equal impact on other variables for both rural and urban groups, some differences emerge in the relative importance of knowledge for the two groups. But, on the whole, regardless of offense type, knowledge appears to be a relatively inconsequential variable.

In most instances, the correlation coefficients are not particularly strong. However, the consistency in the direction and magnitude of these correlations (except between knowledge and agent) suggests that there is a discernible pattern among respondents' knowledge, opinions, and reactions regarding delinquent behavior. This does not mean that these scales are indicative of how people

---

While the present discussion assumes a causal pattern among dimensions, it is not our purpose here to test causal hypotheses. Rather, the path diagrams are presented to highlight the differences or similarities in the patterns of reaction.

†First and second partials (not shown) also suggest that opinion is a significant variable since when it is controlled, either alone or in combination with other factors, substantial and consistent changes in the size of the coefficients among other factors occur. When other factors are controlled, however, few, minimal, or inconsistent coefficients result. SES, it should be noted, is weakly correlated with the various dimensions and has little impact when controlled. Therefore, it is excluded from these analyses.

would react toward individual instances of delinquent behavior. Nor does it suggest that there are no variations in the relationships among these dimensions in each subgroup. Rather, what this analysis suggests is that perceptions of and reactions to delinquency are probably part of a general weltanschauung or cultural ideology. We can expect to find differences in what people perceive as worthy of reaction as well as in the forms that reaction might take. Thus, for instance, one might expect to find that rural and urban respondents will not only react with different degrees of severity to different forms of delinquency, but that the pattern of relationships among the various dimensions of reaction will also differ. This could indicate

TABLE 9.1. *Zero-order Correlations among Dimensions of Reaction by Offense Type and Locality*

Correlations/offense type	Sample		
	Total	Rural	Urban
Knowledge/opinion			
All offenses	.47	.34	.45
Status offenses	.63	.63	.58
Minor property offenses	.54	.38	.50
Major property offenses	.49	.49	.52
Personal offenses	.50	.45	.49
Substance offenses	.31	.42	.32
Knowledge/agent			
All offenses	.04	.16	−.01*
Status offenses	.19	.30	.13
Minor property offenses	.16	.06*	.16
Major property offenses	.12	.14	.13
Personal offenses	.16	.23	.14
Substance offenses	.14	.17	.14
Knowledge/sanction			
All offenses	.21	.15	.13
Status offenses	.41	.25	.33
Minor property offenses	.28	.09*	.21
Major property offenses	.09	.15	.09
Personal offenses	.21	.23	.15
Substance offenses	.07	.20	.09

that our respondents see and, therefore, react to similar aspects of the social world in different ways.

Indeed, the findings presented in this section indicate that the pattern of the relationships between the pairs of dimensions of reaction vary somewhat for offenses of different types among respondents from different communities. In general, regardless of the type of offense, the knowledge people have of the law and their opinions concerning whether or not various forms of illegal behavior should be prohibited are highly correlated. But awareness that particular kinds of activity are illegal does not always mean that respondents would report such conduct to the authorities or state that some type of

TABLE 9.1. *(Continued)*

Correlations/offense type	Sample		
	Total	Rural	Urban
Opinion/agent			
All offenses	.30	.27	.27
Status offenses	.30	.21	.28
Minor property offenses	.33	.25	.34
Major property offenses	.37	.25	.34
Personal offenses	.28	.47	.22
Substance offenses	.34	.47	.31
Opinion/sanction			
All offenses	.49	.37	.38
Status offenses	.46	.17	.42
Minority property offenses	.48	.24	.37
Major property offenses	.42	.45	.37
Personal offenses	.45	.50	.33
Substance offenses	.42	.55	.34
Agent/sanction			
All offenses	.26	.69	.14
Status offenses	.36	.55	.28
Minority property offenses	.35	.58	.29
Major property offenses	.41	.78	.28
Personal offenses	.25	.69	.12
Substance offenses	.36	.71	.28

*Not significant.

formal punishment should be imposed upon offenders. Indeed, when other factors are controlled, the relationships between knowledge and each of the two attitude dimensions (agent and sanction choice) become insignificant in most instances. Although knowledge and opinion appear to have mixed effects on attitudes regarding status offenses, for all other forms of delinquency the opinion people hold as to whether or not the behavior should be prohibited shapes their reactions. Thus, what people say should be done to (or the action *they* would take when encountering) lawbreakers is more a function of what they think about the behavior than a product of their knowledge that such conduct is against the law. But the extent to which, or the manner in which, knowledge and/or opinion shape societal reaction to delinquent conduct is consistent neither for urban and rural respondents nor for various types of such conduct. While both urban and rural respondents exhibit a good deal of congruity in the relationship between knowledge and opinions, in the magnitude of the relationships between their choice of control agent and sanction they differ greatly; and the differences in these relationships are most pronounced when serious property or personal offenses are concerned. Thus, it might be concluded that the form and severity of societal reaction to delinquency, regardless of type, are affected by the perceptions people hold regarding it and, indirectly, by their realization or knowledge that the behavior is illegal.

But the extent to which the interrelationships of these factors influence choice of sanction cannot be determined from correlation analysis. Correlation analysis indicates that various combinations of factors are, or are not, related to one another without any basis for valid assumptions regarding their causality. Path analysis, based on standardized regression coefficients, allows us to assess the order and relative explanatory power of these (or combinations of these) variables. And regression and path analysis more fully reveal the patterns of reactions people exhibit toward different forms of delinquent conduct.

Explaining Reactions

Our aim here is to assess the extent to which variability in reaction (i.e., the choice of sanction) can be explained by differences in the knowledge, opinions, and choice of control agent—together or in various combinations—respondents living in village or urban environments exhibit. That is, it can be hypothesized that some of these

The Structure of Public Reaction

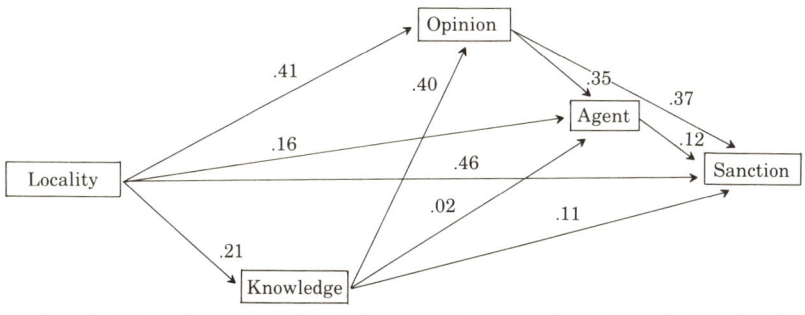

FIGURE 9.1. **Path Model of Sanction Choice Using Location as a Dummy Variable**

factors are independent and that others are intervening variables anteceding the type or severity of the sanctions people say should be imposed on delinquent youngsters. Thus, a significant portion of the variability in choice of sanction may be explained on the basis of the antecedent factors. This is not to say that these variables determine what sanction will, in fact, be recommended. The frequency distributions already indicate a general unanimity in the sanctions Tamil Nadu adults would impose upon specific offense/offenders. Rather, the question here is to what extent do variations in locality produce relative changes in the sanctions recommended. To answer this question, several path models were constructed on the basis of combinations of locality, knowledge, opinion, and choice of control agent and sanction to determine the set of factors which best explain variability in choice of sanction.* These path models visually reveal the similarities or differences in the pattern of relationships among the variables for urban compared to rural respondents.

Figure 9.1 and Table 9.2 highlight the contribution of the residence or locality of respondents in accounting for the variance in sanction preferences. When locality (urban coded as 1 and rural as 0) is treated as a dummy variable and the suppressing effect of SES is eliminated, the independent and intervening variables together explain about 50 percent of the variation in sanction for the total combined sample. This is a substantial increase over the 21 percent of the variance explained by the combination of knowledge, opinion, and agent alone (see Table 9.3, combined sample).

Analysis of the separate path coefficients suggests that locality, followed by opinion, best explains the variance in both choice of agent

---

*Path analyses using SES indicate that it has only a very weak explanatory power and contributes little to the overall explanatory power of the model. Thus, it was excluded from further analysis.

and sanction preferred. On the other hand, knowledge, which has a strong impact on opinion, has a negligible, direct effect on choice of agent and sanction. That is, knowledge alone contributes very little toward explaining choice of agent and sanction. Whatever negligible effect it has is via its impact on opinion. Knowledge is affected by locality to a lesser degree, while locality has a strong impact on opinion. Choice of agent is not affected by the other variables to any great extent, except by opinion, and, in turn, has very little effect on sanction choice. In short, the variation in reaction appears to be best explained by the effects of locality or residence and opinions of respondents. In other words, how people say they would react to delinquent behavior is largely a function of where they live and the effect of such residency on their opinions regarding delinquency laws.

The other dimension of attitude (choice of agent) is not so clearly explained by the antecedent factors included in the model. That is, the total effect of residence and the intervening variables (knowledge and opinion) on choice of control agent is only about .34, explaining less than 12 percent of the variance. Thus, factors not included in this analysis influence who people think should handle delinquent youth. This is surprising since opinions regarding delinquency laws consistently, albeit moderately, affect choice of sanction as well as choice of agent in a positive direction. Since none of the other variables have an equally consistent or as strong a relationship to choice of agent, it is probably understandable that a greater proportion of the variance in sanction is explained by the combinations of these factors. Perhaps among adult Indians in general factors such as residence, SES, and knowledge of the law do not play a major role in shaping their attitudes regarding *who* should be responsible for controlling delinquent youngsters. As the frequency distributions indicate, respondents were quite in agreement in this respect. However, *what* should be done to offenders appears to be more subject to structural and ideological factors so that this dimension of attitude is more varied

TABLE 9.2. **Direct, Indirect, and Total Effects of Locality on Knowledge, Opinion, and Attitudes**

Effect of locality on:	*Direct*	*Indirect*	*Total*
Knowledge	.21	.00	.21
Opinion	.41	.08	.49
Agent	.16	.18	.34
Sanction	.46	.25	.71

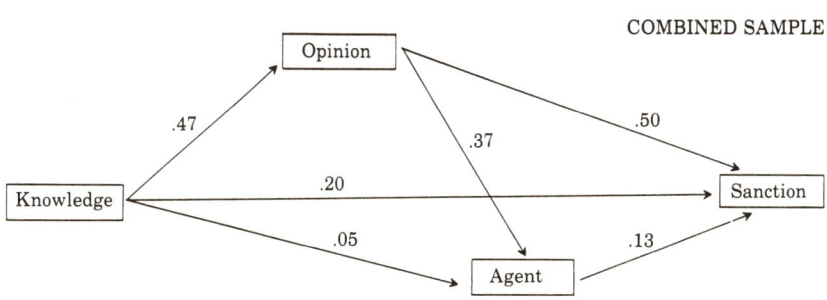
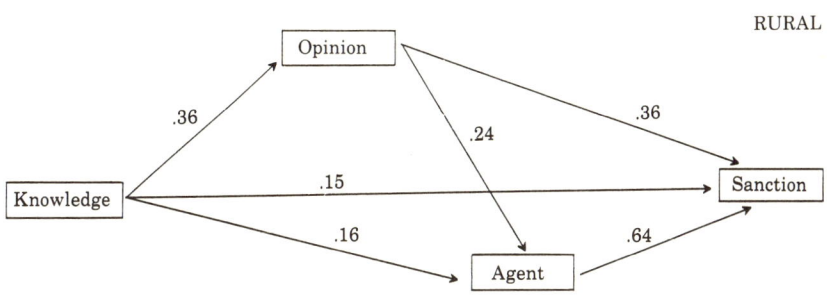
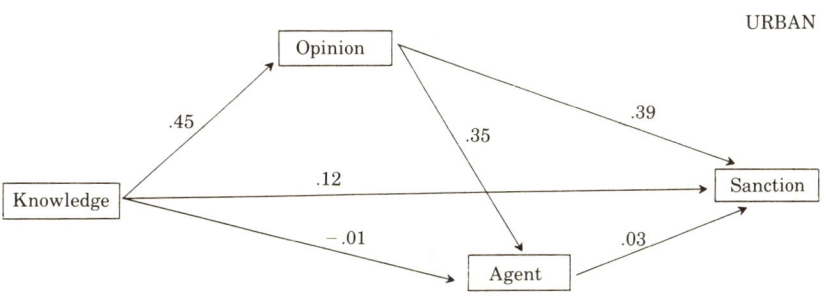

FIGURE 9.2. **Path Models of the Relationships among Knowledge, Opinion, and Attitudes**

depending upon the structural and cultural aspects of their social world.

Separate analysis of the interrelationships among knowledge, opinion, and the two dimensions of attitude for the combined and the rural and urban samples treated separately allows us to assess the relative importance of cultural (i.e., dimensions of ideology) as opposed to social structural (i.e., residence) factors in explaining reactions to delinquency. As indicated by the path models presented in Figure 9.2, only a few substantial differences exist in the relative effects (both direct and indirect) the several variables have on one another, either when the rural and urban samples are combined or treated separately. The overall explanatory power of these variables, in other words, is generally the same. The breakdown table (Table 9.3) shows the amount of variance explained by these variables for the combined and subsamples.

As indicated by path models, opinion is the best single predictor of choice of sanction as well as control agent, although these effects are only moderate when knowledge is controlled. Knowledge is a good predictor of opinion, but its individual and joint effects on either choice of agent or sanction are low. Since all the relationships are direct it suggests that those who are familar with delinquency laws tend to be more repressive in that they more frequently want such behavior to be prohibited by law, report it to formal agents, and

TABLE 9.3. **Direct, Indirect, and Total Effects of Knowledge on the Intervening and Dependent Variable with Combined and Separate Rural and Urban Samples**

Effect of knowledge on:	Direct	Indirect	Total
Combined sample			
Opinion	.47	.00	.47
Agent	.05	.17	.22
Sanction	.20	.26	.46
Rural sample			
Opinion	.36	.00	.36
Agent	.16	.09	.25
Sanction	.15	.29	.44
Urban sample			
Opinion	.45	.00	.45
Agent	−.01	.16	.15
Sanction	.12	.18	.30

prefer more formal sanctions. For the combined sample, these variables together explain about 21 percent of the variance in sanctions recommended by respondents.

A comparison of the models for the rural and urban samples indicates how the relative importance of these factors might differ for different population groups. Level of knowledge has a considerably lower total effect on sanction choice among urbanites compared to rural respondents, even though the direct effects are about the same. However, knowledge is a somewhat better predictor of opinion among the urbanites than among the rural sample. Among the rural respondents, knowledge is weakly related to choice of control agent, whereas for the urbanites this relationship is negligible. Knowledge, along with opinion and choice of agent, explains about 19.4 percent of the variance in sanction choices among rural respondents, whereas for the urban sample the total combined effect of these variables only explains 9 percent of the variance in sanction.

The most noticeable difference between the rural and urban samples is the effect of choice of control agent on sanction. This relationship is high (.64) for the rural respondents, but almost negligible (.03) for the urban sample. As discussed earlier, this reflects the greater homogeneity in attitudes exhibited by the rural respondents. In contrast, whereas opinion and sanction are about equally related for the two groups, the relationship between opinion and choice of control agent is considerably smaller (.24 versus .36) for the rural than for the urban sample. Thus, although opinion in combination with agent explains much of the variance in sanctions for both rural and urban respondents, they do so in different ways.

The path models presented in this section suggest that rural versus urban residence has a strong impact on perceptions of and reactions to delinquent behavior. And variability in sanctioning tendency is a combined result of structural and cultural factors insofar as cultural ideology is related to some aspects of social structure based on location of residence. Identifying exactly what these aspects may be is beyond the scope of the present research. However, the extent to which type of offense behavior is a determination of reaction patterns in these localities can be assessed.

Explaining Reactions to Offense Types

Given that the model described in the preceding section is effective in explaining variations in choice of sanction for delinquency in general, the next task is to pursue the intricacies of these

176   *Delinquency in India*

causal relationships. For it is possible that variation in choice of sanction among the urban and rural respondents is affected by different types or forms of delinquency. To explore the precise patterns of reactions to various forms of delinquency, regression and path analysis were carried out for each of the five offense types for the rural and urban samples separately.*

Path models depicting the interactions among the various dimensions of reactions are presented in Figure 9.3, and the combined breakdown table (Table 9.4) shows the effects of each of the antecedent variables on sanction choice with regard to the offense type and residence of respondents. In order to account for the relative explanatory power of each of the variables, their respective direct, indirect, and total effects are presented. As suggested by the table and figure, variations in sanction choice, within different communities or when different forms of delinquency are considered, are not uniformly affected by the other dimensions of reaction; in some instances the amount of variance explained increases and in others it decreases. Also, it is clear that the variance explained in choice of sanction by choice of agent is consistently related to rural-urban background of the respondents.

STATUS OFFENSES

In both sample groups knowledge and opinion are moderately correlated (Figure 9.3), while knowledge and both choice of agent and sanction are not even weakly related (as was also suggested by correlation coefficients). However, while opinion is weakly related to both choice of agent and sanction among urbanites, these coefficients are negligible for the rural sample. Conversely, the agent and sanction choices of rural respondents are highly related, but only weakly so for the urban sample.

The decomposition table suggests that although the total effect of knowledge on sanction is moderate, it is slightly higher for the urban than for the rural sample. Knowledge has a somewhat greater direct than indirect effect via its interaction through opinion and choice of agent, a fact which suggests that it is a variable of some

*Since residence is an important variable in determining reactions to delinquency in general, it is our intention here to compare and highlight the similarities and differences between rural and urban reactions to types of delinquency. This can be best achieved by path-analyzing the interactions for each group separately. Also, since SES was not found to be a useful variable in explaining overall reactions and is not highly correlated to any of the dimensions when specific offenses are concerned, it was excluded from this analysis.

impact. But the similarity between the rural and urban respondents ends here. Rural residents' opinion of status-offense behavior has virtually no direct or indirect impact on their choice of sanctions. Contrary to this, about 16 percent of the variance in the urbanites' choice of sanction can be explained by their opinion (and via its interaction with choice of agent). This is more a result of the direct rather than the indirect effect of this interaction. Another difference between rural and urban respondents concerns the effect of choice of agent on sanction. Among the rural residents, about 25 percent of the variance in sanction choice is directly accounted for by their choice of control agent, and the effect of agent choice alone is slightly greater than the total effect of knowledge in explaining the variance in their choice of sanction. On the other hand, for the urban group, choice of agent has a weak effect on sanction choice.

In short, the rural respondents' choice of sanctions regarding status-offense behavior is explained to a smaller extent by knowledge or opinion and their interactions compared with choice of agent alone. For the urban sample, to some extent knowledge and its interactions determine choice of sanction.

MINOR PROPERTY OFFENSES

The explanatory ability of the variables included in the path model varies considerably between rural and urban respondents for minor property offenses. In part, this is a function of the differences in their interactions. While agent and sanction choice are strongly related for this offense type among villagers, the two variables are only weakly related for urban respondents. This is quite similar to the locality-based differences for status offenses. In contrast, the relationship between knowledge and opinion is considerably greater for urban respondents than it is for the rural sample. It appears that knowledge of minor property offense laws has a weak impact among the rural sample. Thus, while there is probably greater consistency among the dimensions of reaction to minor property offenses for the urbanites than for the rural respondents, the typically low magnitude of these relationships contributes to the weak explanatory power of the model.

By decomposing the direct, indirect, and total effects of the several antecedent variables on choice of sanction, we can observe that the choice of agent recommended by rural respondents alone best explains their choice of sanction, although the relationship is only moderate as it was with status offenses. In contrast, among the

URBAN SAMPLE

RURAL SAMPLE

STATUS OFFENSES

MINOR PROPERTY OFFENSES

MAJOR PROPERTY OFFENSES

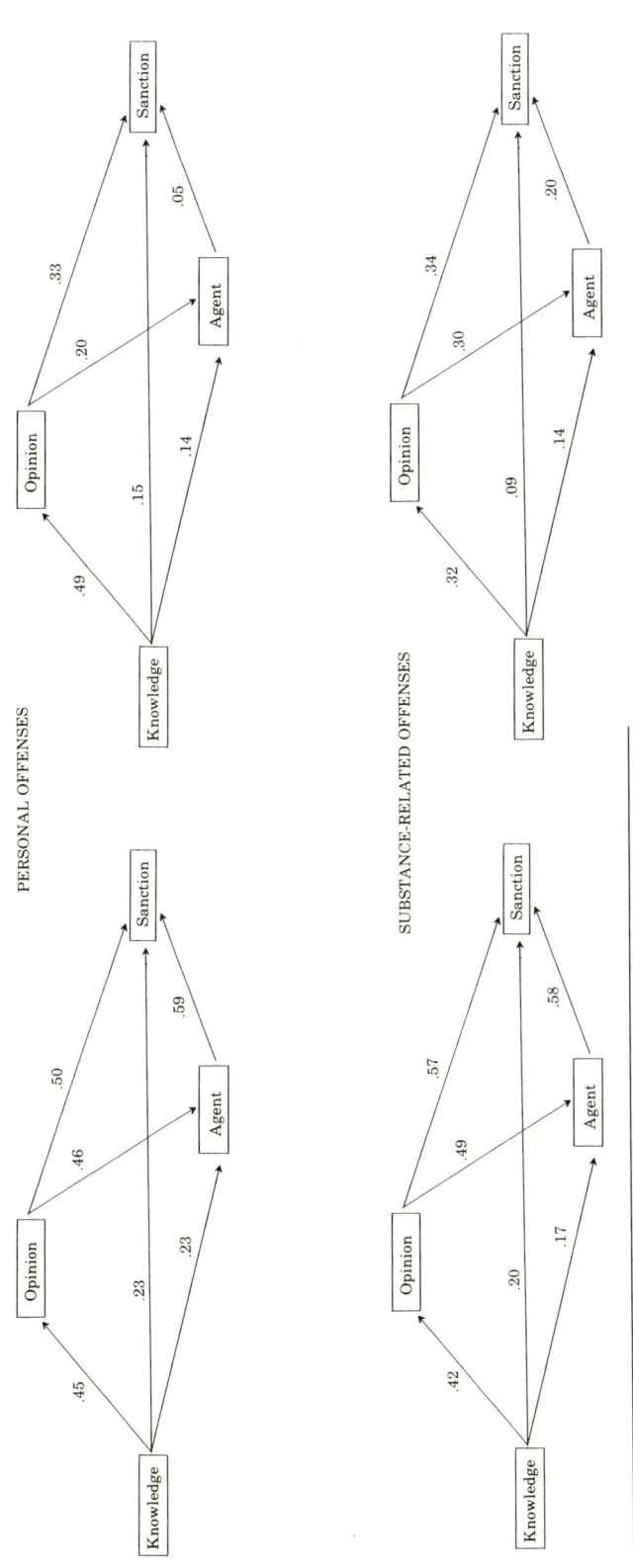

FIGURE 9.3. *Path Models of Sanction Choice by Offense Type and Residence*

TABLE 9.4. **Effects on Choice of Sanction by Type of Offense and Locality**

Offense/dimension	Rural			Urban		
	Direct	Indirect	Total	Direct	Indirect	Total
Status offenses						
Knowledge	.25	.18	.43	.33	.26	.59
Opinion	.02	.02	.04	.34	.06	.40
Agent	.52	—	.52	.18	—	.18
Minor property offenses						
Knowledge	.09	.18	.27	.21	.24	.45
Opinion	.24	.15	.39	.36	.06	.40
Agent	.56	—	.56	.18	—	.18
Major property offenses						
Knowledge	.15	.51	.66	.09	.39	.48
Opinion	.50	.31	.81	.44	.06	.50
Agent	.71	—	.71	.17	—	.17
Personal offenses						
Knowledge	.23	.58	.81	.14	.17	.32
Opinion	.50	.27	.77	.33	.01	.34
Agent	.59	—	.59	.05	—	.05
Substance-related offenses						
Knowledge	.20	.46	.66	.09	.16	.25
Opinion	.57	.28	.85	.34	.06	.40
Agent	.58	—	.58	.20	—	.20

urbanites choice of agent explains a low 3 percent, indicating that their choice of agent has little impact on their choice of sanction where minor property crimes are concerned. Again, this is similar to the patterns found among these variables for status offenses.

Among the urbanites, knowledge and its interactions with opinion and choice of agent have a moderate (20 percent) total effect on choice of sanction. Similarly, the total effect of opinion is 16 percent; adding the indirect effect of opinions accounts for less than 1 percent of the variance in the sanctions urbanites select for minor property offenses. Among the rural respondents, knowledge and its indirect effect on opinion and choice of agent have only a minor total effect (7 percent) on choice of sanction. The total effect of opinion, through its interaction with choice of agent, on choice of sanction is similar for both the urban and rural samples. Among the rural respondents, choice of agent explains 31 percent of the variance in sanction choice. This relationship is a low 3 percent among the urbanites. In the urban group, the pattern of interactions among the four variables for minor property offenses is similar to what we observed for status offenses. As with status offenses, adding the indirect effect of opinions urbanites hold regarding minor property offenses accounts for less than 1 percent of the variance in the sanctions they choose. In general, unlike status offense behavior, opinion appears to be a moderately important variable as far as minor property offenses are concerned; it explains a total of about 15 percent of the variance in sanction choice among both rural and urban respondents.

MAJOR PROPERTY OFFENSES

Although the overall pattern of interactions among the four variables is similar for rural and urban respondents, as far as major property offenses are concerned the ability of the model to explain sanction choice is somewhat greater for the rural than for the urban sample. In large part, this is a function of the considerable difference in the interaction between agent and sanction revealed in the two path models.

Analysis of the direct and indirect effects of the rural and urban respondents' knowledge, opinions, and choice of agent on sanction choice clarifies the pattern of the interactions among these variables. The combination of the variables in the model is more effective in explaining the rural respondents' choice of sanctions than in explaining the reactions of urbanites. The variance in choice of sanction that is accounted for among rural respondents by knowledge, opinion, and choice of agent is quite high—being 44, 66, and 50 percent respectively. But this is not true for the urban sample. Choice of agent explains only about 3 percent of the variance in choice of sanction. Although the direct effect of opinion on choice of sanction is moderate, its indirect effect is almost negligible, as it was for both status and minor property offenses. Opinion explains only a total of 25 percent of the variance in the urban respondents' choice of sanctions. And almost all of the total variance in both sample groups' sanction choice explained by knowledge is accounted for by its indirect rather than direct effect. Also, three of the four indirect effects among the respondents in both samples are quite substantial, suggesting that choice of sanctions may be partly the result of the intervention of opinion and choice of agent rather than a function of knowledge alone.

PERSONAL OFFENSES

For the rural sample one of the most powerful explanatory models considered in this analysis concerns personal offenses. But among urbanites the factors included in the model have a negligible ability to predict sanction choice of this offense type. As in the preceding path model, this difference is a function of the relatively strong interactions between opinion and choice of agent, between opinion and choice of sanction, and between choice of agent and choice of sanction for the rural sample.

Opinion, compared to knowledge, has a greater direct than indirect effect on the rural respondents' choice of sanction. The total variance in their sanction choice explained by knowledge, opinion, and choice of agent each is quite high—66, 59, and 35 percent respectively. In contrast, the variance in the urbanites' choice of sanction is affected only to a low extent by these three variables. The variance in the urbanites' choice of sanction is best explained by opinion, but even then only a low 12 percent is explained. As in other offenses, opinion has a negligible indirect effect. Overall, the variables in the model do not adequately account for the variance in the urbanites' choice of sanction, but for the rural sample the model is quite effective.

SUBSTANCE-RELATED OFFENSES

The interrelationships among the dimensions of reaction analyzed in this discussion in explaining sanction choice are weakest for the urban sample with regard to substance-abuse behavior. Clearly, among both groups of respondents, knowledge of the law has a weak effect on sanction recommendations and on the choice of control agent for this offense type. However, the direct effect of the urbanites' knowledge on choice of sanction is the weakest, accounting for less than 1 percent of the variance in sanction choice.

It is the strong effect of opinion and the compounding impact of knowledge on opinion and choice of agent on sanction among rural respondents that result in the difference between them and the urbanites. But even then, the interactions are explained by the variables included only to a moderate extent.

Looking at the direct and indirect effects of the antecedent variables, it can be observed that there is a direct, locality-based difference in the relative effects of these variables on the choice of sanctions for substance-related behavior. As with major property offenses, the effects of the knowledge and opinions of rural respondents regarding this conduct are moderate, although choice of agent alone also explains about 34 percent of the variance in choice of sanction for this offense type. In contrast, among the urban sample, opinion has the largest direct effect on sanction; but it explains only about 16 percent of the total variance in sanction.

Delinquency, Reaction, and Agrarian Society: Some Observations

The foregoing analysis suggests that the orientations of respondents toward delinquency and its control vary considerably by locality of residence and the type of delinquent conduct involved. Thus, attitudes regarding what should be done to young people who violate different types of laws may indeed be affected by factors relating to the person's social or community environment. But the impact of these factors on the knowledge people have of these laws, the opinions they hold about them, or the agencies they feel should be responsible for controlling young people who violate them may not be the same from one locality to another. Thus, depending upon the specific form of delinquency as well as the urban or rural background of the respondents, we are likely to find differences in the severity of the sanctions people recommend for various offenses/offenders.

VARIABILITY IN REACTION

Generally, it appears that for rural and urban respondents it is the differences in the relationships between who they say should be responsible for controlling different types of delinquent conduct and the types of sanctions they recommend be imposed upon young persons engaging in the behavior that enhance or detract from the ability to predict and explain respondents' choice of sanction. However, of equal importance is the consistent (albeit of small magnitude at times) effect of the opinions that people (particularly urbanites) hold. In short, their *feelings* about such conduct, and their effect on the other combinations of variables, play the most significant role in accounting for the variability in their choice of sanction. In contrast, people's knowledge of delinquency laws does not seem to add to the explanatory ability of the model, since knowledge appears to have an inconsistent, although small, direct effect on the interactions among variables. And overall, it has little impact on choice of sanction.

Thus, among the findings reported in this chapter, the following appear to be most significant:

First, as indicated throughout this study, a number of distinct differences exist in the rural and urban respondents' knowledge of delinquency laws, the opinions they hold regarding them, and the attitudes they exhibit concerning who should deal with young lawbreakers and what should be done to such individuals. Rural and urban respondents also differ in terms of how these dimensions are related to one another concerning delinquent conduct in general or of specific types of delinquent behavior. Generally, urbanites are somewhat more knowledgeable of the law, more often concur with it, and more often feel that formal agents should be involved or that sanctions should be imposed on violators. However, urban respondents are less consistent than rural respondents regarding the choice of sanction and agent of control.

Second, how people say they would react to delinquency is probably more a function of how they "feel" about such conduct. This is suggested by the consistently substantial direct effects of opinion on the other factors as well as the major role it plays in the various path models.

Third, although they are similar in many ways, rural and urban respondents seem to differ somewhat in terms of the structure of their ideological orientations toward delinquent conduct. What rural respondents say should be done to delinquent youth is a function of several things: their opinions, who they think should deal with offending youth, and, to a limited extent, their knowledge of delinquency laws. Among urban respondents, on the other hand, what people say should be done to young offenders is largely a product of their opinions and these, to some extent, are related to their knowl-

The Structure of Public Reaction 185

edge of the law. But sanction preferences cannot be readily predicted from choice of agent, and choice of agent is not a function of the urbanites' knowledge of delinquency laws.

Fourth, residence is not only an important factor in the reactions of respondents to delinquent behavior in general, it also influences how people perceive and respond to specific forms of delinquency. The four-variable path model has greater explanatory power among the rural sample insofar as the type of offense concerned is a major property, personal, or substance-related offense. A reversal of this is to be found among the urbanites, and the path models explain the variability in their choice of sanction to a greater extent when the type of delinquency involves status or minor property offenses. In short, as the locality of residence and type of offense varies, so do the magnitude and pattern of the interaction among respondents' knowledge of juvenile laws, opinions of them, and choice of control agent or sanctions.

In brief, these findings, and the exceptionally high proportion of the variance explained in sanction preferences by the combinations of the factors tested, suggest that the reactions of adult Tamilians to delinquent conduct are probably a function of factors associated with the community of residence and the ideological orientations people within specific communities have regarding illegal behavior, who should be responsible for controlling delinquent youth, and how offenders should be dealt with. In other words, whether or not some form of conduct (delinquent behavior) is or is not likely to be treated as a social problem (other determinants being equal) depends upon who perceives it (e.g., rural versus urban residents) and the views perceivers have of the behavior and the proper responses to it. *That is, the emergence of a delinquency problem is not a mere function of the "objective" occurrence of delinquent behavior.*

As indicated by our analysis of official statistics on delinquency, it appears that the proclivity to react to delinquent conduct exhibited by the respondents in this survey is reflected in their actions. The willingness to attribute criminality to juveniles and to react formally to such conduct is indeed greater among urban people than rural residents if one accepts official statistics on reported delinquency and arrests of young people as measures of *reaction*. However, the differences in these reactions are not readily explained by actual differences in the amount or types of delinquency occurring in the cities and villages of India. Although our self-reported survey of delinquency is hardly adequate for generalization purposes, the delinquency of the village and urban boys in Tamil Nadu does not differ significantly, except insofar as the small sample of village youngsters admit to minor offenses somewhat more frequently than do urban boys.

SOCIAL STRUCTURE, IDEOLOGY, AND
REACTIONS TO DELINQUENCY

It seems that there is something about communities—the structure of social relationships and cultural orientations within them—that affects the genesis of delinquency problems. Research by Taylor et al. (1979) in the United States, for example, suggests that punitive attitudes toward crime (e.g., support of capital punishment and harsher courts) are not related to the salience of crime (e.g., the fear of crime and victimization experiences), although consistency in attitudes is greater in areas where crime is most salient (also see Stinchcombe et al., 1980). In other words, reactions to crime are not necessarily a product of its actual (or perceived) occurrence.

An earlier study by Conklin (1971) compared the perceptions of crime and fear for personal safety of respondents in a high-crime urban community and a low-crime suburban community. According to this study, significant relationships exist among crime rates, perceptions of crime as a problem, and fear for personal safety in that more urban residents preceived crime to be a problem and felt unsafe in their communities. Because of the homogeneity of the individual samples, it was not possible to test the extent to which persons who had ("incorrect") perceptions of low or high crime rates in the two areas respectively felt equally unsafe. However, one can speculate that those who see crime as a problem (regardless of whether it actually is a problem) are likely to exhibit greater fear, but may not as a consequence react to it in a harsher manner (see Taylor et al., 1979, and Stinchcombe et al., 1980). That is, the actual occurrence or experience of crime may heighten perceptions of it as a problem and increase the fear people have of being victimized, but whether people will react to crime in a formal manner as a social problem (e.g., report instances of it to the police and prefer that penal sanctions be imposed on offenders) is not necessarily a product of its occurrence or the fear people have of it. As victimization research indicates, people have a number of (often quite rational) reasons for not reporting crimes. Indeed, among our survey respondents who reported having been victimized and those who said they had not, few differences were found regarding their reactions to various delinquent acts.

The data reported in this and the preceding chapter cannot

directly reveal what factors might explain the reactions of rural and urban Indians to delinquent conduct or the differences and similarities in these reactions, but it is likely that the sociocultural milieus of rural and urban dwellers differ in several important respects so that how youthful misbehavior is perceived by rural and urban Indians (and, indeed, by people generally) and what they feel to be the appropriate reaction to delinquency reflect these differences.

ECONOMIC DEVELOPMENT AND SOCIAL CONTROL

As discussed throughout this book, the differing reactions of rural and urban Indians and of Indians and people in more economically developed nations, such as the United States, might be a function of factors relating to modernization or economic development and the impact these have on the role, power, and status relationships among people. These factors might also affect the reliance of people on various means of social control generally and the place of young people within the dominant socioeconomic order specifically.

Hence, peoples' perceptions of and dependency upon one another, and how they relate and react to each other, are shaped by the requirements of a rural-agrarian versus an urban-industrial economy. In contrast to industrial societies, social life in argarian societies is governed to a much greater extent by persons rather than abstract rules (Beteille, 1974; also see Diamond, 1971). In Indian society social life revolves around the domains of family and locality. As a consequence, violations of group norms or disputes between persons or groups are issues of concern to the family, *jati*, and community. Since urban social life in India more closely resembles that found in the industrialized West, it is not surprising that urbanites' reactions should more closely resemble those of people in economically developed nations. However, since even urban Indians are by no means completely "modernized," their reactions to delinquency are not yet identical to those found in more developed nations.

To be specific, the comparatively nonpunitive attitudes of Indian adults toward juvenile misconduct and the reluctance these people show for controlling such behavior by formal, judicial means can be partially explained by the network of role relationships found in Indian society. Since the state has minimal contact with family or village affairs and little relevance for social relationships, the police and the courts are considered irrelevant as far as ordinary matters of social control are concerned. In fact, although government programs of agricultural and economic development and population control are becoming more widespread and visible in India, the average Indian still has little if any direct contact with the government. In place of government agents or formal sanctions, informal mechanisms of control are relied upon. One's prestige as well as one's socioeconomic chances in life are largely a product of one's family and *jati* membership and the status these have in the community. Thus, the "bad name" one may gain for engaging in deviant or criminal activity reflects upon all members of the group and not on the offender alone (Gough, 1955; Srinivas, 1955; Beals, 1980). As a consequence, such things as gossip, scolding, and the withholding of rewards (e.g., funds for college, a dowry, funeral expenses) are strong informal inducements for conformity and apparently adequate means of social control.

Thus, disputes arising within the family are resolved by family elders rather than outside authorities. Prestigious *jati* elders may be asked to mediate intra-*jati* disputes. And at the village level, problems arising between various groups can be brought to the attention of village elders (usually landowners or respected members of some high-caste group) or the *panchayat* for mediation. Such individuals have no formal authority to sanction, but they have considerable informal power because of the interdependency of Indians and the general subscription to the values of obedience, respect, and deference given to elders or persons of position. To what extent the exercise of their power is fair, equal, or in accord with some sense of due process or the safeguards of procedural law is, of course, a matter that deserves further research. But, in any case, it is rare that the intervention of outsiders would be needed (or tolerated) in what are essentially considered to be private or village matters. For example, a police station is located only two miles from the village of Thamaraikulam; yet, as far as the village residents we interviewed could remember, the police had been "allowed" into the village only once, and this was to record the facts concerning a murder that had taken place in the village. In the case of other serious crimes (e.g., the theft of a bicycle) the police were not contacted; instead the villagers took matters into their own hands by instituting some restitution for the loss. If a "formal" judgment is necessary, typically the matter will be brought to the attention of the village *panchayat*. If all else fails, a host of coercive tactics may be relied upon. For example, water or electricity may be cut off to the offender's land. He may find his tools "broken," or his cow may "get lost" (see Gough, 1955).

Only among the more westernized urban residents who have no strong family ties or no immediate access to informal controls is there a tendency to opt for formal sanctions. Even then, as suggested by the responses of the urban residents to our survey, there is ambivalence in their attitudes; they are as likely to prefer that an offense be reported to the offender's family as to the police or government officials. As Krase and Sagarin (1980: 227) comment:

> With the collapse of traditional informal networks for controlling deviant behavior, the society leans heavily on formal agents of control. However, the newly urbanized population is unready to accept the legitimacy of police and courts.

Thus, even though one may prefer to do otherwise, the lack of options necessitates that officials be called upon to deal with delinquent youth in urbanized areas, thereby increasing the official rate of delinquent behavior recorded in cities.

But perhaps of equal importance is the power that participation in economic activity gives to children or young people in both rural and urban areas of countries such as India. Although they are surely exploited in terms of wages and are low on the universal pecking order, children are still seen as economic assets, both in terms of their immediate as well as their future contributions. To be childless is one of the greatest misfortunes to befall an Indian. "Who will take care of you in your old age?" is a question commonly put to the childless couple, since alternative sources of income for the elderly are practically nonexistent in India. Thus children are treated indulgently and are fretted over to an extent unthinkable in the West. This is not to suggest that children in India are not exploited, abused, mistreated, or in other ways put upon by adults. They surely are, and the threat of the "rod" was quite in evidence in some of the high schools we observed. Still the law is infrequently used either to protect or to control children (and others). Rather, scolding, shaming, and other informal controls are typically used with emphasis placed on the "bad name" a misbehaving child brings to the family—a social control device that derives its significance from the interdependency of child, family, and community.

Since they are integrated into the dominant social and economic structure of the society, Indian youth have little opportunity to deviate from general norms and little reason to establish the subcultural values and behaviors found among adolescents in developed countries. Instead, they actually develop a stake in the status quo. Moreover, since they are members of the socioeconomic system, young people in India are not as likely to be perceived as deviant and in need of control. Indeed, they possess a basis of power (albeit, limited), lost to youth in developed nations, to influence the standards by which these judgments are made.

In short, the different reactions of Indians and Westerners regarding delinquent conduct and the variations in these reactions on the part of rural and urban Tamilians are understandable in light of the socioeconomic characteristics of agrarian and industrial societies. That is, economic development, and the urbanization and industrialization such development requires, alters social arrangements, patterns of behavior, and the contingencies of social control. As a result, in economically developed societies and urban environments, delinquency is likely to emerge as a behavioral problem as well as a societal reaction (or social) problem. India may be spared this consequence of industrial development and modernization as some industrialized nations (e.g., Japan and Switzerland) seem to have been, but it is likely that as the country transforms from an agrarian-village to an industrial-urban society, both the frequency and seriousness of delinquent conduct and the frequency and severity of societal (formal) reaction to it will increase. The latter, however, will be mediated by the cultural ideology held by Indian adults, something that may be shaped by the mass media and the agencies of propaganda and information which help determine beliefs, values, and orientations.

Conclusion

This chapter extends the analysis of the survey data reported in Chapter 8 and the media analysis discussed in Chapter 7. Going on the assumption that together the various dimensions of perception shape peoples' reactions to social phenomena and that these dimensions are affected by the sociocultural milieu in which one is located, we sought to trace the patterns of reaction to juvenile delinquency and to compare these between rural and urban respondents. A number of distinct differences were found in the dimensions of reaction to delinquency as such as well as to specific forms of delinquency. Of the various dimensions, "opinion," either alone or in combination with other variables, appears to be a major determinant of sanction choice. Thus, societal reaction to delinquent behavior is influenced by factors relating to cultural orientations as to what behavior is considered sanctionable, who has the authority or responsibility to take reaction measures, and what type of reaction is thought appropriate.

The Structure of Public Reaction 191

In this respect, we argue that the contrasts in the character of the "delinquency problem" found in rural and urban localities in India, and between developing and developed countries, are the result of profound socioeconomic differences that exist between rural and urban environments and societies with different levels of economic development. The socioeconomic forces associated with urbanization and economic development are important insofar as they influence role definitions, the structure of relationships, social integration, and patterns of power and authority. In this regard, to the extent that informal mechanisms of social control are available and adequate and members of the society are integrated and interdependent, the need or the proclivity to call upon the law and government officials decreases. Black (1980) indicates that as reliance on informal mechanisms of social control decreases, reliance on formal (legal) means increases. And

> with the growth of law and the police . . . the citizenry becomes increasingly dependent upon the state to define and maintain order. As this happens, people increasingly cease to take responsibility for their own security and dispute settlement, and hesitate to help others with matters of this kind (ibid.: 195–196).

In this regard, where informal mechanisms of control are either lacking or not viable and where formal mechanisms are used, the probability increases that deviant conduct such as delinquent behavior will be transformed into a social problem of major proportions.

PART FIVE

Summary and Conclusions

CHAPTER 10

Delinquency, Society, and Social Control

This study was designed as an exploratory effort to investigate the forms, amounts, and distribution of delinquent behavior among Indian youth and to assess the character and extent of societal and legal reaction to that behavior. The limited nature of the research on which the findings presented in the preceding chapters of this volume are based preclude the testing of specific theories of the causes of or societal reaction to delinquent behavior. It was not our intention to engage in such an undertaking, although we hope that the data will throw some additional light on various theories or some aspects of them.

    The major findings of the study suggest that delinquency is (at least relatively speaking) not a social problem in India, either in a behavioral or societal-reaction sense. This is not to suggest that young people throughout India do not misbehave or act in ways that violate the law. They surely do; but, apparently, not to the extent that children in postindustrial or Western societies seem to. Nor do we suggest that Indian officials, or the adult population in general, turn a stoical eye on the misbehavior of their young. Misbehavior on the part of young people in India does indeed receive negative sanctions. But to the extent that it was possible for us to assess it, societal reaction to delinquency in India appears to be not only less extensive than that which occurs in the West, but also less punitive (or less formal). Thus, if social problems are conceptualized as the products of the reactions of groups (societies, organizations) to conditions (or behaviors) they feel harmful or threatening, the "delinquency problem" in India is surely quite unlike that found in the West. Why this is the case remains to be explained.

Although no single study can provide all the empirical evidence required for such an explanation, it is our purpose in this chapter to offer some speculations concerning this issue in light of past research and commentary. The basic argument we attempt to present here is that delinquency is not yet a problem in India because the socioeconomic composition of Indian society either does not allow or, more likely, does not necessitate that it should be an issue of concern.

Summary of Findings

While it would be inappropriate to generalize beyond the limitations of the data gathered in this research, our inquiry suggests that the following general conclusions can be reasonably made with regard to delinquent behavior and reactions to it in India:

I. Official statistics, of arrests and reported crimes, and the results of the self-report survey carried out in Tamil Nadu make it quite apparent that delinquent conduct (as well as crime in general) occurs relatively infrequently in India compared to Western or post-industrialized societies.

    A. It is believed that, in the West, up to approximately 50 percent of all crimes are committed by juveniles, and juveniles are disproportionately arrested for crimes in comparison to adults and to their proportion of the population.

    B. In India crimes attributed to juveniles and arrests of juveniles average about 3 percent each, although this does vary somewhat from state to state. Given that about one-half of the Indian population can be classified as "juveniles," these statistics suggest that officially recognized delinquency is a rarity in most of India.

    C. When compared with similar research carried out in the West, our self-report survey suggests that delinquent conduct is probably much more extensive than official records indicate. But even then involvement in serious forms of delinquency is relatively infrequent among Indian (Tamil Nadu) youth.

    D. Although delinquency itself is comparatively infrequent, the pattern of delinquent behavior among Indian (Tamil Nadu) youth is quite similar to that among Western youth.

        1. Delinquent behavior covers the spectrum of illegality,

but the bulk of delinquency consists of property or status-technical violations.

2. Self-reported delinquent behavior is not class-linked, since youngsters in all socioeconomic groups report such activity. The relative frequency of self-reported delinquency is, however, higher among the lowest socioeconomic groups.

3. Although official delinquency rates are higher in urban areas, self-reported delinquency is found in both urban and rural localities with about the same frequency.

4. As in the West, official (incarcerated) offenders more frequently report involvement in delinquency and more frequent commission of serious offenses.

II. Based on our public attitude survey and unstructured observations and interviews, public reaction to delinquency in Tamil Nadu (and probably India in general) appears to be oriented to informal and comparatively less punitive mechanisms of social control.

A. In general, respondents tended to exhibit consensus regarding the kinds of conduct they felt should be legally prohibited. And knowledge that these acts, at least with regard to the more serious offenses, are in fact legally prohibited was widespread. But considerable variation exists in knowledge and opinions depending upon whether the respondents resided in urban or village communities.

1. Rural respondents tended to favor formal (legislative) prohibition for all offense/offender types less frequently than urbanites.

2. Compared to rural respondents, urbanites tended to be somewhat more knowledgeable of the law.

B. Generally, regardless of offense, rural respondents, compared to urbanites, exhibited a reluctance to involve formal agents of control or to impose formal sanctions against misbehaving youth.

1. Although reaction varied depending upon the specific offense/offender in question, respondents typically preferred that offenders be handled by informal means (e.g., family) and that punitive sanctions (e.g., incarceration) not be imposed on offenders.

2. While rural respondents were consistent in their reactions, urban respondents exhibited incongruity and ambivalence in that they tended to say that informal agents should

be relied upon but that formal sanctions should be imposed on offenders.

C. How people say they will react to delinquency is more a function of how they "feel" (their opinions) about such behavior than it is of their knowledge of the laws concerning it.

    1. While opinions were important factors for both rural and urban respondents, the two groups differed considerably in the structure of their orientations toward delinquency. Among the urbanites, there was relatively little consistency in the factors associated with reactions to delinquency. But among the rural sample, there was a good deal of correspondence among their opinions regarding delinquency, who they thought should control it, and what they thought should be done to offenders.

    2. Socioeconomic status does not appear to be a particularly important factor in explaining general reactive tendencies toward delinquency, either among urban or rural respondents.

D. Residence is not only an important factor in the reactions of our respondents to delinquent conduct in general, it also influences the perceptions and reactions to specific types of offense behavior.

    1. Regardless of type of offense behavior, rural respondents were more consistent than urban respondents in terms of the various dimensions of reaction.

    2. However, the general structure of the interrelationships among the various dimensions of reaction was similar, regardless of residence or type of offense behavior.

    3. Generally, if people knew an act was illegal and were in agreement with its status, they were more likely to say that it should be dealt with formally and receive formal sanction.

III. Official reaction to delinquency appears to reflect the relatively low rates of its occurrence and the general belief that it does not warrant formal intervention by the state.

A. Although comparatively small numbers of offenders receive official reaction, either in the form of arrests or in judicial and correctional processing, those who do warrant such attention tend to correspond to Western "official delinquents" in terms of socioeconomic and other characteristics. They are predominantly males from lower socioeconomic groups and tend to be members of ethnic minorities. In short, they are the more disadvantaged segments of the population.

B. As in the West, comparatively few offenders are placed in correctional facilities; however, those who are so placed receive relatively long sentences, averaging about three years. Compared to the West, youngsters who are processed by the courts are less frequently placed on probation or in other ways remanded to the control of the state. Those who are not incarcerated are typically released to their parents.

C. Correctional officials in Tamil Nadu tend to view their wards as victims of neglect and poverty rather than as "bad" or otherwise aberrant children. Thus correctional programs tend to consist largely of custodial and educational (academic and vocational) activities, and little effort is given either to the punishment or therapy of offenders.

IV. While crime is a staple of the press in Tamil Nadu, the bulk of media coverage concerns political crime and mass demonstrations. Comparatively little attention is given to "street crime." And, most important, delinquency or youth crime is rarely a topic for the media. When it is discussed, delinquency is typically treated as an issue of resource allocation and the provision of care to needy youth.

To summarize, these findings indicate that delinquency is not a problem in India either in terms of (1) its relative occurrence; (2) the orientations of the public toward youthful misconduct; or (3) the activities of official law enforcement and judicial agencies.

Behavior, Reactions, and Social Problems

Independent of its objective harmfulness, any social condition can become a social problem. That is to say, some group(s) within a society or the members of the society collectively can take organized action to abolish, reduce, or control some condition or form of behavior (or those they feel are responsible for it). The same condition existing in any two societies might be treated as a problem in one but not in the other. In this respect, misconduct on the part of young people may be a universal "social problem" insofar as the adult members of every society are "organized" in their activities to "correct" such behavior. What differs is the frequency, extent, and form of this "corrective" action.

The separation of judicial and correctional treatment of young people from that of adults has long been a feature of Indian law and jurisprudence. And the recognition that young people warrant special protection and treatment under the law was institutionalized in parts of India with the passage, as early as 1920, of the various Children Acts. In short, provision for formal (legal) reaction to juveniles as a separate category of miscreants has long existed in Indian law. But to the extent that this research was able to assess it, this form of organized reaction is not only limited in its extent, but also in its frequency. That formal, judicial reaction toward young persons does exist in India suggests, of course, that delinquency is a "social problem" in the sense that the term is used here, but, relatively speaking, it does not seem to be one of major proportions.

Before organized action is taken against any condition or group, those who do, or would, embark upon such action must perceive some threat to their interests and values. Second, they must attribute that threat to some group or condition which they feel they can influence in some way. Third, they must feel that they can "do something" about the threat—i.e., they must believe that their actions will make a difference. Success in "doing something" depends upon the kind and amount of action taken and the relative power of those who embark upon it vis-à-vis those who are to be "influenced." In this regard, the behavior of young people is likely to become a social problem when young people (1) are recognized as a distinct ("out") group; (2) are perceived by others as posing some threat which (3) is believed to be controllable through concerted action; and (4) are relatively powerless to counter the action taken against them. Conversely, when one or more of these conditions are absent, the behavior of young people will *not*, or at least not successfully, be treated as a social problem. And even if all four conditions do exist, the probability that a social problem regarding the young will arise will be affected by the extent to which others are willing either to tolerate the perceived threat or to acknowledge that things can or should be otherwise (Hartjen, 1977: 35–60).

But explaining the creation of a social problem does not account for the form (or extent) of the action taken. That is, the kind of action people take, or the extent of that action, is not directly explained by the factors that stimulate that action in the first place (although, they are, of course, related). In India, delinquency is primarily a family-community matter and, only to a limited extent, a legal-custodial problem. In countries such as the United States, delinquency has largely been treated as a legal-therapeutic problem—a matter to be handled by the police, courts, and psychiatric professions. But why has delinquency not been defined primarily as a moral issue or as one requiring medical intervention? If misbehavior on the part of young people is a universal phenomenon, why do the form, extent, and frequency of control vary from one place or time to another?

Undoubtedly, the relative occurrence of youthful misconduct is an important factor in shaping reactions to it. But as anthropological research shows (e.g., Lemert, 1967), what is perceived as misbehavior, how it is perceived, and what people think should be done or are willing to do about it are not direct functions of its occurrence. That misconduct occurs, and that it is universally "controlled," means that the problem is ubiquitous. Therefore, the existence of "delinquent" behavior does not require explanation. What does require explanation is the relative frequency with which it occurs, the extent to which young people and their behavior are treated as a problem, and the form which societal reaction takes. Such an explanation, we propose, resides in an understanding of the socioeconomic structures of societies and the cultural and value orientations they generate. At several places in this report, we have commented upon a number of socioeconomic factors existent in India which (1) reduce the propensities of young people to deviate; (2) lessen the likelihood that adults will perceive the behavior of young people as warranting intervention, especially by legal authorities; and (3) reduce the extent to which young offenders are reacted to in formal (legal) ways. In the following sections of this chapter we attempt to draw these arguments together in the form of a more general explanation of delinquency and social control in contemporary India.

Explaining Delinquency

The similarities in the types of delinquent conduct found in developed and developing countries, and the apparent similarities in the socioeconomic characteristics of juveniles involved in (or usually apprehended for) such behavior, would tempt one to conclude that the genesis of such conduct stems from common causal conditions. That this may not be the case has been suggested by Defleur (1969).

In her attempt to test Cohen's (1955) subculture theory of delinquency in Cordoba, Argentina, DeFleur found that the kind of "reactive" subcultures Cohen describes as being responsible for delinquent conduct in the United States did not exist in Argentina. Thus, given the lack of a theory with a "sufficiently high level of generality" that could be applied to diverse societies, DeFleur (1969: 39) argues that it is necessary to "develop specific theories which are both consistent with and relevant to particular socio-cultural systems." We are in agreement with this sentiment. However, research accumulated since DeFleur's study offers a number of clues regarding patterns of delinquency within various societies and differences among these societies on which to base a more general conceptual framework and theoretical argument.

Explanations of the epidemiology, the frequency and relative forms of delinquent behavior, and the etiology, or causes, of delinquent acts are probably related, but are not necessarily interchangeable. It may very well be that youngsters who steal in India do so for much the same "reasons" as youngsters who steal in countries like the United States. But this does not tell us why more or less of the juvenile population is engaged in the behavior in the two localities, nor does it tell us why such conduct is treated differently in both localities. To what extent might existing theories pertaining to epidemiology help us understand delinquency rates in India? Of the various schools of thought available, the two discussed below would, on the surface, seem to be the most useful as explanatory models.

Most, if not all, sociological theories of delinquency have, in one or another version, attributed delinquency to some aspect of social "disorganization." Prominent among these are various "anomie" arguments (i.e., Merton, 1956) and their offspring, "opportunity" arguments (i.e., Cloward and Ohlin, 1960). Generally, these arguments attribute delinquency (and other forms of deviance) to the economic inequality which blocks the access of certain segments of the population to legitimate or conventional routes to success and thereby stimulate the development of illegitimate opportunity structures which increases the availability of deviant alternatives.

This line of argument would lead one to expect that crime and delinquency would be most frequent in societies in which members share a success ideology (such as achieving monetary rewards), but in which opportunities (such as jobs or education) to achieve this goal are blocked for some segments of the population. While recognized as prevalent in developed societies, these conditions are likely to become acute in societies that are undergoing rapid modernization, have high levels of poverty, low mobility, and a great disparity among social strata. In this regard, such arguments may be particularly useful in understanding the disparity between urban and rural crime and delinquency rates in developing nations such as India. It is in the city that one's social status is more fully a function of economic wealth (i.e., class) rather than *jati* or family position. It is in the city that at least a greater promise, if not always a greater possibility, of upward mobility exists. But the limited opportunities for many segments of the population to fulfill that promise, even in industrial centers, heighten the probability that a situation of anomie will prevail and that alternatives to achieve economic goals will be sought.*

Similar arguments may also help us understand the higher (official) crime and delinquency rates among certain disenfranchised groups such as Harijans and other minorities who are denied equal opportunity for social mobility. For, in spite of the considerable economic advances that have been made in India and despite the spread of the trappings of modernization in even the most remote localities, the nation remains an impoverished country. The disparity between the rich and the poor is not only great but highly visible. Opportunity to move up the social scale or to even break out of economic deprivation is practically nonexistent, particularly for the more disenfranchised segments of the population. Thus, to the extent that they encounter the promise that modernization brings but experience the reality of economic deprivation, the pressures for them to deviate increase.

But while opportunity arguments may explain *differences* in rates of deviance among various segments of a population, they cannot explain the rates exhibited by the total society. It may very well be that the disadvantaged segments of Indian society are disproportionately engaged in certain forms of illegality, and they may be so engaged for the same opportunity-related reasons that are assumed to apply to people in developed nations. Likewise, the similarities and the differences in the urban and rural crime and delinquency rates found in India and developed countries may be the result of common factors. But these arguments do not adequately explain the magnitude of the rates, nor can they explain the differences in rates found across nations.† Indeed, Clinard and Abbott (1973:172–188) found that anomie, or differential opportunity, arguments cannot explain crime and delinquency rates in the countries they studied. Thus, they argue that differential access to legitimate opportunity structures does not, in itself, appear to generate the differential distribution of criminality found throughout the popu-

---

*The low urban crime and delinquency rates in India, compared to those in developed countries, suggest that stratification based on class has not yet come to dominate in its cities so that the pressures of anomie are not yet great.

†As Durkheim (1964) suggests, various societies may have "normal" rates of crime. But anomie (either in the Durkheimian or Mertonian sense) cannot explain the normal rates. It only addresses changes (either increases or decreases) in normal rates or "abnormally" high rates among specific groups within a population.

lace of these societies. Moreover, access to illegitimate opportunities does not explain criminality as such either, although differential access to these opportunities may determine the forms of deviance exhibited by members of different social-class groups. Thus, opportunity theories may be most applicable to explaining differences in the types of deviant or illegal behavior various segments of the population commit.

A second social-organizational school offers a host of explanations attributing delinquency (and other forms of deviance) to a variety of "disorganizational" features of society which are believed to motivate, or at least to remove impediments to, illegal conduct (see Faris, 1955; Cohen, 1959). Closely akin to this line of thinking are arguments that attribute illegal behavior to the pluralism of modern society which results in value clashes, individualism, social alienation, and impersonality—conditions that are assumed to be conducive to criminality (Barron, 1955).

These arguments would lead one to predict that pluralistic or disorganized societies would generate higher rates of delinquency than socially integrated societies. This argument appears to have some relevance in explaining rates of delinquency in countries such as the United States. Moreover, it also seems to be a reasonable starting point in understanding the differences between rural and urban rates of crime and delinquency in other countries. But, again, the argument is not adequate for explaining the differences in delinquency rates between countries such as the United States and India. If pluralism is a cause of delinquency, as it may be in a highly heterogeneous society like the United States, it should have a similar effect in India as well, for there are probably very few countries more pluralistic than India. Yet its national crime and delinquency rates are low.

Perhaps national delinquency is too broad a phenomenon for the notion of social disorganization to be applicable. That is, while a country as a whole may exhibit a host of characteristics indicative of social pluralism, its rates of delinquency could remain low if the various regions or localities of the country are integrated within themselves. If, for example, specific communities are highly integrated as individual entities, but are different from one another, a country could register a kind of false pluralism simply because of the differences among what are actually homogeneous units. As a nation, India is indeed a pluralistic country. But considerable homogeneity exists within its component states, districts, towns, and villages. In day-to-day life one is surrounded by a commonality of kind, particularly since the country is composed of predominantly isolated agrarian communities. To a South Indian village resident, a visitor from New Delhi is just as much a foreigner as one from another country. Since the people have relatively little sustained contact with "outsiders," it could very well be that the kinds of forces emanating from a pluralistic, individualistic, alienated environment conducive to delinquency are not yet, to any significant extent, operative in India. Indeed, as it has been argued throughout this book, various social and economic factors actually operate to integrate youth into the dominant social system of India rather than to produce the alienating effects of a youth subculture as found in the West.

Even if the residents of communities and villages are separated from one another by caste, religion, and occupation, the requirements of economic interdependence necessitated by an agrarian socioeconomic system help weld otherwise disparate groups into an integrated whole. In fact, much of the violence, in the form of collective assualts on different caste or religious communities, is likely to be related to conflicts that arise from the economic interdependence of various groups or under conditions that serve to upset traditional relationships.

In brief, it is possible that existing epidemiological theories may explain some aspects of delinquency rates in non-Western nations, but they fail to offer specific accounts of national rates or, more importantly, of the apparent differences in the magnitude of these rates between developed and developing countries.

Delinquency and Social Control in "Self-help" Society

As a social problem, delinquency appears to be related to the stage of economic development a country has achieved. Although a number of arguments have been offered which link certain features of sociocultural forms associated with economic development either to the occurrence of crime and delinquency or to societal responses to it (see Quinney, 1977; Chambliss, 1978; Diamond, 1971; Krase and Sagarin, 1980; Shelley, 1981b), the reasons for this linkage have not as yet been satisfactorily determined.

Throughout this book, we have described various aspects of interpersonal and social relationships in Indian society which impede the development of delinquent conduct and inhibit formal-legal reaction to those youths engaged in such behavior. First, we have argued that the integrative structures of family, *jati*, and community serve to block the development of a youth subculture antagonistic to the dominant society and thereby reduce both the motivations and opportunities to deviate. Second, the interpersonal unity produced by these structures inhibit reliance upon formal mechanisms of control and stimulate the use of extralegal, informal measures for dealing with wayward youth. Third, the fact that children are important members of family, *jati*, and community structures reduces the probability that they will be seen as "outsiders" in need of control and, at the same time, gives them a degree of power to affect what is done to them by their elders.

We do not know to what extent these features are to be found in predeveloped societies in general or whether, in fact, they are unique to India. We suspect, however, that India and other premodern societies share a number of characteristics not usually found in developed nations which singularly or in combination help reduce the probability that delinquency will become, or be treated as, a major issue of concern. Because of their social-control practices, Black and Baumgarter (in Black, 1980: 193–208) use the term "self-help" to describe these societies; i.e., the business of dealing with the wayward is nonformalized and is handled at a local level in an informal, conciliatory, rather than a punitive, manner. Accordingly, self-help forms of social control tend to arrive at conciliatory, negotiated settlements that involve compensation rather than penal sanction. Perhaps more important are those who are involved in the settlement of disputes and take responsibility for reacting to the offender. Black and Baumgarter suggest that

> the people immediately involved in a dispute participate in its resolution, and no one else. In other instances, one or both parties may draw upon a network of family, friends, or even situational acquaintances or bystanders for assistance, but this remains much different from the formal organization of law with its headquarters, chains of command, and courts (ibid.: 206).

Since it is the participants and/or their associates who deal with the matter, the dependency on formal agents of social control is reduced and the very norms being challenged are strengthened. As Black and Baumgarter suggest, since the disputants themselves participate in the settlement of the dispute, they play a normative role in one another's lives, validating both the norms and the responsibility and rights of the participants to intervene.

There are other differences between self-help and formal, legal mechanisms of social control, but the two characteristics of informality and normative role involvement generic to self-help social control appear to have major implications for the lack of a delinquency problem in India. Specifically, insofar as social-control activities are treated as local (community, village, *jati*, family) affairs and not as matters for official intervention, official rates of delinquency are likely to be low. An offender may indeed receive some negative sanction, but the offense is not recorded as such in official counts of crime and delinquency. Moreover, to the extent that the intimacy of those involved in resolution of the dispute or reaction to the miscreant leads to the development of a normative role relationship among them, self-help forms of social control serve to integrate the delinquent back into the very community affected by the offense. And to the extent that the person's degree of integration affects his or her propensity to deviate (Hirschi, 1969), the informality and intimacy of self-help social control reduces not only the official, but the actual rates of delinquency.

While Black and Baumgarter attempt to show how such a mechanism of social control could develop in modern societies, the mechanism they describe is the one that prevails in developing or premodern countries—at least it closely resembles the social-control approach typically taken in India. In other words, styles of social control are related to socioeconomic development. The reason for this is not easily ascertainable, but it is quite possible that economic development and its accompanying affluence stimulate a sense of individualism and social isolationism. At the same time they afford a society the means to hire service workers to take care of matters societal members cannot or will not handle themselves. In contrast, the requirements of, and relative poverty caused by, predevelopment economic conditions engender a stronger sense of community and collectivism and necessitate that almost all aspects of life be dealt with by the group acting in unison.

Whatever the case, premodern societies are likely to exhibit sociointeractional forms of mutual aid and self help. People in developed societies are more likely to require and experience control through formal regulation and intervention by government agents. Thus, a social system emphasizing mutual aid and self help is likely to be associated with an altruistic pattern of social interaction. In this type of system, the individual is likely to be frequently involved with others in intimate relationships, and such involvement could heighten the individual's normative acceptance, in part because "being a part of the action," as it were, increases the relevance of the norms for the individual and decreases awareness of and exposure to alternatives. Normative acceptance, in turn, is likely to increase one's "stake in comformity" and consequently decrease one's likelihood of deviation. And the infrequency of deviation itself produces a reduced need for social control of any kind.

In contrast, in developed societies where people are dependent upon the police and courts to manage their disputes and deal with offenders, a kind of social egoism exists in that individuals are neither involved nor intimate with most of the people with whom they interact. People who have little by way of social-moral ties with one another are more likely to experience normative conflict or alienation (either in fact or imagination) and, consequently, are more likely to engage in acts which others perceive as deviant and threatening. Consequently the need for social control increases. And since there is little by way of alternatives, formal agents are called upon to exercise that control. Those persons who are perceived as outsiders and who are relatively powerless—as are the young in modern society—are most likely to experience this control. These patterns are diagrammed in Figure 10.1.

But a self-help style of social control is only likely to work under conditions of political anarchy (Pepinsky, 1976; Black, 1976; Tifft, 1979). Politically anarchic societies are likely to be acephalous societies (Pfohl, 1981). In these societies, members are essentially equal and interdependent upon one another for mutual survival. Interpersonal relationships are structured in terms of a diffused role structure, a kin-based social organization, and a belief system emphasizing collective responsibility (Pfohl, 1981: 80). In these societies, no one has preponderant power to impose his or her will so that the settlement of disputes and control of deviants require either mutual help or are treated as personal matters. As described by Michalowski (quoted in ibid.: 79),

> acephalous societies are small economically cooperative and relatively equalitarian societies with simple technology and divisions of labor based mainly upon age and sex. Stratification in terms of differential access to material goods and political power does not exist. While these societies lack rules or governments with the power to command, direct and correct the behavior of others ... acephalous societies are generally characterized more by order and cooperation than by chaos and competition.

India, of course, is not an acephalous society in the strict sense, although at the village level many of the features of such a society are to be found. Indeed, as described at various points in this book, India is a hierarchical society, stratified on the bases of caste, religion,

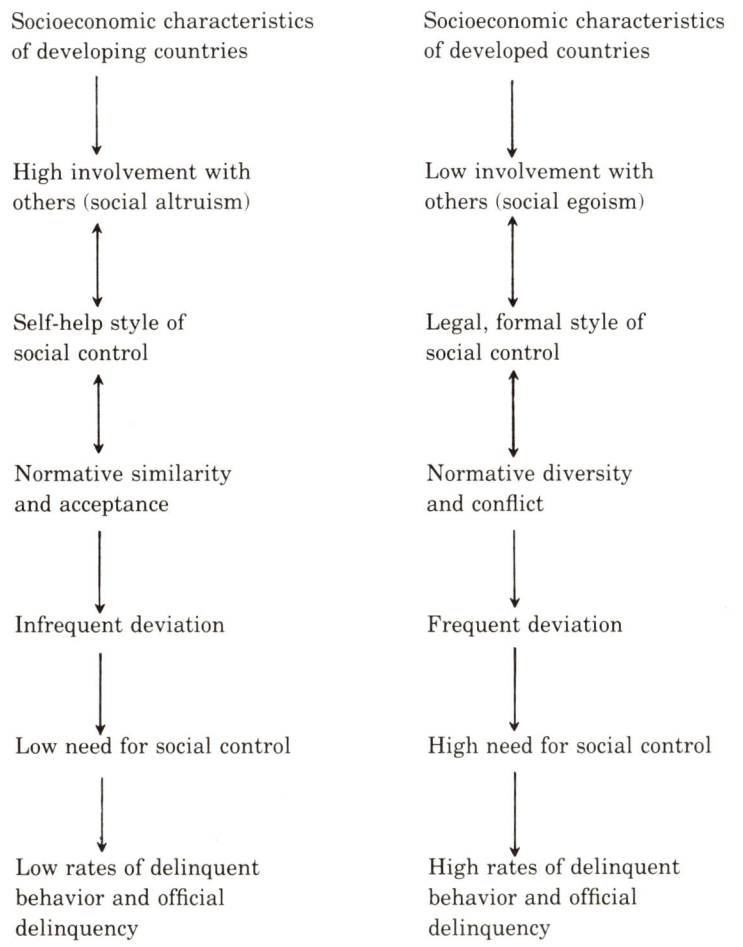

FIGURE 10.1. *Social Systems and Styles of Control*

region, and, increasingly, class. And the rather obvious distinctions among peoples have endured for a considerable length of time and are well recognized (if not always liked) by the populace. This is especially true within the family, *jati*, and community. But at the same time, the degree of governmental, political control characteristic of economically advanced state societies is not to be found in India. At least within the local community, in spite of caste and other distinctions, there exists a degree of egalitarianism and mutual interdependence not found in economically developed societies. At the village level, about the only "government" of any consequence is the *panchayat*, a form of popular judicial institution (Tiruchelvam, 1978: 270), and, while the *panchayat* is not found in urban centers, informal systems of popular justice appear to operate based on "community" ties (family, *jati*, neighborhood). In either case, while "authority" is structured in heirarchical fashion, the commonality of kind and interdependency of the units comprising that structure require that authority be exercised informally and with concession to the desires of group members. Thus, for example, while in the family the senior male may still be dominant and may have the last say in family matters, young people are not, by virtue of their age or employment status, automatically powerless in influencing these decisions. They may not say much directly, but others (relatives) who care about them must be considered. And, indeed, catering to the welfare of subordinates is the principal social-moral obligation of senior members of the family. They would be subject to social disgrace for failing to accomplish this. Similarly, within the village a particular *jati* group may dominate, but it is rare for such a body to impose its will without, at least, the consent of others in the village. Failure to obtain such consent could mean, for example, that workers would be unavailable at harvest time. Also, the gossip that would ensue would be repugnant enough to keep the dominant group in line. And the "bad name" the family or *jati* members might receive for failing to carry out social responsibility could mean that finding mates for their children would be difficult. Indeed, even the need to call upon the authorities is itself an occasion for social disgrace—i.e., it indicates to others that one is incapable of managing one's affairs. In short, India today is very much the kind of society that fosters self-help forms of social control, which, in turn, helps to integrate group members into the kinds of unity and interpersonal involvement such a system of control requires.

This is not to suggest that Indian society functions as an ideal entity overflowing with a sense of commonality and mutual help. The very real chasms among the various segments of Indian society often produce violence and destruction.* And at times police and judicial officials must act to intervene in and control the behavior of con-

---

*The high official rates of and frequent newspaper reports on riots and demonstrations are a clear reflection of this.

flicting groups. But such intervention is comparatively rare at the interpersonal level, and the intergroup riots and disorders that periodically flare up are group-centered rather than individual actions and represent, in some respects, a kind of collective or mass self-help activity directed toward those who are thought to threaten or oppose the group. Hence, more often than not, the deviations of the individual are responded to as matters for the group itself to take care of. This reflects and probably enhances the very unity that allows for the infrequent exercise of such control in the first place.

Although the traditional structures of power and relationships continue to exist in India, there is the possibility that as the country modernizes and "westernizes," these structures will weaken. Particularly in the cities, as class comes to replace family and *jati* as the main basis of stratification, the integrative power of these structures may decrease. Thus, as individuals become "liberated" from the control of family and *jati* and experience the anomie of individualism this would occasion, it is possible that both their desire and opportunity to act in ways they would not otherwise have contemplated may increase. If this should occur to young people as a specific segment of the population, we would then see an increase in the frequency of misconduct on their part. Also, as the society becomes increasingly segregated into autonomous units, we should see increased reliance upon and intervention by formal agents of social control. The consequence could very well be the growth of a delinquency problem comparable to that found in developed or postindustrial societies. Whether this will occur in India, or whether alternative ways of social integration will develop to block the impact of modernization, remains to be seen; but that the development of a delinquency problem may not be inevitable is suggested by the cases of Switzerland (Clinard, 1978) and Japan (Clifford, 1976).

Both Switzerland and Japan are highly urbanized and industrialized, yet their rates of crime and delinquency are uncommonly low. Although somewhat different, both societies appear to have developed or retained a number of institutions and sociointegrative structures which reduce pressures to deviate and, at the same time, allow for the successful repression of the deviance that does occur. For instance, in Switzerland, the exclusion of young people from adult activities found in countries like the United States does not exist. As Clinard (1978: 151) notes,

> along with more open communication lines between the young and the adult population, youth unrest is less in evidence. This is due, in part, to the greater participation at all age levels—for example, in numerous

sports and other activities, as well as the system of national-military service that systematically brings men, aged 20 to 55, together at periodic intervals, from the initial induction into the military service until the suspension of service decades later. As these forces have led to more integration in the society, they have also tended to diminish alienation between age groups.

Similarly, in contrast to the individualism and alienation associated with the economic-urbanization boom that occurred in the United States and Western Europe following World War II, Clifford (1976: 164) suggests that in Japan

> urban concentration has obviously decreased the family role and reduced the older power and authority of parents. However, it has by no means atomized or anonymized the individual who has readily placed himself within other social contexts transferring his family obligations and loyalties to his neighborhood, party, firm, or organization.

In short, even though Japan has developed economically, it has been able to resist or supplant the alienating forces such development seems to generate. As a consequence "the Japanese are still less individualistic than they are group-oriented and, therefore, far more amenable to the pressures to avoid the kinds of individual deviance that would make it easier to commit crimes" (ibid.: 165).

Conclusion

Shelley (1981a: 22) correctly states that "no direct correlation exists between crime and a single social, economic, or political condition. Crime was and continues to be a complex response to intricately connected social forces." Criminologists have long realized that the documentation and unraveling of these social forces would benefit from cross-national or comparative research. Few comprehensive studies of this kind exist, however, indicating the lack of adequate resources to carry out such research and the difficulty involved in its undertaking. The handful of studies now available provide a needed addition to the information we have about criminal phenomena throughout the world. But these studies, like the findings of our own research, shed considerable doubt on the explanations that have been offered and highlight the limitations in our understanding of crime and related phenomena.

In spite of its limited volume, a common theme seems to be emerging from the research conducted in non-Western countries—a theme that may have important implications for our understanding of criminal and delinquent behavior and their control. The key may be the link between economic development or modernization and rates of crime and delinquency. The issue is why these rates increase as a society modernizes.

The major theories of delinquency (and crime) presently available to criminologists may, in fact, be relevant to this question, but none of them alone seems to answer it. However, there is a theme common to the arguments of anomie, opportunity, social pluralism, conflict, and association; and that theme, alluded to in cross-national research, is the degree of social integration a society exhibits. In developed nations where crime seems to be frequent, social integration seems to be minimal. In developing nations the reverse seems to be the case. Thus it may be that the "destruction of the sense of belonging that characterizes contemporary society in most developed nations is particularly conducive to the emergence of increased criminality" (ibid.: 83). Clinard and Abbott (1973: 210), for example, found in their Kampala study that

> the typical offender reveals that although he has not broken his ties with his village completely he has adopted strong urban preferences and behavior patterns. He is neither fully urban nor traditional but rather appears to be a marginal man cut off from supportive family ties.

It was not so much the delinquency of the youngsters we observed in correctional facilities in Tamil Nadu that was responsible for their incarceration, but rather their lack of a home or supportive family ties, which may itself have been partly responsible for their delinquency involvement. Even in economically advanced societies, delinquency rates can be low if the youth of the society are made a meaningful part of its social-interactional system. In short, to the extent that the members of a society are made or allowed to be meaningful participants in its social system, the less likely they are to rebel against or deviate from its norms.

This, of course, has long been recognized by criminologists and has found explicit theoretical expression (i.e., Hirschi, 1969). What is less often recognized is that the same forces that integrate individuals or groups into the dominant society serve to reduce the probability that they will be seen as, and responded to as, offenders (see Erikson, 1966). That is, the extent to which people will engage in delinquency and the likelihood that their behavior will be treated as or labeled delinquent are both affected by the same social forces. As the data and analysis presented in this volume suggest, India may be one instance of a society where these forces operate to reduce both the frequency of delinquency and the severity of societal reaction to it. But investigations of the consequences that seem to follow from modernization and urbanization would lead us to expect that India will experience rising rates of delinquency in the years ahead. This is due to the fact that modernization not only opens up opportunities heretofore nonexistent, but that it also disrupts the unity of traditional relationships. Thus, to the extent that delinquency is indeed linked to or stimulated by various aspects of modernization, and to the extent that these features are intrinsic to a modernized society, we could speculate that in the decades ahead crime and delinquency in India will come to more closely resemble, both in pattern and frequency, the kind of social problem found in the West.

APPENDIX A

Self-report Questionnaire

University of Madras
Indo-American Fellowship Foundation
Adolescent Behavior Study

We are conducting a study that compares the behavior of youngsters in India with young people in other countries. We would appreciate your helping us with this study by filling out the questionnaire given to you by the researcher. You are not identified on the questionnaire in any way and your answers are strictly confidential. So please try to answer each question as honestly as you can. If you have any difficulty with the questions, raise your hand and the researcher will try to help you.

Thank you for your help. Now please turn the page to Part I. Choose only one answer for each question.

Part I

First we would like to know something about the people who have agreed to help us with our study. Given below are several questions. Please check the most appropriate answer for each by placing a check mark (X) in the appropriate blank space provided.

1. How old are you?
    - ___ (1) 8–10 years old
    - ___ (2) 11–13 years old
    - ___ (3) 14–16 years old
    - ___ (4) 17 years old or older

2. How many years of school have you completed?
    - ___ (1) 0–3 years of school
    - ___ (2) 4–6 years of school
    - ___ (3) 7–9 years of school
    - ___ (4) 10–12 years of school

3. Is your father or guardian employed?
    - ___ (1) Yes
    - ___ (2) No
    - ___ (3) Don't know

4. If your father or guardian is employed, what is his/her occupation? Please describe in detail.

   _____

   _____

   _____

5. Approximately, what do you think is his/her income per month?
    - ___ (1) less than Rs.200
    - ___ (2) between Rs.200 and 499
    - ___ (3) between Rs.500 and 999
    - ___ (4) Rs.1000 or more

6. What is your religion?
    - ___ (1) None
    - ___ (2) Hindu
    - ___ (3) Muslim
    - ___ (4) Christian
    - ___ (5) Any other (describe in detail)

Thank you for your answers. Now please turn the page to *Part II* and answer each of the questions in that section.

Part II

Every community has certain rules of conduct that its citizens are expected to follow. However, scientific research shows that irrespective of age everyone violates some standards. Below is a list of acts. We would like to know which, if any of these activities you have engaged in within *the last three years*. Please put a check mark (X) in the appropriate blank space for each act that indicates how many times you have committed the act within the last three years.

Since you cannot be identified by the questionnaire, answer each question accurately and fully.

1. Have you skipped school without a legitimate reason?
    ____ (1) No
    ____ (2) On one or two occasions
    ____ (3) Several times
    ____ (4) Very often

2. Have you taken things worth less than Rs.2/- that did not belong to you?
    ____ (1) No
    ____ (2) Once or twice
    ____ (3) Several times
    ____ (4) Very often

3. Have you ever bought or drank liquor?
    ____ (1) Very often
    ____ (2) Several times
    ____ (3) Once or twice
    ____ (4) No

4. Have you ever intentionally damaged or destroyed public or private property?
    ____ (1) No
    ____ (2) Once or twice
    ____ (3) Several times
    ____ (4) Very often

5. Have you ever defied your parents openly?
   ___ (1) Very often
   ___ (2) Several times
   ___ (3) Once or twice
   ___ (4) No

6. Have you ever run away from home?
   ___ (1) No
   ___ (2) Once or twice
   ___ (3) Several times
   ___ (4) Very often

7. Have you ever taken part in a "gang" fight?
   ___ (1) Very often
   ___ (2) Several times
   ___ (3) Once or twice
   ___ (4) No

8. Have you ever taken things of medium value (worth Rs.2/- to Rs.50/-) that did not belong to you?
   ___ (1) No
   ___ (2) Once or twice
   ___ (3) Several times
   ___ (4) Very often

9. Have you ever driven a car without the owner's permission?
   ___ (1) No
   ___ (2) Once or twice
   ___ (3) Several times
   ___ (4) Very often.

10. Have you ever taken things of large value without the owner's permission (over Rs.50/-)?
    ___ (1) Very often
    ___ (2) Several times
    ___ (3) Once or twice
    ___ (4) No

11. Have you ever used force to get money from another person?
    ____ (1) No
    ____ (2) Once or twice
    ____ (3) Several times
    ____ (4) Very often

12. Have you ever used substances like "ganja"?*
    ____ (1) No
    ____ (2) Once or twice
    ____ (3) Several times
    ____ (4) Very often

13. Have you ever hit or struck one of your parents?
    ____ (1) Very often
    ____ (2) Once or twice
    ____ (3) Several times
    ____ (4) No

14. Have you ever tried to get something by lying about your age or yourself?
    ____ (1) No
    ____ (2) Once or twice
    ____ (3) Several times
    ____ (4) Very often

15. Have you ever gone without permission into the home or onto the property of someone?
    ____ (1) Very often
    ____ (2) Several times
    ____ (3) Once or twice
    ____ (4) No

16. Have you ever been arrested (exclude traffic violations)?
    ____ (1) No
    ____ (2) Once or twice
    ____ (3) Several times
    ____ (4) Very often

*Marihauna.

17. Have you ever appeared before a juvenile judge or magistrate?
    ___ (1) No
    ___ (2) Once or twice
    ___ (3) Several times
    ___ (4) Very often

18. Have you ever been sent to an approved school or Borstal school?
    ___ (1) Five or more times
    ___ (2) Three or four times
    ___ (3) Once or twice
    ___ (4) No

19. Have you ever been placed on probation by a court or magistrate?
    ___ (1) Very often
    ___ (2) Several times
    ___ (3) Once or twice
    ___ (4) No

Thank you for helping us with our study. Please make sure you have answered all the questions.

APPENDIX B

*Public Attitude Questionnaire**

University of Madras
Indo-American Fellowship Foundation
Public Attitude Survey

We are conducting a study of what people think about the behavior of some young people in India today. I will read twenty-five brief stories describing certain acts committed by young people. After each story, I will ask you a series of questions on how you feel about the various acts.

There are no right or wrong answers to any of the questions. What we want to know is how you feel about the behavior. You will not be identified on the questionnaire, so please feel free to respond frankly. Your help in completing this study is very important.

Now I will read the stories:

Part A

1. One day, Palani's friend (the same age as Palani) had gotten a package of cigarettes. Along with several other boys, Palani and his friend decided to smoke the cigarettes.

---

*The twenty-five projective scenarios contained in the public opinion questionnaire are listed here in order. Due to space considerations, the four questions (and response categories associated with each) asked about each scenario are listed only for the first story.

1. Do you think this act should be prohibited by law?
   ___ 1. Yes
   ___ 2. No
   ___ 3. Don't know

2. Is this act prohibited by law?
   ___ 1. Yes
   ___ 2. No
   ___ 3. Don't know

3. To whom (if anyone) would you report this act? (Choose only *one* answer.)
   ___ 1. No one
   ___ 2. Only the person's family
   ___ 3. A church or religious leader
   ___ 4. A doctor or a psychiatrist
   ___ 5. The person's teacher
   ___ 6. A social worker
   ___ 7. The police
   ___ 8. A government official other than the police
   ___ 9. Other (describe)

4. What do you think should be done with the youngster(s) who committed this act? (Choose only one answer.)
   ___ 1. Nothing at all
   ___ 2. Placed on probation
   ___ 3. Psychiatric treatment
   ___ 4. Fined
   ___ 5. Placed in a correctional institution
   ___ 6. Other (describe)

2. Vijay's father was a high-level executive of a large manufacturing firm. He was a very religious man who strongly disapproved of even his colleagues drinking alcohol. Once at a party, some friends produced a bottle of whiskey and urged Vijay to try it, which he did.

3. Balu is a seven-year-old boy. Being big for his age, he had learned early that he could get what he wanted from other boys by being tough and aggressive. One day, he got into a fight with another boy and beat him up very badly.

Appendix B 223

4. Sasi is a thirteen-year-old girl who was very unhappy living at home with her parents. One day she had an argument with her mother that made her very angry. As a result, she just wanted to get away. That night, she packed some of her clothes and caught a train to the next town.

5. For as long as he could remember, Murugan had longed to have a bike of his own. But his father, who had not had a steady job in ten years, could not afford to buy him one. Any money Murugan was able to earn was necessary to help support the family. Once, while walking along the street, he saw an unlocked bike. He jumped on it and pedaled away.

6. Raju is the son of a poor tenant farmer who is barely able to feed his family. Raju did not like village life and often longed to go to the city for excitement. Being poor, he would sneak onto the train and not pay the fare.

7. On a Sunday evening seventeen-year-old Ashok and his friends climbed the large compound wall of an empty house. Playfully they picked up stones and tossed them at the windows, breaking several.

8. Ramesh became associated with a group of other students who frequently smoked marihuana and he also started smoking marihuana often.

9. Eleven-year-old Ram's father had forbidden him to associate with some of the boys in the village. While on an errand for his father, he stopped to chat with some of the youngsters his father had forbade him to be with.

10. Sridhar's father found occasional employment as a coolie at the harbor. Sridhar spotted an unattended car sitting near a warehouse when he and his friends went to the harbor to deliver his father's lunch. On their way home, they broke into the car and, with Sridhar behind the wheel, drove off.

11. Although warnings were posted against unauthorized trespassing on Railway property, Velu and his friends liked to play near the railway yard and would use the objects there as targets for throwing stones.

12. Selvam is the son of an unemployed laborer. Selvam often observed men in his neighborhood drinking arrack and wondered what the stuff tasted like. A friend of his brought him to a house where several men were drinking and Selvam bought a drink with the little money he had earned that day packing things in a grocery store.

13. The parents of a teenage boy were unhappy that their son had been assaulted by a seventeen-year-old boy called Mani. Mani was big for his seventeen years and from childhood used strong-arm tactics on other boys and was often involved in fights.

14. One day Chinthamani was walking down the street with some sharp instrument under his clothing. On closer examination, it was found that he was carrying a dagger.

15. Thirteen-year-old Mohan had a very unhappy home life. After a serious argument with his father, he became very angry and unhappy; so he decided to leave home and packed his few belongings that night. He caught the night train to the next city.

16. Arun Kumar is the son of a high-level civil servant. Once his father's driver did not arrive to pick him up. Arun Kumar became impatient waiting. He started walking home. Halfway, he saw an unlocked bike and he got on it and pedaled away.

17. Singaram did not like school one bit. Even though his parents wanted him to attend school and get an education, Singarum would do his best to avoid attending class and would frequently skip school without his parent's permission.

18. Perumal is the son of a well-to-do landowner in a village. Having little to keep him occupied, Perumal was often bored with the village life and would go to the city under the pretext of visiting relatives. He found it exciting to sneak on the train without paying the fare.

19. Murthy was the youngest son in a large family. He always felt that his parents favored his older brother. Once his mother made him extremely angry by yelling at him for what he thought was an unimportant matter, so he hit her with his fists.

Appendix B 225

20. Murali and four other boys from a new housing colony were involved in a gangfight with boys from a neighboring colony. Every evening Murali and his friends would meet on a particular street corner which they considered their private territory. On that particular day, the boys from the neighboring colony rode up to the street corner on their bikes. Trying to act tough, Murali and his friends started to taunt the intruders. A fight broke out.

21. When Radha was passing through the market, he found a new ball inside the car which was standing there and Radha fearlessly opened the door and took the ball and hid it.

22. One day eight-year-old Pandu and his friends started throwing stones at the windows of a new multistoried building.

23. Muniyamma is sixteen years old. One one occasion, her mother asked Muniyamma to get some water from the well. Muniyamma went, but was gone a long time. When her mother went looking for her, she found Muniyamma playing with a group of girls she was forbidden to associate with.

24. Rajkumar was the son of an officer in a large manufacturing firm. Rajkumar, who was old enough to drive, was never allowed by his father to do so. While walking down the street with some friends, Rajkumar spotted a car left with the key in the ignition. On impulse he persuaded his friends to drive off with him in the car.

25. A large estate with a high wall was directly on the way home from Kantha's school. Even though she read the "No Trespass" sign, she would often sneak onto the estate's grounds and relax in the shade of the many fruit trees located inside the walls.

Part B

Thank you for your answers. In order to better understand the result of our study, we should like to have some information on the people who responded to our questionnaire. Would you please be kind enough to give the following information?

1. *Note*: Interviewer, fill in sex of respondent.
   ____ 1. Female
   ____ 2. Male

2. *Note*: If the respondent insists he doesn't know his/her age, guess approximate age.
   ____ What is your age?

3. How many years of school have you completed?
   ____ 1. Never been to school
   ____ 2. 1–8 years
   ____ 3. 9–11 years
   ____ 4. Some college or technical school
   ____ 5. College graduate
   ____ 6. Post-graduate

4. Are you employed?
   ____ 1. Yes
   ____ 2. No
   (If the individual is a housewife/unemployed/retired person and the answer is No, go to question No. 5)

   a. What is your job title?

   _____

   b. What do you do as part of your job?

   _____

   _____

c. What is your monthly income? (Include all interest on savings, land revenues, rent on buildings and houses owned as well as paychecks.)

_____

_____

5. Is your husband, son, or wife employed?
   ____ 1. Yes
   ____ 2. No

   a. What is his/her job title?

   _____

   _____

   b. What does he/she do as part of his/her job?

   _____

   _____

   c. What is his/her monthly income? (Include all interest on savings, land revenues, rent on buildings and houses owned as well as paychecks.)

   _____

   _____

6. What is your religious affiliation?
   ____ 1. None
   ____ 2. Hindu
   ____ 3. Muslim
   ____ 4. Christian
   ____ 5. Any other
   ____ 6. No answer

7. In the past three years, have you or any member of your household been the victim of a crime?
   ____ 1. Yes
   ____ 2. No

a. Please describe what happened.

_____

_____

b. Was this crime reported to the police or other authorities?
   ___ 1. Yes (If yes, go to question c.)
   ___ 2. No (If no, go to question d.)
c. What was the result?

_____

_____

d. If No, why not?

_____

_____

_____

APPENDIX C

Factor Analysis of Self-report Survey

Status Factor*

CORRELATION COEFFICIENTS

			Variable			
Variable	011	012	013	015	016	024
011 Truancy	1.00	0.32	0.28	0.34	0.45	0.23
012 Petty theft		1.00	0.30	0.30	0.41	0.30
013 Alcohol			1.00	0.28	0.34	0.23
015 Defy parents				1.00	0.43	0.29
016 Runaway					1.00	0.32
024 Lie about self						1.00

	Principal factor with iterations	Factor score coefficients	Percent variance
011 Truancy	.57691	.19877	43.7
012 Petty theft	.56968	.20232	13.2
013 Alcohol	.48760	.15347	12.5
015 Defy parents	.57741	.20478	11.5
016 Runaway	.73293	.37355	10.5
024 Lie about self	.46322	.14311	8.4

*Factor analysis employed = Varimax Rotated, principal factoring with iterations, convergence required seven iterations.

Theft Factor*

CORRELATION COEFFICIENTS

Variable	Variable			
	014	018	020	025
014 Vandalism	1.00	0.43	0.41	0.34
018 Moderate theft		1.00	0.65	0.31
020 Grand theft			1.00	0.38
025 Trespassing				1.00

	Principal factor with iterations	Factor score coefficients	Percent variance
014 Vandalism	.56107	.17862	57.1
018 Moderate theft	.76917	.35886	18.6
020 Grand theft	.80551	.44755	15.8
025 Trespassing	.47681	.13219	8.5

*Factor analysis employed = Varimax Rotated, principal factoring with iterations, convergence required nine iterations.

SES Factor

CORRELATION COEFFICIENT

Variable 008   Variable 009
(Parent's occupation) with (Monthly income) = 0.55

Variable	Principal factor with iterations	Factor score coefficients	Percent variance
008 Parent's occupation	.74155	.47815	77.5
009 Monthly income	.74155	.47815	22.5

APPENDIX D

Factor Analysis of Public Attitude Survey

To determine if reactions toward the various offenses/offenders described in the public attitude survey could be combined to form scales of the knowledge, opinion, and attitude dimensions, the responses of the 803 respondents to the various scenarios were subjected to Guttman-scale analysis and factor analysis. In addition, the respondents' education, income, and occupation were factor-analyzed to provide a weighted SES scale. Each of these procedures was carried out for the combined sample and for the two subsamples individually.

Since the scalogram analysis indicated that not all the criteria for Guttman scales were present, factor analysis was used. While "factors" emerged in this procedure, this analysis also indicated that meaningful factors were not produced. As a rule of thumb, items with a coefficient of .3 and over were considered to be important components of a factor.

As presented in the listing below, for the knowledge dimension, twenty-four of the twenty-five items do form four factors accounting for over 96 percent of the variance in respondents' reactions when the total sample of 803 respondents is considered. But the items contained in the various factors do not suggest a common theme. The same thing occurs when the responses to the opinion, agent, and sanction questions are analyzed. That is, while most of the items do form factors, one would be hard pressed to reasonably combine these items to form scales measuring relations to specific types of offense/offenders. Thus, Factor I and Factor IV for the knowledge items may be considered meaningful, and the same can be said of Factors I and IV, II and III, and I and III for the opinion, agent, and sanction dimensions respectively. But, depending upon the dimension, the component items of these "factors" vary somewhat. Moreover, when the rural and urban subsamples are treated individually, a good deal of variability can be found in the items forming various factors along the four dimensions. Thus, factor analysis failed to clarify, condense, or provide a rationale for combining various items into factors for further analysis. If one's main concern were with public knowledge of, opinions toward, or attitudes regarding various offense types (e.g., property crimes, status offenses), the fact that such factors do not uniformly materialize across dimensions would be a serious drawback. One could, however, address the variance in knowledge, etc. to types of offense behavior without concern for the uniformity of types across the dimensions.

Our main concern in this undertaking, however, was to assess overall reactions to delinquency and to investigate these reactions in terms of the characteristics of respondents. Thus, it was decided that since the various items do largely form factors within each of the four dimensions, responses to all twenty-five "Is," "Should," "Who," and "What" questions could be grouped (or added) to measure overall knowledge, opinions, and attitudes. Second, although the various factors formed by the combinations of these items are not uniform across dimensions and do not always make analytical sense, the factor analysis does suggest that they may be meaningfully combined into offense types as status, property, personal, and substance-related offenses. Correlation coefficients derived for these combined items through both interval and ordinal techniques are very similar, suggesting that the combined responses could be treated as interval data and analyzed in terms of regression and path analysis.

Factor analysis of the education, income, and occupation responses indicated that the three items have more or less equal factor loading (being respectively .62, .74, and .76). Therefore, since each of the items contributes equally to the composite scale, it was decided to dispense with weighting these items and to simply combine the ordinal scores for the component measure.

Appendix D   233

Items Forming Factors for the Knowledge, Opinion, Agent, and Sanction Dimensions*

Knowledge Factors:

	Initial Factor Loadings		Initial Factor Loadings
FACTOR I		**FACTOR II**	
Runaway (boy)	.58	Alcohol use (higher)	.45
Runaway (girl)	.52	Alcohol use (lower)	.38
Smoking	.33	Marihuana use	42
Vandalism (older person)	.38	Ticketless travel (lower)	.49
Vandalism (younger person)	.64	Trespass (boy)	.44
Trespass (girl)	.36	Joyride (lower)	.39
Petty theft	.32	Grand theft (lower)	.57
Assault parent	.43		
Fighting (younger person)	.52		
FACTOR III		**FACTOR IV**	
Ticketless travel (higher)	.46	Truancy	.47
Joyride (higher)	.54	Defy parents (boy)	.53
Grand theft (higher)	.63	Defy parents (girl)	.59
Weapons	.35		
Gangfight	.41		

Opinion Factors:

FACTOR I		**FACTOR II**	
Truancy	.48	Alcohol use (lower)	.37
Defy parents (boy)	.54	Ticketless travel (higher)	.50
Defy parents (girl)	.66	Joyride (higher)	.49
Trespass (girl)	.49	Grand theft (higher)	.58
Assault parent	.48	Grand theft (lower)	.37
Fighting (older person)	.32	Gangfight	.46
FACTOR III		**FACTOR IV**	
Marihuana use	.50	Runaway (boy)	.50
Trespass (boy)	.50	Runaway (girl)	.47
Joyride (lower)	.40	Vandalism (younger person)	.57
Weapons	.36	Vandalism (older person)	.36
		Petty theft	.36
		Fighting (younger person)	.46

Appendix D

Agent (Whom):	Initial Factor Loadings		Initial Factor Loadings
FACTOR I		**FACTOR II**	
Alcohol use (lower)	.31	Truancy	.39
Vandalism (older person)	.49	Runaway (boy)	.46
Trespass (boy)	.35	Runaway (girl)	.44
Joyride (higher)	.41	Assault parent	.45
Joyride (lower)	.45	**FACTOR III**	
Grand theft (lower)	.38	Defy parents (boy)	.47
Fighting (older person)	.34	Trespass (girl)	.37
Gangfight	.51	Fighting (younger person)	.33
		Weapons	.34

Sanction (What) Factors:

FACTOR I		**FACTOR II**	
Truancy	.45	Marihuana use	.43
Runaway (boy)	.39	Ticketless travel (higher)	.41
Runaway (girl)	.48	Ticketless travel (lower)	.33
Smoking	.45	Trespass (boy)	.45
Alcohol use (higher)	.44	Joyride (lower)	.35
Alcohol use (lower)	.41	Weapons	.37
Vandalism (older person)	.41	Gangfight	.44
Vandalism (younger person)	.53		
Assault parent	.48		
Fighting (older person)	.33		
FACTOR III		**FACTOR IV**	
Defy parents (boy)	.61	Petty theft	.50
Defy parents (girl)	.53	Joyride (higher)	.38
Trespass (girl)	.38	Grand theft (higher)	.49

*Varimax Rotated, principal factoring with iterations was used in all cases.

Bibliography

Adorno, Theodore M.; Frenkel-Brunswick, Elise; Levison, Daniel J.; and Nevitt Sanford, R.
    1950   *The Authoritarian Personality.* New York: Harper.
Akers, Ronald L.
    1964   "Socio-Economic Status and Delinquent Behavior: A Retest." *Journal of Research in Crime and Delinquency* 1: 38–46.
Akman, Dogan K.; Normandeau, Andre; and Turner, Stanley
    1967   "The Measurement of Delinquency in Canada." *Journal of Criminal Law, Criminology and Police Science* 58: 330–337.
Allport, Gordon W.
    1958   *The Nature of Prejudice.* Garden City, New York: Doubleday.
    1967   "Attitudes." In Martin Fishbein (ed.), *Readings in Attitude Theory and Measurement,* pp. 1–13. New York: John Wiley.
Altheide, David L.
    1974   *Creating Reality: How T.V. News Distorts Events.* Beverly Hills: Sage.
Baig, Tara Ali
    1978   "The Seeds of Crime." *The Indian Express,* October 9, p., 8.
Barrett, Marvin, ed.
    1973   *The Politics of Broadcasting.* New York: Thomas Y. Crowell.
Barron, Milton L.
    1955   *The Juvenile in Delinquent Society,* New York: Knopf.
Batta, I. D.; McCulloch, J. W.; and Smith, N. J.
    1975   "A Study of Juvenile Delinquency Among Asians and Half Asians." *British Journal of Criminology* 15: 32–42.
Bayley, Davis H.
    1969   *The Police and Political Development in India.* Princeton: Princeton University Press.
Beals, Alan R.
    1980   *Gopalpur: A South Indian Village.* New York: Holt, Rinehart and Winston.

Becker, Howard S.
  1963 *Outsiders: Studies in the Sociology of Deviance.* New York: The Free Press.
  1966 *Social Problems: A Modern Approach.* New York: John Wiley.
Bendix, Reinhard, and Lipset, Seymour Martin, eds.
  1966 *Class, Society and Power.* New York: The Free Press.
Berger, Peter L., and Luckmann, Thomas
  1967 *The Social Construction of Reality.* New York: Doubleday.
Berk, Richard A., and Rossi, Peter H.
  1977 *Prison Reform and State Elites* (appendix). Cambridge, Mass.: Ballinger.
Bernstein, Basil
  1958 "Some Sociological Determinants of Perception." *The British Journal of Sociology* 9: 159–173.
Beteille, André
  1974 *Studies in Agrarian Social Structure.* Delhi: Oxford University Press.
Bittner, Egon
  1980 *The Function of the Police in Modern Society.* Cambridge, Mass.: Oelgeschlager, Gunn, and Hain.
Black, Donald
  1976 *The Behavior of Law.* New York: Academic Press.
  1980 *The Manners and Customs of the Police.* New York: Academic Press.
Blackmore, John
  1974 "The Relationship Between Self-Reported Delinquency and Official Convictions Among Adolescent Boys." *British Journal of Criminology* 14: 172–176.
Boggs, Sarah L.
  1971 "Formal and Informal Crime Control: An Exploratory Study of Urban, Suburban, and Rural Orientations." *Sociological Quarterly* 12: 319–327.
Braithwaite, John
  1981 "The Myth of Social Class and Criminality Reconsidered." *American Sociological Review* 46: 36–57.
Bureau of Police Research and Development
  1977 *Crime in India, 1974.* New Delhi: Ministry of Home Affairs, Government of India.
Carter, Timothy J., and Clelland, Donald
  1979 "A Neo-Marxian Critique, Formulation and Test of Juvenile Dispositions as a Function of Social Class." *Social Problems* 27: 96–108.
Cavan, Ruth S., and Cavan, Jordan T.
  1968 *Delinquency and Crime: Cross-Cultural Perspectives.* Philadelphia: Lippincott.

Census of India: Tamil Nadu Series 19—Tamil Nadu—Part II A
    1973   New Delhi: Government of India.
Central Bureau of Correctional Services
    1970   *Juvenile Delinquency: A Challenge.* New Delhi: Department of Social Welfare, Government of India.
    1976   *Social Defence: A Statistical Handbook.* New Delhi: Department of Social Welfare, Government of India.
Chambers, Carl D., and Inciardi, James A.
    1971   "Deviant Behavior in the Middle East: A Study of Delinquency in Iraq." *Criminology* 9: 291–315.
Chambliss, William J.
    1978   "Toward a Political Economy of Crime." In Charles E. Reasons and Robert M. Rich (eds.), *The Sociology of Law: A Conflict Perspective,* pp. 191–212. Toronto: Butterworths.
_____, and Seidman, Robert B.
    1971   *Law, Order, and Power.* Reading, Mass.: Addison-Wesley.
Chauhan, S. K.
    1978   "'Court' That Dispenses Sympathy." *The Hindustan Times,* April 24, pp., 1–4.
Chein, Isidor
    1967   "Behavior Theory and the Behavior of Attitudes: Some Critical Comments." In Martin Fishbein (ed.), *Readings in Attitude Theory and Measurement,* p. 51–57. New York: John Wiley.
Christie, Nils
    1978   "Youth as a Crime-Generating Phenomenon." In Barry Krisberg and James Austin (eds.), *The Children of Ishmael: Critical Perspectives on Juvenile Justice,* pp. 221–230. Palo Alto: Mayfield.
Chung, Kevin
    1980   "TV Violence and Children." *The Asian Messenger* (Spring): 63–64.
Clark, John P., and Tifft, Larry L.
    1966   "Polygraph and Interview Validation of Self-Reported Deviant Behavior." *American Sociological Review* 31: 516–523.
Clelland, Donald, and Carter, Thomas J.
    1980   "The New Myth of Class and Crime." *Criminology* 18: 319–336.
Clifford, William
    1976   *Crime Control in Japan.* Lexington, Mass.: Lexington.
Clinard, Marshall B.
    1978   *Cities with Little Crime.* New York: Cambridge University Press.
_____, and Abbott, Daniel J.
    1973   *Crime in Developing Countries.* New York: John Wiley.
Cloward, Richard A.
    1959   "Illegitimate Means, Anomie and Deviant Behavior." *American Sociological Review* 24: 164–176.

Bibliography

———, and Ohlin, Lloyd
1960 *Delinquency and Opportunity.* New York: The Free Press of Glencoe.

Cohen, Albert K.
1955 *Delinquent Boys: The Culture of the Gang.* New York: The Free Press.
1959 "The Study of Social Disorganization and Deviant Behavior." In Robert K. Merton, Leonard Broom, and Leonard S. Cottrell, Jr. (eds.), *Sociology Today*, pp. 474–481. New York: Basic Books.

Conklin, John B.
1971 "Dimensions of Community Response to the Crime Problem." *Social Problems* 18: 373–384.

Davis, James F.
1952 "Crime News in Colorado Newspapers." *American Journal of Sociology* 57: 325–330.

DeFleur, Lois B.
1967 "Ecological Variables in the Cross-Cultural Study of Delinquency." *Social Forces* 45: 556–570.
1969 "Alternative Strategies for the Development of Delinquency Theories Applicable to Other Countries." *Social Problems* 17: 30–39.

Demos, John, and Demos, Virginia
1973 "Adolescence in Historical Perspective." In Michael Gordon (ed.), *The American Family in Historical Perspective*, pp. 209–221. New York: St. Martin's Press.

Dentler, Robert A., and Monroe, Lawrence J.
1961 "Social Correlates of Early Adolescent Theft." *American Sociological Review* 26: 733–743.

Dewey, Richard
1960 "The Rural-Urban Continuum: Real But Relatively Unimportant." *American Journal of Sociology* 66: 60–65.

Diamond, Stanley
1971 "The Rule of Law Versus the Order of Custom." *Social Research* 38: 42–72.

Durkheim, Emile
1964 *The Rules of Sociological Method.* Translated by Sarah A. Solovay and John H. Mueller and edited by George E. G. Catlin. New York: The Free Press.
1967 *The Division of Labor in Society.* Translated by George Simpson. New York: The Free Press.

Elliott, Delbert S., and Ageton, Suzanne S.
1980 "Reconciling Differences in Estimates of Delinquency. *American Sociological Review* 45: 95–110.

Empey, LaMar T.
1982 *American Delinquency: Its Meaning and Construction.* Homewood, Ill.: Dorsey Press.

———, and Erickson, Maynard L.
- 1966 "Hidden Delinquency and Social Status." *Social Forces* 44: 546–554.

Epstein, Edward Jay
- 1973 *News from Nowhere: Television and the News.* New York: Basic Books.

Erikson, Kai T.
- 1964 "Notes on the Sociology of Deviance." In Howard S. Becker (ed.), *The Other Side*, pp. 9–21. New York: The Free Press.
- 1966 *Wayward Puritans.* New York: John Wiley.

Europa Year Book: A World Survey, vol. 2
- 1978 London: Europa Publications.

Faris, Robert E. L.
- 1955 *Social Disorganization.* New York: Ronald Press.

Federal Bureau of Investigation
- 1979 *Uniform Crime Reports in the United States.* Washington, D.C.: U.S. Government Printing Office.

Festinger, Leon
- 1957 *A Theory of Cognitive Dissonance.* Stanford, Calif.: Stanford University Press.

———, Riecken, Henry W., Jr.; and Schachter, Stanley
- 1956 *When Prophecy Fails.* Minneapolis: University of Minnesota Press.

Fishbein, Martin, ed.
- 1967 *Readings in Attitude Theory and Measurement.* New York: John Wiley.

Friday, Paul C.
- 1980 "International Review of Youth Crime and Delinquency." In Graeme R. Newman (ed.), *Crime and Deviance: A Comparative Perspective*, pp. 100–129. Beverly Hills: Sage.

———, and Hage, Jerald
- 1976 "Youth Crime in Postindustrial Societies: An Integrated Perspective." *Criminology* 14: 347–368.

Garafalo, James
- 1977 *Public Opinion about Crime, Report SD-VAD-1.* Washington, D.C.: National Criminal Justice Information and Statistical Service, LEAA.

Gerbner, George, and Gross, Larry
- 1976 "Living with Television: The Violence Profile." *Journal of Communication* 26: 173–200.

Gibbons, Don C.
- 1981 *Delinquent Behavior.* 3d ed. Englewood Cliffs, N.J.: Prentice-Hall.

———; Jones, Joseph F.; and Garabedian, Peter G.
- 1972 "Gauging Public Opinion about the Crime Problem." *Crime and Delinquency* 18: 134–146.

Gibson, H. B.
1971 "The Factorial Structure of Juvenile Delinquency: A Study of Self-Reported Acts." *British Journal of Clinical Psychology* 10: 1–9.
———; Morrison, Sylvia; and West, D. J.
1970 "The Confession of Known Offenses in Response to a Self-Reported Delinquency Schedule." *British Journal of Criminology* 10: 277–280.
Gough, Kathleen E.
1955 "The Social Structure of a Tanjore Village." In McKim Marriott (ed.), *Village India: Studies in the Little Community*, pp. 36–52. Chicago: University of Chicago Press.
Greenberg, David F.
1978 "Delinquency and the Age Structure of Society." In Peter Wickman and Phillip Whitten (eds.), *Readings in Criminology*, pp. 66–86. Lexington, Mass.: D. C. Heath.
1979 *Mathematical Criminology*. New Brunswick, N.J.: Rutgers University Press.
Gusfield, Joseph R.
1963 *Symbolic Crusade: Status Politics and the American Temperance Movement*. Urbana, Ill.: University of Illinois Press.
Hackler, James C.; Ho, Kwai-Yiu; and Ross, C. Urquhart
1974 "The Willingness To Intervene: Differing Community Characteristics." *Social Problems* 21: 328–344.
Hardt, Robert H., and Peterson-Hardt, Sandra
1977 "On Determining the Quality of the Deliquent Self-Reported Method." *Journal of Research in Crime and Delinquency* 14: 247–261.
Hartjen, Clayton A.
1977 *Possible Trouble: An Analysis of Social Problems*. New York: Praeger/Holt, Rinehart and Winston.
1978 *Crime and Criminalization*. 2d ed. New York: Holt, Rinehart and Winston.
1981 "Crime as Commonsense Theory." *Criminology* 18: 435–452.
Heider, Fritz
1946 "Attitudes and Cognitive Organization." *Journal of Psychology* 21: 107–112.
Higgins, Patricia B., and Ray, Marla W.
1978 *Television's Action Arsenal: Weapons Use in Prime Time*. Washington, D.C.: U.S. Conference of Mayors.
Hindelang, Michael; Hirschi, Travis; and Weis, Joseph
1979 "Correlates of Delinquency: The Illusion of Discrepancy Between Self-Report and Official Measures." *American Sociological Review* 44: 995–1014.
1981 *Measuring Delinquency*. Beverly Hills: Sage.

Hirschi, Travis
    1969   *Causes of Delinquency.* Berkeley: University of California Press.

Hollingshead, August B., and Redlich, Frederick C.
    1953   "Social Stratification and Psychiatric Disorders." *American Sociological Review* 18: 163–169.

Holzner, Burkart
    1968   *Reality Construction in Society.* Cambridge, Mass.: Schenkman.

Hubbard, Jeffrey C.; DeFleur, Melvin L.; and DeFleur, Lois B.
    1975   "Mass Media Influence on Public Conceptions of Social Problems." *Social Problems* 23: 22–34.

Hudson, Daniel, and Brady, Kenneth W.
    1959   "Problems and Methods of Cross-Cultural Research." *Journal of Social Issues* 15: 5–19.

Inkeles, Alex
    1968   "Society, Social Structure and Child Socialization." In John A. Clausen (ed.), *Socialization and Society*, pp. 73–129. Boston: Little, Brown.

Jensen, Gary F., and Rojek, Dean G.
    1980   *Delinquency: A Sociological View.* Lexington, Mass.: D. C. Heath.

Katz, Daniel, and Braly, Kenneth W.
    1967   "Verbal Stereotypes and Racial Prejudice." In Martin Fishbein (ed.), *Readings in Attitude Theory and Measurement*, pp. 32–38. New York: Wiley.

Kitsuse, John I., and Cicourel, Aaron
    1963   "A Note on the Use of Official Statistics." *Social Problems* 11: 131–139.

Klopper, Joseph T.
    1960   *The Effects of Mass Communication.* New York: The Free Press of Glencoe.

Kohn, Melvin
    1959   "Social Class and Parental Values." *American Journal of Sociology* 65: 337–351.

Krase, Jerome, and Sagarin, Edward
    1980   "Formal and Informal Control in Cross-Cultural Perspective." In Graeme R. Newman (ed.), *Crime and Deviance: A Comparative Perspective*, pp. 211–235. Beverly Hills: Sage.

Krisberg, Barry, and Austin, James
    1978   *The Children of Ishmael: Critical Perspectives on Juvenile Justice.* Palo Alto: Mayfield.

Krishnamurti, S., and Alagamalai, K.
    1975   *A Hand Book of Criminal Law*, 12th ed. Madras: S. Subbiah Chetty & Co.

Krohn, Marvin; Akers, Ronald L.; Radosevich, Marcia J.; and Lanza-Kaduce, Lonn
    1980   "Social Status and Deviance: Class Context of School, Social Status, and Delinquent Behavior." *Criminology* 18: 303–318.

Labovitz, Sanford
  1967 "Some Observations on Measurement and Statistics." *Social Forces* 46: 151–160.
  1970 "The Assignment of Numbers to Rank Ordered Categories." *American Sociological Review* 35: 515–524.
Larkin, Ralph W.
  1979 *Suburban Youth in Cultural Crises.* New York: Oxford University Press.
Lee, Alfred McClung
  1946 "The Press in the Context of Intergroup Tensions." *The Annals of American Academy of Political and Social Science* 244: 163–167.
Lemert, Edwin M.
  1967 *Human Deviance, Social Problems, and Social Control.* Englewood Cliffs, N.J.: Prentice-Hall.
Lerner, Daniel
  1958 *The Passing of Traditional Society: Modernizing the Middle East.* New York: The Free Press.
Lester, Marilyn
  1980 "Generating Newsworthiness: The Interpretive Construction of Public Events." *American Sociological Review* 45: 984–994.
Lipset, Seymour Martin
  1959 *Political Man: The Social Bases of Politics.* Garden City. N.Y.: Doubleday.
Liska, Allen E.
  1974 "Emergent Issues in the Attitude-Behavior Consistency Controversy." *American Sociological Review* 39: 261–272.
Littrell, W. Boyd
  1979 *Bureaucratic Justice: Police, Prosecutors, and Plea Bargaining.* Beverly Hills: Sage.
McDonald, Lynn
  1969 *Social Class and Delinquency.* London: Farber & Farber.
Maccoby, Eleanor E.; Johnson, Joseph P.; and Church, Russell A.
  1958 "Community Integration and the Social Control of Juvenile Delinquency." *Journal of Social Issues* 15: 38–51.
Maddison, Angus
  1971 *Class Structure and Economic Growth: India and Pakistan since the Moghuls.* New York: W. W. Norton.
Mandelbaum, David G.
  1970 *Society in India.* Vol. 2: *Change and Continuity.* Berkeley: University of California Press.
Marsh, Robert M.
  1967 *Comparative Sociology.* New York: Harcourt, Brace and World.
Martin, John M.
  1973 "Toward a Political Definition of Juvenile Delinquency." In R. Serge Denisoff and Charles H. McCaghy (eds.), *Deviance, Conflict, and Criminality*, pp. 345–360. Chicago: Rand McNally.

Matza, David
    1969   *Becoming Deviant*. Englewood Cliffs, N.J.: Prentice-Hall.
Mencher, Joan P.
    1970   "A Tamil Village: Changing Socioeconomic Structure in Madras State." In K. Ishwaran (ed.), *Change and Continuity in India's Villages*, pp. 197–218. New York: Columbia University Press.
Merton, Robert K.
    1956   *Social Theory and Social Structure*. New York: The Free Press.
Miller, Walter B.
    1958   "Lower-Class Culture as a Generating Milieu of Gang Delinquency." *Journal of Social Issues* 14: 5–19.
Mishra, Vishwa Mohan
    1970   *Communication and Modernization in Urban Slums*. New York: Asia Publishing House.
Molotch, Harvey, and Lester, Marilyn
    1974   "News as Purposive Behavior: On the Strategic Use of Routine Events, Accidents, and Scandals." *American Sociological Review* 39: 101–112.
Murphy, Fred J.; Shirley, Mary M.; and Witmer, Helen Q.
    1946   "The Incidence of Hidden Delinquency." *American Journal of Orthopsychiatry* 16: 686–695.
Myrdal, Gunnar
    1944   *An American Dilemma*. New York: Harper and Row.
Natt, B., and Malik, P. C.
    1973   *Law and Material on the Code of Criminal Procedure*. Lucknow: Eastern Book Co.
Newman, Donald J.
    1957   "Public Attitudes toward a Form of White-Collar Crime." *Social Problems* 4: 228–232.
Newman, Graeme R.
    1974   "Acts, Actors and Reactions to Deviance." *Sociology and Social Research* 58: 434–440.
    1976   *Comparative Deviance: Perspectives on Law in Six Countries*. New York: Elsevier.
Normandeau, Andre
    1966   "The Measurement of Delinquency in Montreal." *Journal of Criminal Law, Criminology and Police Science* 57: 172–177.
Nyrop, Richard F.; Benderly, Beryl Lieff; Cover, William W.; Cutter, Milissa J.; and Parker, Newton B.
    1975   *Area Handbook for India*. Washington, D.C.: United States Government Printing Office.
Osgood, Charles E., and Tannenbaum, Percy H.
    1955   "The Principle of Congruity in the Prediction of Attitude Change." *Psychological Review* 62: 42–55.
Parker, Howard A.
    1970   "Juvenile Court Actions and Public Response." In Peter G.

Garabedian and Don C. Gibbons (eds.), *Becoming Delinquent*, pp. 252–265. Chicago: Aldine.

Pepinsky, Harold E.
   1976   *Crime and Conflict*. New York: Academic Press.

Pfohl, Stephen J.
   1981   "Labeling Criminals." In H. Laurence Ross (ed.), *Law and Deviance*, pp. 65–98. Beverly Hills: Sage.

Phillips, Barbara C.
   1977   "Approaches to Objectivity: Journalistic versus Social Science Perspective." In Paul M. Hirsch, Peter Miller, and F. Gerald Kline (eds.) *Strategies for Communication Research*, 6: 63–77. Beverly Hills: Sage.

Platt, Anthony
   1969   *The Child Savers*. Chicago: University of Chicago Press.

Porterfield, Austin L.
   1943   "Delinquency and Its Outcome in Court and College." *American Journal of Sociology* 44: 199–208.

Priyadarsini, S., and Hartjen, Clayton A.
   1981   "Delinquency and Corrections in India." In Gary F. Jensen (ed.), *Sociology of Delinquency: Current Issues*, pp. 109–123. Beverly Hills: Sage.

Quinney, Richard
   1970   *The Social Reality of Crime*. Boston: Little, Brown.
   1974   *Critique of Legal Order*. Boston: Little, Brown.
   1975   *Criminology*. Boston: Little, Brown.
   1977   *Class, State, and Crime*. New York: Longman.

Ranchhoddas, R., and Thakore, D. K.
   1953   *Law and Crime*. 18th. ed. Bombay: The Bombay Law Reporter Office.

Rao, P. Venugopal
   1978   "Juvenile Delinquency and the Law—I." *The Indian Express*, March 1.

Reiss, Albert, Jr., and Rhodes, Albert Lewis
   1961   "The Distribution of Delinquency in the Social Class Structure." *American Sociological Review* 26: 720–732.

Ritchie, Oscar, and Koller, Marvin R.
   1964   *Sociology of Childhood*. New York: Appleton-Century-Crofts.

Robertson, Priscilla
   1974   "The Home as a Nest: Middle-Class Childhood in Nineteenth Century Europe." In Lloyd de Mause (ed.), *The History of Childhood*, pp. 229–257. New York: The Psychohistory Press.

Rooney, Elizabeth A., and Gibbons, Don C.
   1966   "Societal Reaction to 'Crimes without Victims.'" *Social Problems* 13: 400–410.

Rosen, Bernard C.
 1956 "The Achievement Syndrome: A Psychocultural Dimension of Social Stratification." *American Sociological Review* 21: 203–211.
Rosenberg, Charles E., ed.
 1975 *The Family in History*. Philadelphia: University of Pennsylvania Press.
Roshco, Bernard
 1975 *Newsmaking*. Chicago: University of Chicago Press.
Ross, Robert, and Staines, Graham L.
 1972 "The Politics of Analyzing Social Problems." *Social Problems* 20: 18–41.
Rossi, Peter H.; Bose, Christine E.; and Berk, Richard E.
 1974 "The Seriousness of Crimes: Normative Structure and Individual Differences." *American Sociological Review* 39: 224–237.
Sarma, I. R. K.
 1980 "Household Income—Structure and Distribution." *Quarterly Journal, National Council of Applied Economic Research* (April): 31–37.
Schachter, Stanley
 1954 "Interpretive and Methodological Problems of Replicated Research." *Journal of Social Issues* 10: 52–60.
Schur, Edwin M.
 1965 *Crimes without Victims*. Englewood Cliffs, N.J.: Prentice-Hall.
 1973 *Radical Nonintervention*. Englewood Cliffs, N.J.: Prentice-Hall.
Schwartz, T. P., and Leitko, Thomas
 1977 "The Rise of Social Problems: Newspapers as 'Thermometers.'" In Armand L. Mauss and Julie C. Wolfe (eds.), *This Land of Promises: The Rise and Fall of Social Problems in America*, pp. 427–436. Philadelphia: Lippincott.
Scott, John W., and Tilly, Louise A.
 1975 "Women's Work and the Family in Nineteenth Century Europe." In Charles E. Rosenberg (ed.), *The Family in History*, pp. 145–178. Philadelphia: University of Pennsylvania Press.
Sellin, Thorsten, and Wolfgang, Marvin E.
 1964 *The Measurement of Delinquency*. New York: John Wiley.
Shane, Paul G.
 1980 *Police and People: A Comparison of Five Countries*, St. Louis: Mosby.
Shanmugam, T. E.
 1980 *Psychosocial Factors Underlying Juvenile Delinquency*. Madras: University of Madras.
Shelley, Louise I.
 1981a *Crime and Modernization: The Impact of Industrialization and Urbanization on Crime*. Carbondale, Ill.: Southern Illinois University Press.

Bibliography

1981b   *Readings in Comparative Criminology.* Carbondale, Ill.: Southern Illinois University Press.

Shapland, Joannna M.
- 1978   "Self-Reported Delinquency in Boys Aged 11–14." *British Journal of Criminology* 18: 255–266.

Sherizen, Sanford
- 1978   "Social Creation of Crime News: All the News Fitted to Print." In Charles Winick (ed.), *Deviance and Mass Media*, pp. 203–224. Beverly Hills: Sage.

Short, James F., and Nye, F. Ivan
- 1958   "Extent of Unrecorded Juvenile Delinquency: Tentative Conclusions." *Journal of Criminal Law, Criminology and Police Science* 49: 296–302.

Shukla, K. S.
- 1978   "Wiping That Stigma." *Indian Express*, April 20, p. 9.

Simmel, George
- 1957   "The Metropolis and Mental Life." In Paul Hatt and Albert J. Reiss, Jr. (eds.), *Cities and Society*, pp. 635–647. New York: The Free Press.

Singh, S. D.
- 1966   *Sohoni's The Code of Criminal Procedure*, vol. 3. 12th. ed. Allahabad: Law Book Co.

Smith, M. Brewster
- 1967   "The Personal Setting of Public Opinion: A Study of Attitudes Toward Russia." In Martin Fishbein (ed.), *Readings in Attitude Theory and Measurement*. New York: John Wiley.

Spector, Malcolm, and Kitsuse, John I.
- 1977   *Constructing Social Problems.* Menlo Park, Calif.: Cummings.

Srinivas, M. N.
- 1955   "The Social Structure of a Mysore Village." In McKim Marriott (ed.), *Village India: Studies in the Little Community*, pp. 1–35. Chicago: University of Chicago Press.

Stinchcombe, Arthur L.; Adams, Rebecca; Heimer, Carol A.; Scheppele, Kim Lane; Smith, Tom W.; and Taylor, D. Garth
- 1980   *Crime and Punishment—Changing Attitudes in America.* San Francisco: Jossey-Bass.

Stone, Lawrence
- 1977   *The Family, Sex and Marriage in England, 1500–1800.* New York: Harper and Row.

Sundeen, Richard A.
- 1981   "Juvenile Arrests in Papua New Guinea." In Gary F. Jensen (ed.), *Sociology of Delinquency: Current Issues*, pp. 124–142. Beverly Hills: Sage.

Taylor, D. Garth; Scheppele, Kim Lane; and Stinchcombe, Arthur L.
- 1979   "Salience of Crime and Support of Harsher Criminal Sanctions." *Social Problems* 26: 413–425.

Tifft, Larry L.
    1979   "The Coming Redefinition of Crime: An Anarchist Perspective." *Social Problems* 26: 392–402.

Tiruchelvam, Neelan
    1978   "The Ideology of Popular Justice." In Charles E. Reasons and Robert M. Rich (eds.), *The Sociology of Law: A Conflict Perspective*, pp. 263–280. Toronto: Butterworths.

Tittle, Charles R.; Villemez, Wayne J.; and Smith, Douglas A.
    1978   "The Myth of Social Class and Criminality." *American Sociological Review* 43: 643–656.

Toby, Jackson
    1963   "The Prospects for Reducing Delinquency Rates in Industrial Societies." *Federal Probation* 27: 23–25.
    1979   "Delinquency in Cross-Cultural Perspective." In LaMar T. Empey (ed.), *Juvenile Justice: The Progressive Legacy and Current Reforms*, pp. 105–149. Charlottesville: University Press of Virginia.

Tuchman, Gaye
    1978   *Making News: A Study in Construction of Reality.* New York: The Free Press.

Tucker, M. J.
    1974   "The Child as Beginning and End: Fifteenth and Sixteenth Century English Childhood." In Lloyd deMause (ed.), *The History of Childhood*, p. 229–257. New York: The Psychohistory Press.

Vaz, Edmund W.
    1962   "Juvenile Delinquency in Paris." *Social Problems* 10: 23–31.

Vaz, Edmund M., and Casparis, John
    1981   "A Comparative Study of Youth Culture and Delinquency: Upper Middle-Class Canadian and Swiss Boys." In Louise L. Shelley (ed.), *Readings in Comparative Criminology*, pp. 56–77. Carbondale, Ill.: Southern Illinois University Press.

Voss, Herman L.
    1966   "Socio-Economic Status and Reported Delinquent Behavior." *Social Problems* 13: 314–324.

Walsh, Warren B.
    1944   "What the American People Think of Russia." *Public Opinion Quarterly* 8: 513–522.

Warwick, Donald P. and Lenninger, Charles A.
    1975   *The Sample Survey: Theory and Practice.* New York: McGraw-Hill.

Weinberg, S. Kisson
    1964   "Juvenile Delinquency in Ghana: A Comparative Analysis of Delinquents and Non-Delinquents." *Journal of Criminal Law and Police Science* 55: 471–481.

Weinstein, Jay A.
    1976   "Madras: Theoretical, Technical and Empirical Issues." In Giri Raj Gupta (ed.), *Main Currents in Indian Sociology*, vol. 1: Con-

temporary India: Some Sociological Perspectives, pp. 258–278. Durham, N.C.: Carolina Academic Press.

Wiebe, Paul D.
 1976 "Social Life in a Madras Slum." In Giri Raj Gupta (ed.), *Main Currents in Indian Sociology*, vol. 1: *Contemporary India: Some Sociological Perspectives*, pp. 278–298. Durham, N.C.: Carolina Academic Press.

Williams, Jay R., and Gold, Martin
 1972 "From Delinquent Behavior to Official Delinquency." *Social Problems* 20: 209–229.

Wilson, James Q.
 1968 *Varieties of Police Behavior*. Cambridge, Mass.: Harvard University Press.

Winick, Charles, ed.
 1978 *Deviance and Mass Media*. Beverly Hills: Sage.

Wirth, Louis
 1938 "Urbanism as a Way of Life." *American Journal of Sociology* 44: 1–24.

Wiseman, Jacqueline P.
 1970 *Stations of the Lost*. Englewood Cliffs, N.J.: Prentice-Hall.

Zeldes, Ilya
 1980 "Juvenile Delinquency in the USSR: A Criminological Survey." *International Journal of Comparative and Applied Criminal Justice* 4: 15–29.

Index

Abbott, Daniel J., 203
acephalous societies: characteristics of, 208; and India, 208–209; social control in, 205–212
adolescent subculture: and delinquency, 75, 76; in developed societies, 75, 76, 117–119; in developing societies, 79, 119–121; and economy, 75–76, 81; and employment, 75–76
agrarian society: and delinquency, 77–82; and integration of youth, 80–82; reactions of public in, 183–190; social control in, 119–121; social relationships in, 77–79; and work, 79–80
alcohol use: arrests for, 86, 88; attitudes toward, 143, 151; rates of, 48, 51, 53; self-admitted, 58–65
alienation, 75–77, 81, 208
anomie theory, 202, 203
approved schools: junior, 44, 111–112; private, 22, 112–115; programs in, 108–116; public, 22, 110–112; senior, 44, 110–111. *See also* corrections, juvenile
arrests: of approved school and high school boys, 95–99; characteristics of offenders, 92–94; in India, 86–90; juveniles as percent of, 87; in Madras and Tamil Nadu, 90–92; and social class, 96–99
assault: attitudes toward, 143, 154; of parent, 61; self-reported, 58–65
attitudes, public: congruence in, 157, 160; survey of, 25–32; toward agent of control, 156, 158–160; toward sanction, 156, 157–160

Baumgarter, M. P., 206
Black, Donald, 76, 191, 206–207

Chengalpattu (approved school), 110-11
child labor: amount of, 80; in developed societies, 75–76; in developing societies, 79–80; and delinquency, 75–80. *See also* work
children: neglected, 41; uncontrollable, 42
children acts: enforcement of, 135; India, 40–42; Tamil Nadu, 40, 43–46
Christie, Nils, 117, 119
class, social: and delinquency, 67–74; and judicial contact, 96–99; SES scale, 66–67

Index

Clifford, William, 211–212
Clinard, Marshall B., 203, 211, 213
Code of Criminal Procedure, 40, 41, 43
Cognitive congruence and dissonance, 157–159
Conklin, John B., 186
Cordoba, Argentina: delinquency in, 201
corrections, juvenile: facilities, 106–109; personnel, 34, 115–116; programs, 109–115. *See also* approved schools
Crime in India, 46
crime news. *See* mass media
crime rates: in India, 47–49; 50–54; juvenile as percentage of, 49–54
criminal justice: news of, 33, 131–133
criminal law: news of, 33
cross-national (comparative) research, 7–12

DeFleur, Lois B., 201
defying parents: attitudes toward, 143, 150; self-reported, 59
delinquency laws. *See* laws
delinquency problem: creation of, 4, 75–76; in developed societies, 5, 74–77; in developing societies, 77–81
delinquent behavior: amount of, 6, 8, 49–54, 58–65, 196–197; in developed societies, 9; in developing societies, 9, 10, 75–81; and youth crime, 8
demonstrations. *See* riots
destitute children: laws regarding, 41–44; treatment of, 104–106
Dina Tanthi, 33, 127–130

Friday, Paul C., 75, 76

gambling: arrests for, 86, 89; rates of, 48, 53

Gandhi, Indira, 34, 128, 133
Gandhigram Institute, 17
gangfighting: attitudes toward, 143, 155; self-reported, 61
grand theft: arrests for, 88; attitudes toward, 143, 154; rates of, 48, 50; self-reported, 60
Greenberg, David F., 75, 77

Hage, Jerald, 75, 76
high schools (described), 22
Hindu, The, 23, 127–130
Hubbard, Jeffrey C., 126

Immoral Traffic in Women and Children Act: arrests for violations of, 86, 89; rates of violation, 48, 49, 51
India: characteristics of, 13–15
Indian Express, The, 33, 127–130
Indian Penal Code, 40, 41, 43, 46, 47; arrests for violations of, 86–92
industrialization: and delinquency, 74–77; and social control, 117–119

Japan: crime and delinquency in, 75, 211–212
jati (subcaste), 18; and integration of youth, 75–79, 81; and social control, 119–121, 187–190
joyriding: attitudes toward, 143, 153; self-reported, 60
judicial: authorities, 34; processing, 7, 102–106
judicial contact: and offense behavior, 96–98; rates of, 95; scale of, 96–99; and SES, 96–99
juvenile corrections. *See* corrections, juvenile
juvenile court: in Madras and Tamil Nadu, 102–106

knowledge (of delinquency laws): effect on attitudes and opinions, 170–183; by locality, 148; by

offense type, 143; variations in, 147, 148
Krase, Jerome, 189

laws: in India, 39–46; *Indian Penal Code,* 40, 43; special and local, 46, 47, 51; in Tamil Nadu, 42–46. *See also* children acts
legal proceedings. *See* juvenile court

Madras (city of): attitude survey in, 28–29; characteristics of, 16–17; crime and delinquency in, 51–54
Madurai University, 17
Maharashtra, 50
marihuana use: attitudes toward, 143, 151; self-reported, 59
Martin, John M., 118
mass media: characterization of crime and delinquency in, 126; content of, 130–134; content analysis of, 32–34; coverage, 127–130; delinquency news in, 134–137; impact of, 125–127
modernization, 11, 75

neglected children: laws regarding, 41–44; treatment of, 104–106
Nekkunram (approved school), 113–115
Newman, Graeme R., 10, 141
newspapers. *See* mass media

official reaction to delinquency: arrests, 86–92; and dispositions, 102–106; and self-reported delinquency, 94–99; and staff ideology, 115–116
opinions, public: effects on attitudes, 174; by offense type, 143, 175–183; by residence, 144, 145, 175; variations in, 146–147, 170–171
opportunity (theory), 202, 204

panchayat, 18, 188, 210
perceptions: of delinquency and deviance, 7; dimensions of, 139–142, 167–170
personal crime: arrests for, 88; in media, 33, 131–134; rates of, 48, 50; self-reported, 63, 65
police: arrest behavior, 87–88; size of force, 87
political crime: media reports of, 33, 130–133
postindustrial society: and delinquency, 74–75; and role relationships, 76–77; and youth, 75–76
probation, 108
Prohibition Act: arrests for violations of, 89–92; attitudes toward, 143–161; rates of violations of, 48–54; self-reported, 58–65
property crimes: arrests for, 86, 88; attitudes toward, 156, 160; media coverage of, 33, 131–133; rates of, 48, 50; scale of, 66; self-reported, 61–74; and SES, 67–74

Ranipet (approved school), 111–112
reception homes, 107–108
residence: effects on perceptions and reactions, 170–186
riots: arrests for, 88; media reports of, 33, 130–132; rates of, 48, 50
Rossi, Peter H., 165
running away from home: attitudes toward, 143, 150–151; self-reported, 59

Sagarin, Edward, 189
salience of crime: and attitudes toward control, 186–187
sanctions: attitudes toward, 172–183; choice of, 149–157; variations in choice of, 159–161
self-help societies. *See* acephalous societies

self-reported delinquency: frequency of, 58–75; research on, 19; survey of, 19–25
sentencing: alternatives, 44–45; in India, Tamil Nadu, and Madras, 102–106; laws governing, 44–45
Shaligram (approved school), 112–113
Shelley, Louise I., 212
Sherizen, Sanford, 126
smoking cigarettes: attitudes toward, 143, 151
social altruism, 207–209
social control: in acephalous societies, 205–212; choice of agent, 149–157; and delinquency, 140–141; in developed societies, 117–119; in developing societies, 119–121; and economic development, 187–190, 205–212; types of, 205–211; variations in choice of, 159–161, 172–183
social disorganization and delinquency, 202, 204
social egoism, 208–209
social integration: and deliquency, 80–81; in developed societies, 74–75; in developing societies, 80–81; and social control, 117–121
social problem: creation of, 125; delinquency as, 4, 5, 195
societal reaction: to crime and delinquency, 6, 197–198; dimensions of, 165, 167; by offense type, 166, 175–183; variations in, 183–186
status offense: attitudes toward, 149–156, 160, 161; scale of, 66–74; self-admitted, 61–74; and SES, 67–74, 96–99
substance abuse offense: arrests for, 89; attitudes toward, 143, 151; rates of, 48, 51; self-reported, 63
Switzerland: crime and delinquency in, 75, 211–212

Tamil Nadu (state of): characteristics of, 15–16; crime and delinquency in, 50–54
Tanjore (approved school), 111–112
Taylor, D. Garth, 186
Thamaraikulam (village of): attitude survey in, 30–31; characteristics of, 17–18
theft. See property crimes
ticketless travel: attitudes toward, 143, 152
trespass: attitudes toward, 143, 153; self-reported, 60
truancy: attitudes toward, 143, 150; self-reported, 59

uncontrollable children: laws regarding, 44–46
Uniform Crime Report, 46
urbanization: and delinquency, 74–77; and social control, 117–119

vandalism: attitudes toward, 143, 152; self-reported, 60

weapon, concealed: attitudes toward, 143, 154
West Bengal, 50
Wiebe, Paul D., 17
work and juveniles, 75, 79–80. See also child labor

youth problem. See delinquency problem; social problem
youthful offender, 41–44